MUSLIMS UNDER LATIN RULE,

1100–1300

MUSLIMS UNDER LATIN RULE, 1100–1300

James M. Powell, Editor

PRINCETON UNIVERSITY PRESS

PRINCETON, NEW JERSEY

COPYRIGHT © 1990 BY PRINCETON UNIVERSITY PRESS
PUBLISHED BY PRINCETON UNIVERSITY PRESS, 41 WILLIAM STREET,
PRINCETON, NEW JERSEY 08540
IN THE UNITED KINGDOM· PRINCETON UNIVERSITY PRESS,
OXFORD
ALL RIGHTS RESERVED

LIBRARY OF CONGRESS CATALOGING-IN-PUBLICATION DATA
MUSLIMS UNDER LATIN RULE, 1100–1300 / JAMES M. POWELL,
EDITOR.
P CM.
ISBN 0-691-005586-6
1. MUSLIMS—EUROPE—HISTORY. 2 ISLAM—RELATIONS—
CHRISTIANITY 3. CHRISTIANITY AND OTHER RELIGIONS—ISLAM. 4.
LATIN ORIENT.
I. POWELL, JAMES M.
DS36.96.M87 1990 940'.0882971—DC20 90-34238 CIP

PUBLICATION OF THIS BOOK HAS BEEN AIDED BY THE WHITNEY
DARROW FUND OF PRINCETON UNIVERSITY PRESS

THIS BOOK HAS BEEN COMPOSED IN LINOTRON GALLIARD

PRINCETON UNIVERSITY PRESS BOOKS ARE PRINTED
ON ACID-FREE PAPER, AND MEET THE GUIDELINES FOR
PERMANENCE AND DURABILITY OF THE COMMITTEE ON
PRODUCTION GUIDELINES FOR BOOK LONGEVITY
OF THE COUNCIL ON LIBRARY RESOURCES

PRINTED IN THE UNITED STATES OF AMERICA BY
PRINCETON UNIVERSITY PRESS,
PRINCETON, NEW JERSEY

1 3 5 7 9 10 8 6 4 2

CONTENTS

ABBREVIATIONS vii

INTRODUCTION 3
James M. Powell

ONE
The Mudejars of Castile and Portugal in the Twelfth and Thirteenth Centuries 11
Joseph F. O'Callaghan

TWO
Muslims in the Thirteenth-Century Realms of Aragon: Interaction and Reaction 57
Robert I. Burns, S.J.

THREE
The End of Muslim Sicily 103
David S. H. Abulafia

FOUR
The Subjected Muslims of the Frankish Levant 135
Benjamin Z. Kedar

FIVE
The Papacy and the Muslim Frontier 175
James M. Powell

CONCLUSIONS
A Comparative Note 205
James M. Powell

NOTES ON THE CONTRIBUTORS 209

INDEX 211

ABBREVIATIONS

AHR	*American Historical Review*
BAE	*Biblioteca de Autores Españoles*
CLC	*Cortes de los antiguos reinos de León y Castilla*
COD	*Conciliorum Oecumenicorum Decreta*
CODOM	*Colección de documentos para la historia del reino de Murcia*
ES	*España Sagrada*
H.-B.	J.L.A. Huillard-Bréholles, *Historia diplomatica Friderici secundi*
HID	*Historia, Instituciones, Documentos*
IP	Paul F. Kehr, *Regesta Pontificum Romanorum: Italia Pontificia*
Mansi	J. D. Mansi, *Sanctorum Conciliorum Nova et Amplissima Collectio*
MGH	*Monumenta Germaniae Historica*
MGH, Epp.	*Epistolae*
MGH, SS.	*Scriptores*
MHE	*Memorial Historico Español*
Partidas	*Las Siete Partidas*
PMH	*Portugaliae Monumenta Historica*
RHC	*Recueil des Historiens des Croisades*
RHC, Lois	*Lois*
RHC, Occ.	*Historiens Occidentaux*
RHC, Or.	*Historiens Orientaux*
RISS	C. A. Garufi, *Rerum Italicarum Scriptores*, 2d ser.
VI	*Corpus Iuris Canonici*: Liber Sext
X	*Corpus Iuris Canonici*: Decretales

MUSLIMS UNDER LATIN RULE,

1100–1300

INTRODUCTION

James M. Powell

THE INCEPTION OF THIS VOLUME goes back to a session at the meeting of the American Historical Association in December 1985, devoted to "Medieval Mediterranean Society in Comparative Perspective," in which all of the contributors participated. The focus on Muslims under Latin rule in the twelfth and thirteenth centuries emerged from the papers and comments at that session. However, the essays here go well beyond the beginnings made in the session. It is to the credit of the contributors that they have remained faithful to the format outlined at that time.

The essays presented here do not include all facets of the topic. Benjamin Z. Kedar has elsewhere written about the Muslims of Hungary, calling attention to existing research on the subject and himself discussing the presence of Hungarian Muslims in Jerusalem at the time of the Fifth Crusade. He also alludes to their prominence in the Hungarian polity in the next decades of the thirteenth century.[1] More might have been written about this interesting group and others, but the lack of sufficient earlier research and the difficulty in finding willing collaborators have made these efforts unfeasible.

Although a vast literature exists on Muslim-Christian relations, significantly less attention has been paid to Muslim minorities in Christian lands. Of course, the important work on Muslims in the realm of Aragon by Robert I. Burns is well known. Likewise, the contributions of Joshua Prawer and the Jerusalem School, of which Benjamin Z. Kedar is a leading member, have attracted widespread attention as have the studies by John Boswell and Henri Bresc, though these lie chiefly

---

[1] Benjamin Z. Kedar, "Ungarische Muslime in Jerusalem im Jahre 1217," *Acta Orientalia Academiae Scientiarum Hungaricae* 40 (1986): 325–27.

outside of the period considered here. There is, therefore, a growing body of historical literature that illustrates the depth of interest in this topic. The justification for this collection of essays lies in their effort to place the relations between dominant Christians and subject Muslims into a comparative perspective across a geographical spectrum that extends from Spain to the Near East. The result is a complex picture of common themes and regional diversities involving not merely the continued existence of Muslim minorities in newly conquered lands, but the building of new Latin societies, the restoration of churches and ecclesiastical institutions, and the forging of new ways of life between enemies.

Since the seventeenth century, the Western idea of toleration has taken on new meanings. The literature on Muslim-Christian relations has long focused on differences between the two groups in their approaches to religious minorities, vacillating between romantic and apologetic descriptions of mutual respect and toleration and the hard-boiled realism of tensions and conflicts between dominant groups and minorities. If, in the course of this discussion, Muslim tolerance has often been contrasted with Christian intolerance, it may be because the debate has centered more often on Muslim treatment of minorities than on subject Muslims under Latin rule. It has been easy enough, though often misleading, for scholars to single out elements, events, and characteristics that seemed to support their divergent views. As this discussion has matured, however, there has been a growing realization of the inadequacy of the modern idea of toleration to explain the experience of premodern societies. In a nutshell, tolerance meant something very different to them than it does to us. That difference becomes very clear in these essays. In fact, it might be enough to say that that difference is central to much of the work undertaken here.

The matrix of medieval ideas of toleration lay in a view of community that is chiefly familiar in the writings of anthropologists and ancient historians, but which has not been utilized by medievalists until recently. The difference in status between members of a community and strangers, the regulation of behavior toward both, and the idea of the guest and the conferral of religious protection on the latter speak of ideas of tolerance far removed from our own. However, it was against this background in Greco-Roman antiquity that both Christian and, later, Muslim views developed. What has been too seldom emphasized is the degree to which these views were related to one another, whether by common experience and heritage or by direct borrowing. The attitudes and practices described in the subsequent chapters of this book were not merely the result of the conquest of one people by another and the imposition of minority status, but emerged from some shared ideas about the nature of communities. Fundamental to these ideas was the notion that no one should be forced to change his religion by force and against his will. Learned opinion in both communities generally opposed forced conversions, but, in the popular mind, as evidenced in such sources as the *Song of Roland*, it was often endorsed. In practice, this principle was often breached, but it remained theoretically intact. Religious identity represented the core of a community. For this reason, the ultimate act against any community was the destruction of its religious identity through forced conversion. Only, it seems, when a community lost its rights completely might some justify forced conversion, but such was not a generally accepted view.

Defeat in war, which certainly deprived the vanquished of their lands and property, as well on occasion of their freedom, did not usually result in a change of religion or a total destruction of their status as members of another community. Only acceptance and later rejection of the religion of the conqueror led to the forfeiture of one's right to practice his own religion and to the penalty of death. Under these circumstances, it becomes clear that tolerance between Muslims and Christians, between peoples long at war with one another, sharing the Mediterranean as a frontier, can hardly be described in abstract terms. Though certain principles continued to influence relations between them, experience and changing circumstances brought about significant changes in treatment. By the end of the period treated here, Muslim minorities were more often severely restricted or had suffered expulsion than had been the case earlier. Scholars examining the position of Christian minorities in lands under Muslim rule have also noted increased severity of treatment and suggested that it was a result of the Crusades. While these essays offer no alternative answer to this latter question, their response to the first may lead to an examination of other factors, particularly the perception by the dominant group of the danger represented by a religious minority.

Perhaps the most important contribution to be made by these essays is the explanation they offer of the diversity of treatment of Muslims under the various regimes studied here. Joseph F. O'Callaghan and Robert I. Burns show how this diversity even extends to regions under the same rule. The experience of the tiny Muslim remnant in Catalonia bears only a general resemblance to that in the kingdom of Aragon or in the more recently conquered lands of the kingdom of Valencia. The importance of colonization by Latin Christian immigrants is well illustrated by David S. H. Abulafia for the kingdom of Sicily, but bears on Aragon as well. On the other hand, a shortage of colonists marks portions of Portugal and Castile, as well as the Latin lands of the Levant. The experience of eastern Sicily is rather different from that of the western part of the island. Palermo and Messina became melting-pots of immigrants. Both ecclesiastical and secular leaders tended to view Muslim minorities in terms of their *utilitas*, thus setting up a tension between economic interests and religious concerns in dealing with the threat posed by Muslim minorities to nearby Christian groups. Long-established Muslim communities presented a far different challenge to leaders in both church and state than did the temporary arrangements resulting from the changing military frontier.

Conversion was long advocated as the solution to this problem. No wonder that all of these essays deal in some degree with conversionary efforts. While the difficulty in securing converts from Islam, even under the conditions discussed here, is not surprising, the lack of emphasis on full-scale missionary attempts at least until the end of our period does raise interesting questions in the minds of the contributors. Significantly, the issue of Muslim intransigence, which has often been central in other discussions, occupies much less space here. The *utilitas* of

Muslim peasants and craftsmen to their Christian masters and the opposition of those masters to their conversion assumes a larger role. Canon law was forced to compromise with the demands of secular and ecclesiastical lords, who were unwilling to lose the service of their Muslim slaves through conversion.

By no means were subjected Muslims always or even usually enslaved. The institution of slavery itself arose from the military situation rather than from politico-religious ideas. Muslim slaves, serfs, and freemen were found side by side, but slavery was not evenly distributed in all these societies. The example of Majorca and Minorca, with their different reaction to the conquerors, seems to illustrate the reason for this diversity. Negotiation of surrender terms served as a basis for the preservation of the rights of Muslim communities and of individuals to emigrate or to remain as peasants or freemen. Prolonged resistance led to death or enslavement. However, *utilitas* explains the regional importance of the slave trade as a means of meeting labor needs.

Given their proximity to Muslim-ruled territories, why did so many conquered Muslims choose to remain? Of course, many, chiefly members of the elite groups, fled. This seems especially to have been true of urban dwellers. In the countryside, peasants clung to the soil. They attempted to weather the storm under the shelter of their community and its officials, who had the delicate task of dealing with the Latins. As the period of dominance lengthened, undermining to some degree their confidence in Islam's capacity to triumph, pressures from surrounding Latin society increased. The example of Lucera shows how a community could resist such pressures until its fragmented remains were ultimately absorbed into the Christian milieu of its southern Italian surroundings. On the other hand, some peasants, such as the Ḥanbalīs from the area around Nablus, finally yielded to intense pressures and fled. Abulafia suggests how often this occurred in Sicily from the late eleventh century throughout our period.

From the picture presented here, it would be easy enough to stress the oppression of a minority by the dominant Latins. Of course, others would find ample evidence for *convivencia*, a term that finds little support in the chapters presented here. Neither approach really characterizes the situation seen in a comparative perspective; both have a certain validity at particular times and places. Muslims were sometimes oppressed; indeed their very status as conquered minorities made that inevitable. Muslims also lived in peaceful and even mutually beneficial relations with their Christian neighbors. Muslim peasants and Christian peasants might find more in common on some matters than either had with their lords. But we must try to see beyond the usual ways of putting the question of tolerance for religious minorities to the difficulties that posed themselves to any attempt to create conditions where enemy communities could live together in peace, if only in a prolonged truce.

What forms the basis of our discussion here is nothing else than the records of prolonged attempts to find solutions to this problem and to exercise the limited options implicit in their life situation. The record demonstrates weaknesses within the framework in which both Muslims and Latin Christians worked as well as the near total breakdown of the communitarian principles that served to protect, at least in theory, the rights of both societies. What we are witnessing are societies in severe stress, sometimes in agony. But it would be a mistake to see this stress only as it affects the minorities; ultimately, it serves to reshape the thinking of the majority as well. The search for solutions does not lead to the rationalist view of toleration by any direct path. Its more direct path is through the purgatory of persecution and expulsion. But defense of the rights of the majority—the preservation of the faith of simple Christians from contamination—does not settle the problem of the rights of the minority. From the middle of the thirteenth century on, the tension between the rights of both groups becomes a central theme in the canonistic literature dealing with Muslims and Jews. There is no easy solution. Contemporary arguments are found supporting expulsion and greater isolation of minorities, but these are usually hedged about by safeguards for the religious and property rights of these groups. Though an increasingly defensive mentality marks both the thought and the practices of this period, Latin Christianity was unable to turn its back on those principles of tolerance that marked the teachings of Christ and that found reiteration in the writings of contemporary canonists like Oldradus da Ponte.

The chapters that follow are much more the stories of the spectrum of human experience against the background of two cultures than arguments in continuation of old debates about toleration and oppression. What is striking is the degree to which religious ideas and communitarian traditions worked together to blunt the harsh realities of the relations between victors and vanquished. But even more noteworthy is the tendency of both religious and secular leaders to view their relations to Muslims (and Jews) narrowly in terms of the needs and interests of their own communities. In a real sense, the chapters that follow show no evidence of the evolution of Muslim and Jewish policies in Latin Christian societies; there were only policies that regulated the relationship of these societies to their own. Though the kernels for a policy of religious toleration were always present and even nurtured to a limited degree, they did not serve as the basis for any coherent policy. Their importance was chiefly as a check or restraint on actions based on utter intolerance of the rights of minorities.

But, if we pose no solutions, we do suggest that the comparative approach offers the foundation for a richer understanding of the problems we have discussed. Though it would be presumptuous to suggest that others have not already reached the same or similar conclusions on these issues, these essays explore the obstacles in the way of generalization at the same time as they suggest the validity of some generalizations.

1

THE MUDEJARS OF CASTILE AND PORTUGAL IN THE TWELFTH AND THIRTEENTH CENTURIES

Joseph F. O'Callaghan

EVER SINCE Francisco Fernández y González published his study of the social and political condition of the Mudejars of Castile in the late nineteenth century, scarcely any new work has focused attention on this theme. To be sure, Isidro de las Cagigas published a study of the Mudejars as a religio-ethnic minority in 1948–1949, but his emphasis was essentially upon the progress of the reconquest and he did not significantly expand our knowledge. More recently, Miguel Ángel Ladero Quesada studied the Mudejars at the close of the Middle Ages and published a collection of documents illustrating their status during the reign of Isabel the Catholic. Similarly, Juan Torres Fontes contributed several articles relative to the Mudejars of the kingdom of Murcia, while Manuel González Jiménez recently considered the fate of the Andalusian Mudejars. Little has been written, however, about the Mudejars of Portugal.[1]

---

[1] Robert I. Burns, "Mudejar History Today: New Directions," *Viator* 8 (1977): 127–43; Francisco Fernández y González, *Estado social y político de los mudejares de Castilla* (Madrid, 1966); Isidro de las Cagigas, *Minorías étnico-religiosas de la edad media española: Los mudejares*, 2 vols. (Madrid, 1948–1949); Miguel Ángel Ladero Quesada, *Los mudejares de Castilla en tiempos de Isabel I* (Valladolid, 1969); idem, "Los mudejares de Castilla en la baja edad media," *HID* 5 (1978): 257-304; Juan Torres Fontes, *Los mudejares murcianos en el siglo XIII* (Murcia, 1961); Manuel González Jiménez, *En torno a los orígenes de An-*

The present essay attempts to establish the essential framework for the study of the Mudejars in the twelfth and thirteenth centuries in the kingdoms of Castile and Portugal. An overview of the current state of our knowledge will likely encourage other more detailed studies.

As is well known, medieval Spain was a land of three religions, a land where Christians, Muslims, and Jews often lived side by side with one another, though not necessarily in harmony. The differences among them were all-inclusive, touching on every aspect of life, making it impossible for the three religions to be assimilated in any more than a purely superficial way. Toleration was officially sanctioned, but the likelihood of eventual social integration was remote, so long as the three groups lived according to different legal systems.[2]

Thus, in the years of Muslim dominance, Christians and Jews were tolerated minorities, enjoying the protection of the Islamic state but governed by laws totally different from those of the Muslims. The Mozarabic Christians, for example, still lived according to the Visigothic Code, administered by their own magistrates. When ascendancy passed to the Christians, they adhered to a similar policy of toleration, allowing Muslims and Jews to practice their respective religions and to use their own laws. In the minds of all, however, there was no question that the distinctions among the three religious groups would always remain.[3]

---

dalucía, 2d ed. (Seville, 1988), pp. 67–78. I want to thank González Jiménez for allowing me to read his manuscript, "Los mudejares andaluces (siglos XIII–XIV)," soon to be published with the proceedings of the V Coloquio de Historia Medieval Andaluza. His forthcoming *Diplomatario andaluz de Alfonso X* contains valuable documentation relative to the history of the Mudejars. María José Pimenta Ferro, "Judeus e mouros no Portugal dos séculos XIV e XV (Tentativa de estudo comparativo)," *Revista de Historia económica e social* 9 (1982): 75–89, is a sketch.

[2] Joseph F. O'Callaghan, *A History of Medieval Spain* (Ithaca, 1975); Jocelyn N. Hillgarth, *The Spanish Kingdoms, 1250–1516*, 2 vols. (Oxford, 1976–1978); Angus MacKay, *Spain in the Middle Ages: From Frontier to Empire, 1000–1500* (New York, 1977).

[3] Isidro de las Cagigas, *Minorías étnico-religiosas de la edad media española: Los mozarabes*, 2 vols. (Madrid, 1947–1948); Eliyahu Ashtor, *The Jews of Moslem*

After the disintegration of the Caliphate of Córdoba in 1031, as the kings of León, Castile, and (in the twelfth century) Portugal made significant advances in the reconquest, they were faced with the task of integrating large numbers of Moors (as the Spanish Muslims were commonly called) into their kingdoms. Those who submitted to Christian rule in this manner came to be known as Mudejars, a word derived from *al-mudajjan*, meaning "those allowed to remain."[4]

Surrender Agreements

In confronting the Moors, the Christian rulers adopted various policies, depending on the manner in which a town or fortress was brought under Christian rule. In some instances this was accomplished by assault, or else by blockade and siege, resulting in the eventual submission of a population on the verge of starvation. In the case of forcible conquest, the Christians were more likely to slaughter the defenders and to reduce the survivors to slavery. Thus when Fernando I of León-Castile (1035–1065) seized Viseu and Lamego in 1055, the Moors of Viseu were treated as booty, while in Lamego many were killed and others were compelled to labor in the repair of churches.[5]

When a city or large town was taken, it was often following a siege and negotiations whereby the defenders were persuaded to surrender. No surrender pacts (*pactum, pleitesía*) have come down to us, but the terms of many are reported by contemporary historians. Thus the Moors of Coimbra, after a siege of six

---

Spain, 2 vols. (Philadelphia, 1973–1979); Yitzhak Baer, *A History of the Jews in Christian Spain*, 2 vols. (Philadelphia, 1961); Thomas Glick, *Islamic and Christian Spain: Comparative Perspectives on Social and Cultural Formation* (Princeton, 1979).

[4] Fernández y González, *Estado social y político*, pp. 1–7, prefers *mudajalat*, i.e., one who entered into dealings with another; Cagigas, *Mudejares*, 1:58–64, and Robert I. Burns, *Islam under the Crusaders: Colonial Survival in the Thirteenth-Century Kingdom of Valencia* (Princeton, 1973), p. 64, favor *mudajjan*, recorded in Ramon Martí's thirteenth-century Arabic glossary.

[5] Justo Pérez de Urbel and Atilano González Rúiz-Zorrilla, eds., *Historia Silense* (Madrid, 1959), chaps. 86–87, pp. 189–90.

months, appealed to Fernando I, in July 1064, asking him to grant them their lives in return for the surrender of the city and all their goods. The king compelled all the Moors to depart beyond the river Mondego dividing Galicia and Portugal; another source recorded that more than five thousand Moors were sent into captivity.[6]

When Alfonso VI of León-Castile (1065–1109) took possession of Toledo on May 6, 1085, after a prolonged siege, he agreed that the Moors could remain in the city and retain their houses and possessions, provided that they served him as king and paid him the tributes previously owed to the Muslim rulers. Those who wished to leave could do so, taking their movable goods; if they should wish to return later, they would be allowed to do so. Despite this conciliatory policy, many of the Moors chose to abandon the city, hoping to return once the Almoravids triumphed over Alfonso VI. Although the king also assured the Moors of continued possession of the great mosque, they eventually were deprived of it.[7]

Christian expansion was halted for another generation as a consequence of the Almoravid invasion following the fall of Toledo. The disintegration of the Almoravid Empire, however, allowed Alfonso VII of León-Castile (1126–1157), who counted the Moorish king, Zafadola, among his vassals, to capture Oreja in October 1139; according to the terms of the *pactum*, the Moors, carrying their movable goods but leaving behind their arms and Christian captives, were given safe-conduct to Calatrava. The Moors of Coria, seeing that the Almoravids could not assist them, asked for terms and surrendered in June 1143, and the "city was cleansed of the barbarian people and of the contamination of Muḥammad."[8]

---

[6] *Historia Silense*, chaps. 87–90, pp. 189–94; *Chronicon Complutense*, in *España Sagrada*, ed. Enrique Flórez, 51 vols. (Madrid, 1754–1759), 23:317.

[7] Rodrigo Jiménez de Rada, *De rebus Hispaniae*, in *Opera*, ed. Francisco Lorenzana (Madrid, 1793; repr. Valencia 1968), bk. 6, chap. 22, pp. 135–36; Louis Barrau-Dihigo, ed., *Chronique latine des rois de Castille* (Bordeaux, 1913), chap. 2, p. 21; Julio González, *Repoblación de Castilla la Nueva*, 2 vols. (Madrid, 1975), 1:77–79; Bernard F. Reilly, *The Kingdom of León-Castilla under King Alfonso VI (1065–1109)* (Princeton, 1988), pp. 171–72, 183.

[8] Luis Sánchez Belda, ed., *Chronica Adefonsi Imperatoris* (Madrid, 1950), bk. 2, chaps. 151–54, 159–61, pp. 117–20, 123–25.

Meanwhile, Afonso I, the first king of Portugal (1128–1185), captured Santarém on the Tagus River on March 15, 1147, killing and expelling the Muslim inhabitants. With the aid of a northern fleet on its way to the Holy Land, he besieged Lisbon for nearly five months. The archbishop of Braga, sent to persuade the defenders to surrender, indicated that they would be permitted to retain their liberties and customs, "unless some of you may freely be added to the church of God." When the Moors surrendered on October 24, 1147, the *pactum* allowed them to depart, giving up their arms, gold and silver, horses and mules, and clothing. Even so the city was sacked and many were killed.[9]

These successes were checked by the arrival of the Almohads who reestablished the unity of Islamic Spain. After a half-century of armed struggle, Almohad rule began to break down following the Christian victory at Las Navas de Tolosa in 1212. As Christian forces advanced through the Campo de Calatrava, en route to Las Navas, they slaughtered the Moorish garrison in Malagón and accepted the surrender of Calatrava, whose defenders wished to escape a similar fate. After the battle of Las Navas, the Moors fled from Baeza, though some unwisely took refuge in the mosque where they were burned to death. The defenders of nearby Úbeda offered one million gold pieces if the Christians would leave them in peace, but the archbishops of Toledo and Narbonne opposed any compromise. Following a general assault, the city was taken and its inhabitants were enslaved. The Christians shortly abandoned both Baeza and Úbeda, which the Moors then reoccupied.[10]

The Christian triumph at Las Navas hastened the collapse of the Almohad Empire and opened Andalusia, Murcia, and the Algarve to conquest. The rapid advances made by Fernando III

[9] Charles David, ed. and trans., *De expugnatione Lyxbonensi: The Conquest of Lisbon* (New York, 1936), pp. 117–19, 173–81; Duodechinus, *Epistola ad Cunonem, abbatem in Montem Sancti Dysibodi*, in *MGH, Scriptores*, 17:28; Arnulfus, *Epistola ad Milonem, Episcopum Tarvanensem*, in *Recueil des historiens de la Gaule et de la France*, 14:327; *Annales D. Alfonsi Portugallensium regis*, in Monika Blöcker-Walter, *Alfons I von Portugal* (Zürich, 1966), p. 157.

[10] Jiménez de Rada, *De rebus Hispaniae*, bk. 8, chaps. 5, 12, pp. 180, 188–89; *Chronique latine*, chaps. 22, 25, pp. 63, 72; *Anales Toledanos I, ES*, 23:397.

of Castile-León (1217–1252) were due in part to the acceptance of his suzerainty by various Muslim leaders vying for supremacy in Al-Andalus. Among them were Abū Zayd, governor of Valencia, and his brother, Al-Bayasī, who controlled Baeza and Córdoba until he was assassinated in 1226 because of his close dependence upon the Christian king. Ibn Hūd of Murcia acknowledged Fernando III's overlordship as well, but he too was assassinated in 1238. Ibn al-Aḥmar, the first Naṣrid king of Granada, also became a vassal of Fernando III, promising to pay an annual tribute.[11]

The conquest of Andalusia was achieved in various ways. Some Muslim strongholds, such as Andújar (1225), were surrendered by agreement with their lords, but the Moors retained possession of their property. When other places, such as Quesada (1231), were taken by assault, the persons and goods of the defenders were treated as booty. The most important cities and towns, such as Baeza (1226), Úbeda (1233), Córdoba (1236), Jaén (1246), and Seville (1248), capitulated on specific terms (*pleitesía*), usually after a siege. When Úbeda surrendered, the Moors were permitted to leave, taking their movable goods under safe-conduct to Muslim territory. Three years later the Moors of Córdoba capitulated and were guaranteed a secure departure, carrying their belongings. Whatever property they left behind would be disposed of by the king, who endeavored to repopulate the city with Christians. Then the "patrician city was cleansed of the filth of Muḥammad," and the mosque was transformed into a cathedral. The bells of Compostela, which Almanzor (Al-Manṣūr) had carried off and placed in the mosque two hundred years before, were now returned to the Galician shrine. The small towns and villages depending on Córdoba simply acknowledged the king's sovereignty and so the inhabitants were able to remain in possession of their lands and goods.[12]

---

[11] Julio González, *Reinado y diplomas de Fernando III*, 3 vols. (Córdoba, 1980–1986), 1:319, 361–62; 2:244–45, 247–49, nos. 203, 205–6; Ramón Menéndez Pidal, ed., *Primera crónica general*, 2 vols. (Madrid, 1955), chap. 1070, 2:746.

[12] Jiménez de Rada, *De rebus Hispaniae*, bk. 9, chaps. 16–17, p. 206; *Chro-*

A few years later, in order to avert the threat of subjection by Ibn al-Aḥmar or perhaps by the emir of Tunis, the family of Ibn Hūd decided to accept Fernando III as their overlord and protector of their dominions in Murcia. As he was ill at the time, Fernando sent his oldest son Alfonso to receive the submission of the Murcian towns in 1243. In accord with the *pleitesía*, the Murcian lords, in return for protection, became vassals of Castile and surrendered half the public revenue to the king. Otherwise they continued to govern their towns as in the past, coining money and maintaining military forces. When the Moors of Mula, Lorca, and Cartagena offered resistance, Alfonso expelled them, but allowed some to remain in the suburbs.[13]

In 1246, after a long siege, Ibn al-Aḥmar agreed to the surrender of Jaén, promising to pay an annual tribute of 150,000 *maravedís*, to serve Fernando III in war and peace, and to attend his cortes. The Moors withdrew from the city, the mosque was transformed into a cathedral, and Christian settlers moved in. Two years later, after long negotiations, Seville capitulated. The Moors evacuated the entire city, leaving buildings and other property intact; taking their movable goods, money, and arms, they were given safe-conduct to Jerez or to Ceuta in North Africa. After three days the king entered the vacant city and the chief mosque was consecrated as a cathedral. Many of the towns in the surrounding countryside, including Alcalá de Guadaira, Carmona, Jerez, Arcos, and Medina Sidonia, by means of a *pleitesía* accepted Fernando III's authority while retaining their property, law, and religious liberty.[14]

As a consequence, the Christian reconquest of Andalusia was

---

nique latine, chaps. 64, 72–73, pp. 137, 147–49. For other instances of *pleitesías*, see *Primera crónica general*, chaps. 1057, 1063, 1069, 1072, 1076, 1077, 1090, 2:740, 743, 746, 748–49, 754; González Jiménez, *En torno*, pp. 25–29; Derek W. Lomax, *The Reconquest of Spain* (New York, 1978), pp. 142–47.

[13] *Primera crónica general*, chaps. 1060, 1065, 2:741–42, 744; González, *Fernando III*, 1:340–53; Antonio Ballesteros, *La reconquista de Murcia por el Infante Don Alfonso de Castilla* (Murcia, 1959).

[14] *Primera crónica general*, chaps. 1069–71, 1123–24, 1130, 2:746–47, 766–67, 770; González, *Fernando III*, 1:363–94; González Jiménez, *En torno*, pp. 25–28.

nearly complete. Some cities and towns were largely evacuated by the Moors, while elsewhere the Mudejars were still in the majority. Ibn al-Aḥmar, king of Granada, Ibn Hūd, king of Murcia, and Ibn Maḥfūt, king of Niebla to the west of Seville, all vassals of Castile, acknowledged Castilian suzerainty.

Farther west, the Portuguese under Sancho II (1223–1248) and Afonso III (1248–1279), aided by the military orders, completed the reconquest of Alentejo and the Algarve, but there is a paucity of information about the process. More than likely, when the Moors yielded castles, cities, and towns, many withdrew to other Muslim areas in Spain or in North Africa.[15]

Geographical Distribution of the Mudejars

Prior to the fall of Toledo in 1085, the Moors had either been expelled or had elected to abandon their settlements. Indeed, Muslim jurisconsults argued that the faithful were required to withdraw rather than to submit to Christian authority.[16] As the reconquest progressed from the Tagus river valley to the Guadalquivir, the Christians encountered an increasingly larger Muslim population. The policy adopted in Toledo, whereby the Moors had the option of remaining where they were under the protection of their Christian conquerors or of gathering their movable goods and withdrawing to still independent Muslim territory, was often implemented upon the surrender of other Muslim cities. Although the Crown needed workers to cultivate the fields and to continue the crafts and commerce that made the cities of Islamic Spain the great prizes that they were, many aristocrats, merchants, and well-to-do craftsmen

---

[15] Aleixandre Herculano, *História de Portugal desde o começo da monarquia até o fim do reinado de D. Afonso III*, 9th ed., 8 vols. (Lisbon, n.d.), vols. 4–5; Joaquim Veríssimo Serrão, *História de Portugal*, 2d ed., 2 vols. (Lisbon, 1978), 1:27–29, 137–40; H. V. Livermore, *A New History of Portugal* (Cambridge, 1966), pp. 70–71, 75, 80; A. H. de Oliveira Marques, *History of Portugal*, 2d ed., 2 vols. (New York, 1976), 1:63–65, 73–75.

[16] Cagigas, *Mudejares*, 1:65–70, citing an opinion of Ibn Rushd (Averroes) extracted by Al-Wansharīsī.

emigrated to the kingdom of Granada or to North Africa; others, perhaps chiefly agricultural workers, as well as the poor, the aged, and the infirm remained on their ancestral lands.

The scarcity of sources makes it difficult to do more than give an overall impression of the geographical distribution of the Mudejar population. In the eighth century the Moors had abandoned the northernmost reaches of the peninsula and the Duero Valley had remained a no-man's land for two hundred years before Christian repopulation began in earnest.[17] Fernando I, according to the chroniclers, had expelled the Moors beyond the Mondego River. The royal accounts for 1294 mention the *morerías* or Moorish communities in the kingdom of León, in the diocese of Palencia, and in the cities of León and Burgos.[18] The most recent studies of Burgos and Valladolid suggest that the Moorish population of the towns and the surrounding countryside was scant indeed.[19] Thus the Mudejar population in Galicia, Asturias, Leon, Old Castile, and northern Portugal apparently consisted of a few individuals or families in and around the principal towns.[20]

In Castilian and Leonese Extremadura, where the great municipalities were established, there is some evidence of the presence of small groups of Moors in the towns. Once again the royal accounts of 1294 refer to the *morerías* of the archdiocese of Toledo, the bishoprics of Ávila, Segovia, Plasencia, and Cuenca, and the towns of Coria, Madrid, Almoguera, Santa Olalla, Cauncis (?), and San Gil. In Ladero Quesada's judg-

[17] Juan Ignacio Rúiz de la Peña, "Siervos moros en la Asturias medieval," *Asturiensia medievalia* 3 (1979): 139–61; Claudio Sánchez Albornoz, *Despoblación y repoblación del valle del Duero* (Buenos Aires, 1966).

[18] Asunción López Dapena, *Cuentas y gastos (1292–1294) del Rey D. Sancho IV el Bravo (1284–1295)* (Córdoba, 1984), pp. 197–99, 636–37.

[19] Carlos Estepa Díez, "De fines del siglo IX a principios del siglo XIII," and Teófilo Rúiz, "El siglo XIII y primera mitad del siglo XIV," in *Burgos en la edad media*, ed. Julio Valdeón Baruque (Valladolid, 1984), pp. 51–52, 153–54, respectively; Adeline Rucquoi, *Valladolid en la edad media. Génesis de un poder*, 2 vols. (Valladolid, 1987), 1:230.

[20] José Leite de Vasconcellos, *Etnográfia portuguesa*, 4 vols. (Lisbon, 1933–1958), 4:335–36; Veríssimo Serrao, *História de Portugal*, 1:192–93; Oliveira Marques, *History of Portugal*, 1:79–80.

ment, the Mudejar population of these northern and central regions was not a remnant surviving from the conquest, but was probably the result of a northward emigration in the later twelfth and thirteenth centuries from the kingdom of Toledo. Although Alfonso VI in 1085 allowed the Moors to remain in Toledo and the other towns of the Tagus river valley, their situation deteriorated in the course of time, as the guarantees given in the capitulation were altered. As a consequence some Mudejars migrated northward, while others went southward to Andalusia or to the southeastern region where the *fuero* of Cuenca offered them security in their holdings as well as juridical equality with Christian settlers. Julio González concluded that the Mudejar population of Toledo was minimal and those mentioned in the documents tended to be persons of humble status.[21]

In the sparsely settled Guadiana river valley, La Mancha, the Campo de Calatrava, and the Alentejo, an area largely held in lordship by the military orders of Santiago, Calatrava, Alcántara and Avis, it is likely that only small pockets of Moors were found there, mainly in rural areas, as there were few towns of consequence. The *fuero* of Coria which was widely used in that region, however, offered a more advantageous situation to the Mudejars.[22]

In Andalusia, the Algarve, and Murcia, the picture changed remarkably. The number of major cities and towns was considerably greater and the Muslim population had always been densest there. Seville, Córdoba, Jaén, Faro, Loulé, Ayamonte, Mértola, Murcia, Lorca, and Cartagena were all well-populated towns, with many smaller towns dependent upon them.

Even though many Moors departed after the conquest of the

[21] López Dapena, *Cuentas y gastos*, pp. 197–99, 636–37; Rafael Ureña y Smenjaud, ed., *El Fuero de Cuenca* (Madrid, 1935), art. 11.19–23, pp. 314–16; Juan Gutiérrez Cuadrado, ed., *Fuero de Úbeda* (Valencia, 1979), tit. 2, p. 256; Juan Gutiérrez Cuadrado, ed., *El Fuero de Béjar* (Salamanca, 1975), arts. 14, 31–32, pp. 45, 48; Ladero Quesada, "Mudejares," pp. 259–70; González, *Repoblación*, 2:127–29, 132, 137.

[22] José Maldonado y Fernández del Toro, ed., *El Fuero de Coria* (Madrid, 1949); Ladero Quesada, "Mudejares," pp. 266–70.

great cities of Andalusia, still others remained in virtue of the surrender agreements. As the Moors were forced to vacate the city of Seville in 1248, Alfonso X gave the properties that they abandoned to the city council and authorized it to purchase others from Moors who wished to sell them.[23] In the years immediately following there are signs of the Mudejar presence, as settlers from other towns established their houses and shops in the center of the city, chiefly in the parishes of San Pedro, San Salvador, Santa Catalina, and San Isidro. The Mudejars also possessed a cemetery outside the walls. In the kingdom of Seville by virtue of *pleitesías* concluded with the Crown, Moors remained in Tejada, Sanlúcar, Guillena, Alcalá del Río, Alcalá de Guadaira, Marchena, Carmona, Arcos, Lebrija, Osuna, Cazalla, and Écija. In 1254 Alfonso X, anxious to strengthen the Christian position near the Granadan frontier, compelled the Moors of Morón to sell their houses and lands to Christian settlers and move to Silibar. Many towns in the kingdom of Córdoba, namely, Baena, Cabra, Luque, Almodóvar, Palma del Río, Rute, Aguilar, Santaella, Castro del Río, and Zuheros, also had a Mudejar population. On the upper Guadalquivir in the old Muslim kingdom of Jaén, there were Mudejar communities in Jaén, Alcaudete, Arjona, Porcuna, Jodar, and Zambra. Many Moors were settled in the countryside in small villages and on farms.[24]

The situation of the Andalusian Mudejars changed radically following their revolt in 1264. Two years before Alfonso X had seized Niebla, dispossessing the Muslim king, Ibn Maḥfūt, and forcing the Moors to evacuate the city. Then in 1263 the king expelled the Mudejars from Écija and initiated the Christian

[23] Fernández y González, *Estado social y político*, nos. 28 (June 21, 1253), 32 (March 28, 1254), pp. 334–36, 340; Manuel González Jiménez, Mercedes Borrero Fernández, and Isabel Montes Romero-Camacho, *Sevilla en tiempos de Alfonso X el Sabio* (Seville, 1987), pp. 79–80; Miguel Ángel Ladero Quesada, *Historia de Sevilla: La ciudad medieval*, 2d ed. (Seville, 1980), pp. 19–21.

[24] Antonio Ballesteros, *Sevilla en el siglo XIII* (Madrid, 1913), pp. 101–16; Julio González, *Repartimiento de Sevilla*, 2 vols. (Madrid, 1951), 2:308–12, 525–43; Manuel González Jiménez, "Orígenes de la Andalucía cristiana," in *Historia de Andalucía*, ed. Antonio Domínguez Ortiz, 8 vols. (Madrid, 1980–1981), 2:250–53; González Jiménez, *En torno*, pp. 69–70.

repopulation of the city.²⁵ Fearful of the steady encroachment of Castile upon the kingdom of Granada, Ibn al-Aḥmar incited the Mudejars of Andalusia and Murcia to rebel, probably in May 1264. While the Moors of Arcos, Lebrija, Medina Sidonia, and other towns responded to the call to arms, those of Jerez, who had been forced earlier to admit a Castilian garrison into the citadel, now ejected the enemy troops. In due course, Jerez, Vejer, Medina Sidonia, Rota, Sanlúcar, Lebrija, and Arcos were compelled to surrender, but Alfonso X determined that the secure retention of these frontier towns required the expulsion of the Moors and their replacement by Christians. Although the *Libro del repartimiento de Jerez* redacted after the surrender recorded the presence of twenty-seven Mudejar families there, they were newcomers from other areas of Andalusia, who were permitted to settle in the town by reason of a personal privilege granted by the king. The Mudejars also emigrated from Marchena, Carmona, and other towns of the regions surrounding Córdoba and Seville.²⁶

The continuance of hostilities between Castile and Morocco and Granada in the latter part of the thirteenth century and in the first half of the fourteenth century, until Alfonso XI's great victory at Salado in 1340, probably resulted in a continued decline of the Mudejar population. Consequently, González Jiménez and Ladero conclude that the Mudejars, save for a few enclaves here and there, disappeared almost entirely by the end of the thirteenth century. The royal accounts of 1294 reveal organized communities (*morerías*) in Seville, Córdoba, and Constantina, paying an annual tribute to the Crown. The sums indicate that these communities were greatly reduced in size and vastly inferior to the Jewish communities. The evidence of a Mudejar presence in the Andalusian towns from the second

[25] *Crónica de Alfonso X*, chap. 6, in *BAE*, 66:6; María José Sanz, "Repartimiento de Écija," *HID* 3 (1976): 542–50.
[26] *Crónica de Alfonso X*, chaps. 10–14, pp. 9–11; Manuel González Jiménez and Antonio Gómez González, *El libro del repartimiento de Jerez de la Frontera. Estudio y edición* (Cádiz, 1980), pp. lxxxi–lxxxiii, lxv–lxviii; González Jiménez, *En torno*, pp. 72–79; idem, *La repoblación de la zona de Sevilla durante el siglo XIV. Estudio y documentación* (Seville, 1975).

half of the thirteenth century on probably should be attributed to migration from other regions of Christian Spain, such as the Tagus river valley.[27]

The Moorish population in the vassal kingdom of Murcia was quite substantial, as little effort was made to displace the people after their initial submission to Fernando III in 1243. Many Moors apparently left Lorca, so that Alfonso X authorized Christians to purchase Moorish property there. At the same time, he assured the Moors of Aledo and other towns that he would observe the agreements (*pleitos, cartas de posturas*) that he had concluded with them.[28] The Murcian Mudejars, however, joined in the conspiracy with Granada against Alfonso X in 1264. Preoccupied with the subjugation of the rebels in Andalusia, he called upon his father-in-law, James I of Aragón, to assist him in suppressing the uprising in Murcia. In the fall of 1265 James I invaded the kingdom, forcing the Moors of Elche and other towns to submit. They were guaranteed possession of their houses and fields, the right to worship freely, and the right to be judged according to their own law by their own judges. The city of Murcia surrendered on similar terms at the end of January 1266 after a short siege. James I's only demand was that the Muslims give up the great mosque adjacent to the *alcazar* so that it could be transformed into a Christian church. After rewarding his followers with lands and castles and providing for the defense of Murcia, he returned to his own realm, restoring the city and kingdom to Alfonso X.[29]

---

[27] González Jiménez, "Orígenes," 2:254, 256; idem, *En torno*, pp. 72–79; idem, "La gran propieded en Andalucía del siglo XIII," *En la España medieval. Estudios dedicados al profesor D. Julio González González* (Madrid, 1980), pp. 143–55; Ladero Quesada, "Mudejares," pp. 271–75; López Dapena, *Cuentas y gastos*, pp. 122–23, 197, 635.

[28] Juan Torres Fontes, *Colección de documentos para la historia del reino de Murcia*, 5 vols. (Murcia, 1963–), 3:41, 43–45, 47–48, nos. 29, 30 (March 28, 1257), 32 (April 14, 1257); idem, *Repartimiento de Lorca* (Murcia, 1977), p. 65, no. 5 (October 2, 1260).

[29] J. M. Casacuberta and E. Bagüe, eds., *Crònica de Jaume I*, 9 vols. (Barcelona, 1926–1962), chaps. 379–93, 409–33, 439–56, 7:36–60, 82–98, 8:1–48; Juan Torres Fontes, *La reconquista de Murcia en 1266 por Jaime I de Aragón* (Murcia, 1965); Burns, *Islam*, p. 129.

"Recognizing the error that the Moors of Murcia committed against" Alfonso X, representatives of the *aljama* of Murcia renewed their allegiance to him on June 23, 1266, humbly asking his pardon, mercy, and favor. The king's brother, Infante Manuel, who was lord of Elche, allowed those who wished to depart to do so safely; those who remained were guaranteed their property, customs, and laws.[30]

The policy that Alfonso X followed in the reconstruction of the kingdom of Murcia was quite different from that of James I. Whereas the latter in effect had confirmed the status quo ante bellum, Alfonso X, concerned to eliminate the possibility of a Mudejar uprising in the future, decided to encourage extensive Christian settlement there. He ordered the Mudejars to evacuate the city of Murcia and to remove to the suburb of Arrixaca within forty days. In order to prevent Christians and Muslims from coming to blows, a wall was erected between the city and the suburb. Assigned half the municipal district, the Moors were also assured of religious liberty and the right to be governed by their own laws and customs. During the remaining eighteen years of Alfonso X's reign, the number of Christian settlers steadily increased, while the more well-to-do Mudejars emigrated to Granada or North Africa. Fernando IV in 1305 emphasized the paucity of Mudejars in the kingdom of Murcia when he reported that "the greater part of the Moors are dead and the others flown." As Juan Torres Fontes points out, the political and economic situation of those who remained was depressed, as they were mostly peasants, cultivating the soil and lacking prestige and authority.[31]

Thus it appears that in Andalusia and Murcia the Mudejar population suffered a steady attrition after the revolt of 1264. Pressured by efforts to establish a strong Christian presence there and threatened by the hazards of war on an increasingly

---

[30] *CODOM*, 2:21–22, 27–28, nos. 22 (August 20, 1265), 30 (June 23, 1266); Fernández y González, *Estado social y político*, pp. 361–62, no. 47.

[31] Juan Torres Fontes, "El estatuto concejíl murciano en la epoca de Alfonso X el Sabio," *CODOM*, 2:xxi–lxxvi; idem, *Repartimiento de Murcia* (Madrid, 1960), pp. v–xi; idem, *Repartimiento de Lorca*, pp. xxi–xxiv; Burns, *Islam*, pp. 145–46.

hostile frontier, those Mudejars who could do so opted to emigrate, leaving their less fortunate brethren behind.

The Juridical and Social Status of the Mudejars

Contemporary legal texts enable us to portray the juridical and social characteristics of the Mudejars, but one must keep in mind that in actuality the laws may not always have been enforced. More than likely there was always some disparity between the strictures of the law and the reality of daily life. There are few documentary indications concerning the application of these laws.

Municipal *fueros*, the law codes of Alfonso X, the enactments of the cortes, conciliar legislation, and individual charters often mention the Moors. Although most Castilian *fueros* refer to the Moors only incidentally, several charters (*forais*) were granted to Moorish communities in Portugal. In March 1170, for example, Afonso I granted a *foral* to the free Moors (*mouros forros*) of Lisbon, Almada, Palmela, and Alcácer, which became the model for the status of the Mudejars in that kingdom. Afonso II confirmed it in 1217. Afonso III granted essentially the same charter to the free Moors of Silves, Tavira, Loulé, and Faro in the Algarve in 1269, and four years later to those of Évora.[32]

Title 25 of *Partida* 7 is devoted to the Moors, but on the whole the Alfonsine law codes have much more to say about the Jews—surely a reflection of the greater numbers and influence of Jewish communities in the cities.[33] Also of importance

[32] *Portugaliae Monumenta Historica, Leges et Consuetudines*, 2 vols. in 3 pts. (Lisbon, 1856–1858; repr. Nendeln, Liechtenstein, 1967), 1:396–97, 715–16, 729–39.

[33] Real Academia de la Historia, ed., *Las Siete Partidas del Rey Don Alfonso el Sabio*, 3 vols. (Madrid, 1801; repr. 1972). There is no title on the Moors in the *Espéculo*, though it seems likely that one was included in one of the missing books of this code. The *Fuero Real* (4.2) has a title on the Jews but not on the Moors. For these codes, see Real Academia de la Historia, ed., *Opúsculos legales del Rey Don Alfonso el Sabio*, 2 vols. (Madrid, 1836); Dwayne Carpenter, "Alfonso el Sabio y los moros: Algunas precisiones legales históricas y textuales con respecto a *Siete Partidas* 7.25," *Al-Qantara* 7 (1986): 229–53.

is the *Leyes de moros del siglo XIV*, a compilation in Castilian (divided into 308 titles) of Islamic law relating to marriage, inheritance, sharecropping, sales, crimes, and the like.[34]

Freemen and Slaves

Broadly speaking, the Moorish population was divided into two classes, freemen and slaves. A third group, intermediary between the other two, were freedmen. Whatever their status, as Alfonso X pointed out, "the Moors who are in all our realms are ours and we have to guard and protect them and to have our rights from them in whatever place they may live."[35]

The subject Moors, whether in Castile or Portugal, were under the protection of the king who dealt directly with them. The charters granted by Afonso I in 1170 to the Moors of Lisbon and the adjacent towns, as well as those later issued by Afonso III to Évora and the towns in the Algarve were given to freemen.[36] Many of the Moors residing in the towns and forming part of the municipal *aljama* were freemen. The Mozarabic documents of Toledo in the twelfth and thirteenth centuries do not reveal any Muslims of distinguished rank, but do mention bricklayers, potters, and butchers.[37] There are references in 1260, for example, to the shopkeepers, artisans, and sharecroppers of Alicante. In Seville the names of a merchant (*trompero*) and a saddle maker (*albardero*) are known, and in Burgos a dyer sold houses in 1305. The master mason who

---

[34] *Leyes de moros del siglo XIV*, in "Tratados de legislación musulmana," in *Memorial Histórico Español*, ed. Pascual de Gayangos, 48 vols. (Madrid, 1851–1918), 5:428–48. Isa Jedih, *muftí* and *alfaquí* of the Moors of Segovia in 1462, compiled a *Suma de los principales mandamientos y devedamientos de la ley y çunna*, which he wrote in Castilian because the Castilian Moors had lost their Arabic schools.

[35] *CODOM*, 3:74–75, no. 55 (June 30, 1260); Galo Sánchez, ed., *El Fuero de Madrid* (Madrid, 1963), art. 96, p. 65.

[36] José Mattoso, *Identificação de um país. Ensaio sobre as origens de Portugal, 1096–1325*, 2 vols. (Lisboa, 1985), 1:371–75.

[37] Ángel González Palencia, *Los mozárabes de Toledo en los siglos XII y XIII*, 4 vols. (Madrid, 1929–1930), 1:151–52, 233–41.

built the castle of Alandroal for the military order of Avis in 1298 left an inscription testifying to his achievement.[38]

Those Moors who had the misfortune to be captured in battle or after a siege usually were reduced to slavery. The chronicles often refer to the number (often exaggerated) of Moors taken captive and enslaved during the wars of the reconquest.[39] Documentary evidence of the presence of *mauri captivi* in Asturias extends from the late tenth century to the middle of the twelfth century.[40] In Portugal the number of slaves increased during the twelfth-century invasions of the Almohads, but the supply of slaves was curtailed after the completion of the reconquest by the middle of the thirteenth century.[41] Hostilities along the frontier between Castile and Granada and in the Straits of Gibraltar continued to supply slaves and it is likely that some of them eventually were sold in Portugal. The Portuguese charters specified that the toll charged for the sale of a Moor should be half a *maravedí*; in Alicante in 1258 it was eight *burgaleses*.[42] Moorish slaves were considered as chattels to

[38] *CODOM*, 3:74–75, nos. 39, 55; Ballesteros, *Sevilla*, p. xlix, no. 44; Rúiz, "El siglo XIII y primera mitad del siglo XIV," p. 154; Leite de Vasconcellos, *Etnográfia portuguesa*, 4:315; González, *Repoblación*, 2:130–31.

[39] *Anales Toledanos I*, *ES*, 23:389, 397, capture of 10,000 in 1142, 60,000 in 1212 at the taking of Úbeda; *Chronicon de Cardeña*, *ES*, 23:373–74, capture of 17,000 in 1225; *Primera crónica general*, chap. 1076, 2:749, capture of 700; Ibn ʿIdhārī, *Al-Bayān al-Mugrib*, trans. Ambrosio Huici, 2 vols. (Tetuán, 1953–1954), 2:268–70, sale of 53 captives taken at Salé in 1260. See also Leite de Vasconcellos, *Etnográfia portuguesa*, 4:300–301; María del Carmen Carlé, *Del concejo medieval castellano-leonés* (Buenos Aires, 1968), pp. 55–56; Rafael Gibert, *El concejo de Madrid* (Madrid, 1949), p. 655; Heath Dillard, *Daughters of the Reconquest: Women in Castilian Town Society, 1100–1300* (Cambridge, 1984), pp. 21, 50, 105, 158.

[40] Rúiz de la Peña, "Siervos moros" pp. 141–43; Manuel González Jiménez, "Esclavos andaluces en el reino de Granada," in *Actas del III Coloquio de Historia medieval andaluza: La Sociedad medieval andaluza: Grupos no privilegiados* (Jaén, 1984), pp. 327–38; Charles Verlinden, *L'esclavage dans l'Europe médiévale: Péninsule ibérique. France* (Bruges, 1955).

[41] Mattoso, *Identificação*, 1:251–53; 373; idem, *Le monachisme ibérique et Cluny. Les monastères du diocèse de Porto de l'an mille a 1200* (Louvain, 1968), pp. 237–40.

[42] FSantarém (1179), FLisbon (1179), FCoimbra (1179), FMonforte (1257), FExtremoz (1258), FTerena (1262), FSilves (1266), FVillaviçosa

be bought and sold, as the many examples in the Mozarabic documents of Toledo reveal.[43] They could even be given in pledge. In 1284 sixty-four slaves from Aledo were given as a pledge for six thousand *maravedís*; fifty six of them were later sold.[44]

Many lords and religious houses owned slaves who performed household services for them or worked in the fields. Alfonso X, for example, commemorating his birthday on the feast of St. Clement, gave the convent of San Clemente in Toledo eight Moors for service.[45] In 1292 Mayor Petrez, a nun of San Clemente, with the consent of her abbess, emancipated her slave Fatima, who paid a fee for redemption. Until her mistress died, Fatima would remain in her service; if she were to flee and were caught, she would be enslaved again.[46] Owners were responsible for their slaves' actions and received any fines (*calumnia, coima*) for injuries inflicted upon them.[47] The *Siete Partidas* (3.18.90) contains a form letter of emancipation of a Moorish slave, his wife, and children, in return for one hundred gold *doblas*. Sometimes when slaves were freed, they became Christians but remained in dependence upon their former masters. The *fuero* of Sepúlveda (art. 248), for example, provided that if a Moorish freedman or freedwoman died without chil-

---

(1270), FCastro Marim (1277), *PMH Leges*, 1:407, 412, 416, 670, 680, 698, 706–8, 717, 734, 759; Juan Manuel del Estal, *Documentos inéditos de Alfonso X el Sabio y del Infante, su hijo Don Sancho* (Alicante, 1984), p. 181, no. 5.

[43] González Palencia, *Mozarabes de Toledo*, 2:231, 234–35, 265–67, 298, 318, nos. 630, 634, 664, 690, 703.

[44] *CODOM*, 2:76, no. 84; FZorita, art. 692, p. 308; FBéjar, arts. 928, 987–88, pp. 159, 165; González Palencia, *Mozarabes de Toledo*, 3:223, no. 934.

[45] *MHE*, 1:43, no. 22 (May 25, 1254); Fernández y González, *Estado social y político*, pp. 343–44, no. 34; Leite de Vasconcellos, *Etnográfia portuguesa*, 4:304–5; Mattoso, *Identificação*, 1:373–75. FBéjar, art. 946, p. 161, awarded a Moorish captive to the municipal chaplain and another to the scribe if they accompanied the host into battle.

[46] González Palencia, *Mozarabes de Toledo*, 3:67, no. 795; 3:55–67, nos. 785–94.

[47] FSepúlveda, art. 44, in *Los Fueros de Sepúlveda*, eds. Emilio Sáez et al. (Segovia, 1953), p. 77; FTomar (1174), FTorres Novas (1190), *PMH Leges*, 1:479; FCoria, arts. 97, 119, pp. 37, 45; Ladero Quesada, "Mudejares," p. 278.

dren, the former owner would inherit all the goods of the deceased. Slaves also sought freedom in flight. In the Portuguese towns the reward for finding a wandering slave was half a *maravedí*, and a Moor who had fled would suffer the loss of his foot.[48] If anyone stole or sold a Moor belonging to another, the *Fuero Real* (4.14.1) required that he be fined four times the value.

Moorish slaves sometimes were purchased so they could be exchanged for Christians who were held captive. The municipal *fueros*, as James W. Brodman has remarked, were much concerned with this method of ransoming captives. By providing that the price of a Moor purchased for this purpose should be only one-third of the usual amount, the *fuero* of Escalona (1130) tried to make it easier for parents to redeem their children in captivity.[49] As a further inducement, Alfonso VII declared in the *fuero* of Toledo (1118) that no toll (*portazgo*) should be collected when a Moor was purchased in order to redeem a Christian. Alfonso X applied this law to Alicante in 1252.[50] The *fuero* of Cuenca and several others of the same family did not levy the royal tax on booty (*quinto*) on Moors purchased for this reason.[51]

---

[48] FSepúlveda, art. 248, p. 149; FCoria, art. 400, p. 106; FSalamanca, art. 265; and FLedesma, art. 179, in *Fueros leoneses de Zamora, Salamanca, Ledesma y Alba de Tormes*, eds. Américo Castro and Federico de Onís (Madrid, 1916), pp. 173, 247; González Palencia, *Mozárabes de Toledo*, 1:243; González, *Repoblación*, 2:132–34; Leite de Vasconcellos, *Etnográfia portuguesa*, 4:343–45; Mattoso, *Identificação*, 1:373–75.

[49] James W. Brodman, "Municipal Ransoming Law on the Medieval Spanish Frontier," *Speculum* 60 (1985): 318–30; idem, *Ransoming Captives in Crusader Spain: The Order of Merced on the Christian-Islamic Frontier* (Philadelphia, 1986), pp. 1–8; FEscalona, in Tomas Muñoz y Romero, *Colección de Fueros municipales y cartas pueblas de los reinos de Castilla, León, Corona de Aragón y Navarra* (Madrid, 1847), p. 487; FBéjar, arts. 30, 927, pp. 47–48, 159; FÚbeda, tít. 6, p. 259; González Palencia, *Mozárabes de Toledo*, 1:246–47.

[50] Muñoz y Romero, *Colección de Fueros*, p. 364; *CODOM*, 3:17, 126, nos. 13 (October 5, 1252), 114 (August 20, 1271).

[51] FCuenca, art. 30.21, pp. 684–49; FAlarcón, art. 611; and FAlcaraz, art. 10.21, in *Les Fueros d'Alcaraz et d'Alarcón*, ed. Jean Roudil (Paris, 1968), p. 430; Jean Roudil, ed., *El Fuero de Baeza* (The Hague, 1962), p. 193; FBéjar, art. 915, p. 157; Rafael Ureña y Smenjaud, ed., *Fuero de Zorita de los Canes*

In order to encourage owners to sell their Moors for possible redemption of a Christian, the *fuero* of Cuenca and others gave the owner ten *maravedís* in addition to the sale price. The Leonese and Portuguese *fueros* specified that the price for captured Moors purchased before auction for purposes of exchange should be thirty *maravedís*, and after auction, one hundred. Otherwise, Moors could be bought privately at one and a half times their auction price. If it were not possible to effect the ransom, the former owner could buy back his slave if he wished.[52]

Social Restraints

Inasmuch as the Moors were regarded as an alien element in Christian society, steps were taken to curtail their contacts with Christians. In this respect, comparable regulations were enacted for both Moors and Jews; for example, municipal baths were segregated so that persons of different religious groups would not encounter one another in that intimate setting.[53] So that Christians could recognize Moors on sight and thus keep their distance from them, and in order to prevent the Moors from presenting themselves as persons of high social position, the cortes of Seville in 1252 (art. 40) forbade Moors living in Christian towns to wear certain types of clothing or certain col-

(Madrid, 1911), art. 628, p. 288. Alfonso VIII gave the military order of Santiago half the redemption of Moorish captives worth one thousand gold coins or more (March 10, 1190); Julio González, *El reino de Castillo durante la época de Alfonso VIII*, 3 vols. (Madrid, 1960), 2:931, no. 543.

[52] FCuenca, art. 30.21–23, pp. 648–49; FBéjar, art. 927, p. 159; FBaeza, art. 24, p. 60; FAlba de Tormes, art. 91, in *Fueros leoneses de Zamora, Salamanca, Ledesma y Alba de Tormes*, art. 91, p. 324; FCoria, arts. 125, 173, 251, pp. 46, 57, 75; Pedro Lumbreras Valiente, ed., *Los Fueros municipales de Cáceres* (Cáceres, 1974), art. 132; Rafael de Ureña y Smenjaud and Adolfo Bonilla y San Martín, eds., *Fuero de Usagre (Siglo XIII) anotado con las variantes del de Cáceres* (Madrid, 1907), art. 134, p. 50; see also the customs of Castel-Rodrigo, Alfaiates, Castello-Bom, and Castello Melhor in *PMH Leges*, 1:759, 765, 804, 889, 893–94, 932.

[53] James F. Powers, "Frontier Municipal Baths and Social Interaction in Thirteenth-Century Spain," *AHR* 84 (1979): 649–67.

ors such as white, red, and green, or white or gilded shoes, on penalty of thirty *maravedís* or imprisonment at the king's mercy. In addition, they were required to wear their hair cut about or parted, without a topknot (art. 40). The cortes of Valladolid in 1258 (art. 27) and Seville in 1261 (art. 30) repeated this, but added that Moors should wear long beards as required by their religion. The use of red stockings or gilded, white, or black scalloped shoes was prohibited by the assembly of Jerez in 1268 (art. 8) on penalty of one hundred *maravedís* for the first offense, and two hundred for the second.[54]

The law also attempted to safeguard Christian women from possible seduction by the Moors and to restrict social relationships that might otherwise have led to intermarriage between persons of different religions. No Christian woman was permitted to nurse a Moorish or Jewish child nor were Moorish or Jewish women to nurse Christian children, on penalty of ten *maravedís* for each day that this was done.[55] Extending these restrictions further, the assembly of Jerez in 1268 (art. 30) forbade a Christian woman to live with Moors or Jews or to serve them in any way, on penalty of being enslaved. Christian women who had intercourse with Moors were treated with great severity. In the case of a virgin or a widow, the *Siete Partidas* (7.25.10) stipulated that for the first offense, she would

---

[54] Antonio Ballesteros, "Las Cortes de 1252," *Anales de la Junta para Amplicación de Estudios e Investigaciones científicas* 3 (1911): 140; Ismael García Ramila, "Ordenamientos e posturas y otros capítulos generales otorgados a la ciudad de Burgos por el rey Alfonso X," *Hispania* 5 (1945): 219–20; Antonio López Ferreiro, *Fueros municipales de Santiago y de su tierra* (Santiago de Compostela, 1895), p. 385; Matías Rodríguez Díaz, *Historia de la ciudad de Astorga*, 2d ed. (Astorga, 1909), pp. 719–20; Real Academia de la Historia, ed., *Cortes de los antiguos reinos de León y Castilla*, 5 vols. (Madrid, 1861–1903), 1:59, 69. These regulations were repeated in the cortes of Palencia in 1313 (arts. 27, 35, 42), Burgos in 1315 (art. 24), Valladolid in 1322 (art. 54), and the assembly of Burgos in 1338 (art. 43), *CLC*, 1:225, 231, 244, 280, 353, 451; Ladero Quesada, "Mudejares," pp. 284–85.

[55] Ballesteros, "Las Cortes de 1252," p. 141; García Ramila, "Ordenamientos," p. 220; López Ferreiro, *Fueros municipales*, p. 385; cortes of Seville in 1261 (art. 25), Rodríguez Díaz, *Historia de la ciudad de Astorga*, p. 718; cortes of Valladolid in 1258 (art. 38), Jerez in 1268 (art. 31), Palencia in 1313 (art. 42), *CLC*, 1:62, 77, 244; FSepúlveda, art. 215, p. 134.

lose half her goods, while her lover would be stoned; for the second all her property would be confiscated and she would be executed. A married woman would be turned over to her husband to be burned, or repudiated, or punished in whatever way he wished. A prostitute and her lover would be whipped publicly, but executed after a second offense. The penalty of stoning, presumably to death, was considered sufficient to deter a Moor from engaging in such liaisons with Christian women.[56] By contrast, anyone who raped a Muslim woman escaped with his life but had to pay 10 percent of the fine due to a Christian victim of the same crime. In the *Cantigas de Santa María*, Alfonso X told of a Christian woman who committed adultery with a Moorish slave, but was saved from the flames by the Virgin Mary, while her paramour was totally burned.[57]

One final restriction should be noted. The assembly of Jerez in 1268 (art. 7), while proscribing certain types of clothing for Jews, also prohibited them from assuming Christian names. Although article 8 limiting the Moors manner of dress did not include the prohibition against the use of Christian names, it is likely that it was intended. The cortes of Palencia in 1313 (art. 42) made it explicit.[58]

Morerías and *Aljamas*

The Moors were dispersed in the country areas and in towns and cities. Where the urban population was large enough, they

[56] *CLC*, 1:77. FZorita, arts. 247, 272, pp. 146, 155, provided the penalty of burning for both the man and the woman and enslaved a Christian who had a child by a Moorish woman; FSepúlveda, art. 68, p. 89; FÚbeda, tit. 29.2, pp. 303–4; FBéjar, arts. 280, 317, 350, pp. 80, 85, 88. *Fuero Real* (4.11.1) legislated the death penalty for a Christian woman who married a Moor or a Jew. See also Afonso II's law of 1211 in *PMH Leges*, 1:178; Ladero Quesada, "Mudejares," p. 287; González, *Repoblación*, 2:132.

[57] FCuenca, art. 11.22–23, p. 316; FBaeza, art. 246, p. 105; FBéjar, art. 316, p. 85; FAlarcón, art. 231, p. 218; FAlcaraz, art. 4.22–23, p. 218; Alfonso X, *Cantigas de Santa María*, ed. Walter Mettmann, 2 vols. (Vigo, 1981), 1:601–3, no. 186; Dillard, *Daughters of the Reconquest*, pp. 188–90, 206.

[58] See also cortes of Burgos in 1315 (art. 24), Valladolid in 1322 (art. 54); *CLC*, 1:68–69, 244, 280, 352.

were organized in communities called *morerías* or *aljamas*. Though they may have tended to live in certain neighborhoods later known as *morerías*, laws restricting them to those districts were enacted only in the fifteenth century. In Toledo, for example, they were scattered among the Christians; nor did they occupy a separate quarter in Seville.[59] On the other hand, as already noted, Alfonso X ordered a wall erected in Murcia to separate the Moorish quarter, the Arrixaca, from the Christian population. Similar measures may have been adopted in other towns. In 1272 the king allowed the Moors to settle in Orihuela, but ordered a suburb (arrabal) beyond the bridge set aside where they could do so.[60] In Lisbon the Moors occupied a separate *arrabal dos mouros*. In many smaller places, where they were few in number, they probably were intermingled with the rest of the population.[61]

Where they were allowed to settle, the Moors were assured of security in their property holdings. Fernando III in 1222 promised the Moors settling in Tudejen near the Navarrese frontier security and whatever other rights they had elsewhere in the kingdom of Castile, provided they paid the customary tribute to the Crown. In the charter cited above, Alfonso X guaranteed the safety of the Moors coming to settle in Orihuela, together with their wives, children, and belongings. In the *Partidas* (7.25.1) the king affirmed the security of Moors living among Christians and forbade anyone to take anything

---

[59] Burns, *Islam*, pp. 145–46; González Palencia, *Mozarabes de Toledo*, 1:151–52; Gibert, *Madrid*, p. 68; González, *Repartimiento*, 1:365; idem, *Repoblación*, 2:130; González Jiménez, "Origenes," 2:250–51; González Jiménez et al., *Sevilla*, pp. 81, 83; Ladero Quesada, "Mudejares," p. 286; Carlé, *Concejo medieval*, pp. 55, 59–60.

[60] Rúiz, "El siglo XIII y primea mitad del siglo XIV," p. 153; Estal, *Documentos inéditos*, p. 104, no 2; Torres Fontes, "Estatuto concejíl murciano," *CODOM*, 2:xxi–lxxvi.

[61] King Dinis granted Fatima, "moura da rainha," a house in the *arrabal dos mouros*. Jorge Gaspar, "A cidade portuguesa na Idade media: Aspectos da estructura física e desenvolvimiento funcional," in *La ciudad hispánica durante los siglos XII al XVI*, eds. Emilio Sáez et al., 2 vols. (Madrid, 1985), 1:136. Pedro I of Portugal confirmed the separation of districts in the cortes of Elvas in 1361; Leite Vasconcellos, *Etnográfia portuguesa*, 4:328.

from them by force.⁶² While the king might extend his protection to the Moors in order to encourage their settlement in certain areas, their right to acquire property occasionally was curtailed for other reasons. In 1238, for example, Fernando III forbade the sale of property in Madrid to Moors, Jews, and religious orders because the revenues of the municipality were thereby depleted. This did not mean that they could not own property in Madrid, but rather that they could not acquire additional holdings. In the cortes of Valladolid in 1293 Sancho IV, in a measure probably directed primarily at the Jews, forbade Moors and Jews to acquire property once belonging to Christians and to sell what they had already acquired.⁶³

The *aljama* or *morería*, as the Mudejar community was called, had its own officials, with whom the Crown could treat of essential matters, independently of the government of the town where the Moors lived. For example, Ibn Sabah, *alcayde de Moros*, acting on behalf of the elders (*los vieios*) and the entire *aljama* of Morón, made an agreement in 1254 with the royal judge providing for the transfer of his people to Silibar. Manuel González Jiménez counts eight *aljamas* in the old kingdom of Jaén, fifteen in the kingdom of Córdoba, and twenty in the kingdom of Seville before the Mudejar revolt of 1264.⁶⁴ Alfonso X dealt with the *aljama* of the Moors of Alicante and recognized similar *aljamas* in the lands of his brothers Manuel and Luis in the kingdom of Murcia. Manuel's widow, Beatriz, settled a dispute in 1285 between the aljama of Elche and the

---

⁶² González, *Fernando III*, 2:181, no. 149; Estal, *Documentos inéditos*, p. 104, no. 2.

⁶³ González, *Fernando III*, 3:155, no. 622; *CLC*, 1:115 (art. 26 for Castile), 128 (art. 23 for León).

⁶⁴ Fernández y González, *Estado social y político*, pp. 346–48, no. 36. *Aljamas* in the kingdom of Seville: Seville, Marchena, Carmona, Écija, Morón-Silibar, Alcalá de Guadaira, Constantina, Matrera, Bornos, Osuna, Niebla, Gibraleón, Huelva, Saltes, Arcos, Lebrija, Cazalla, Chist. In the kingdom of Córdoba: Córdoba, Hornachuelos, Moratalla, Benamejí, Vierben, Baena, Luque, Cabra, Castro del Rio, Almodóvar, Santaella, Lucena, Zuheros, Rute, Aguilar. In the kingdom of Jaén: Cabra de Santo Cristo, Santiesteban, Porcuna, Alcaudete, Albendín, Baeza, Quesada, Andújar. González Jiménez, *En torno*, pp. 70, 187–90.

town council concerning water rights. The aljamas of the Extremaduran towns of Badajoz, Moura, Serpa, Valencia, Hornachos, Magacela, Benquerencia, and Alcántara, as well as others in the lands of the military orders, were cited in the chancery registers of Sancho IV for 1284/85.[65]

Thus, while they dwelled in Christian cities and towns, the Moors, organized in their own community or *aljama*, were always considered a people apart and did not participate in municipal government.[66] The principle, already established in canon law, that no non-Christian should have authority over Christians, effectively excluded Moors from any role in urban administration. In the *fuero* of Escalona in 1130 Alfonso VII affirmed that no Jew or Moor should sit as a judge in cases involving Christians. The *fuero* of Sepúlveda (art. 16b) denied the right of a Moor to be a toll collector (*portazguero*) or administrative agent (*merino*) in the town. Afonso II of Portugal similarly declared in 1211 that no Moor or Jew could be a royal fiscal agent (*ouençal*) or entrusted with any responsibility whereby Christians would be aggravated in any way. In like manner in 1271 Alfonso X refused to permit any non-Christian to hold office in Lorca.[67] While it is very clear that, despite these prohibitions, the king employed Jews in various official capacities (e.g., the tax farmer Zag de la Maleha), there seems to be no evidence that Moors were similarly engaged. As they were so often described as "enemies of the cross of Christ," it would have seemed especially objectionable if they were given any authority over Christians.

Just what authority the once independent kings of Murcia (who continued to be recorded as vassals confirming Castilian royal charters) exercised over their fellow Muslims is uncertain. ʿAbd Allāh, *rey de los moros del Arrixaca*, disposed of property

---

[65] *CODOM*, 2:78–79, nos. 87–88; 3:77, 156, nos. 59, 146; Mercedes Gaibrois de Ballesteros, *Historia del reinado de Sancho IV*, 3 vols. (Madrid, 1922), 1:153–54, 179–80.

[66] Gibert, *Madrid*, p. 66; idem, "Estudio histórico-jurídico," in Sáez, *Fueros de Sepúlveda*, p. 423.

[67] Muñoz y Romero, *Colección de Fueros*, pp. 485–86; *FSepúlveda*, art. 16b, p. 66; *PMH Leges*, 1:178; *CODOM*, 3:123, no. 114.

there in 1279, as did Ibrāhim Abū Isḥaq ibn Hūd, who bore the same title in 1295. The title "king of the Moors of the Arrixaca of Murcia," in any case, suggests that their authority was much more circumscribed than before.[68]

The ordinary magistrate in the *aljama* was the alcalde, a word derived from Arabic *al-qāḍī*, meaning "judge." Sometimes he was called *alcaide* or *alcayat*, both terms coming from *al-qā'id* ("military commander"). The similarity of the terms, even though their meanings were quite distinct, easily resulted in confusion in Christian minds. Although most Castilian texts refer to the *alcalde*, and the Portuguese to the *alcaide*, in practice their functions seem to have differed little.[69] Afonso I in 1170 allowed the free Moors of Lisbon, Almada, Palmela, and Alcácer to elect an *alcaide* to judge them and declared that no Christian should have any power to injure them. Afonso III repeated this in his charters to the free Moors of Silves, Loulé, Tavira, Faro, and Évora.[70] After the conquest of Seville, Fernando III appointed the *alcalde* of the Moors, ʿAbd al-Haqq al-Bayasī. Ibn Sabah was described in 1254 as the *alcayde* of the Moors of Morón. The names of other *alcaldes* of the Andalusian Moors are also known.[71]

Litigation

The Moorish *alcaldes* were responsible for administering justice among the Mudejars. Alfonso X reminded the citizens of Cartagena in 1257 that pleas between Moors resident in the city should be adjudicated by the *alcalde moro*, but if he did not do

---

[68] *CODOM*, 2:64–65, 108–9, nos. 69, 110.

[69] González, *Repartimiento*, 1:310; Burns, *Islam*, pp. 368–73.

[70] *PMH Leges*, 1:396, 715–16, 729–30; Leite de Vasconcellos, *Etnográfia portuguesa*, 4:306–9.

[71] Ibn Khaldūn, *Histoire des Berbères*, trans. Baron de Slane, 4 vols. (Paris, 1852–1856), 2:322; Fernández y González, *Estado social y político*, pp. 346–48, no. 36. Other Moorish *alcaldes* were Suleman of Carmona; Hamet aben Pasay of Alcalá de Guadaira; Ali el Gordo of Rute; Hamet aben Xayt of Santaella; Aboambre and Aben Porcoz of Écija. The *algayeci* of Cabra and the *alcalde* of Osuna are mentioned but not named. González Jiménez, *En torno*, pp. 69–70.

so, the communal *alcaldes* should compel him. In some cities such as Burgos, where the Moors did not have their own judges, the municipal *alcaldes* had jurisdiction over their suits, as Sancho IV declared in 1293. The same principle was applied in litigation between Moors and Christians. Establishing the policy that would be followed in the future, Alfonso VII, in the *fuero* given to Toledo in 1118, commanded that pleas between Christians and Moors or Christians and Jews should be heard by a Christian judge. This principle was subsequently applied in Andalusia, where the *fuero* of Toledo was granted to Córdoba and other cities, and also in the kingdom of Murcia. Alfonso X assured the citizens of Alicante (1252) and Lorca (1271) that only a Christian judge had jurisdiction over litigation between Christians and Moors.[72] Although the Portuguese customs of Santarém and Beja provided that in such instances the Moorish litigant should make his case before the Christian judges, the *alcayde dos mouros* was also expected to be present. It is not likely that the Muslim and Christian judges were intended to share jurisdiction equally, but the Moor who was party to the suit would have the comfort and possible assistance of a Muslim judge.[73]

Alfonso X forbade Mudejars to act as attorneys or advocates except in cases involving members of their own religious group. A law attributed to Afonso III of Portugal, while admitting the right of Moors to give testimony in suits involving other Moors, forbade them to be procurators, advocates, or witnesses in suits in which only Christians were participants.[74]

In cases involving members of different religious groups, the law usually required proof by witnesses representing each reli-

---

[72] Sancho IV's order was confirmed by Fernando IV in 1295 and 1314. Emiliano González Díez, *Colección diplomática del concejo de Burgos (884–1369)* (Burgos, 1984), pp. 245–48, 280–81, nos. 153–54, 168; Muñoz y Romero, *Colección de Fueros*, p. 366; Estal, *Documentos inéditos*, p. 170, no. 2.4; *CODOM*, 3:17, 57–58, 126, nos. 13, 40, 114; Ladero Quesada, "Mudejares," p. 281.

[73] *PMH Leges*, 2:24, 71–72.

[74] *Espéculo*, 4.9.2; *Fuero Real*, 1.9.4; *Partidas* 3.6.5; *PMH Leges*, 1:307–10; FLedesma, art. 176, p. 247; FSalamanca, art. 259, p. 170.

gion, but the inferior status of the Muslims was manifest. The *fuero* of Sepúlveda (art. 70), for example, stipulated that in a civil action, the oath of a Christian should be supported by two Christians and a Moor, or by two Moors and a Christian, or by three Moors. A Moor, conversely, should be aided by two Christians and a Moor, or three Christians (but not by two Moors and a Christian). In the same manner, two Christians and a Moor were necessary to prove that a Christian had committed a crime against a Moor (art. 40) or that a Moor had injured a Christian (art. 41). Alfonso X, in a charter given to Cartagena in 1257, set down similar requirements. In the *Espéculo* (4.7.5) and the *Partidas* (3.16.9), he ordered that neither a Moor nor a Jew nor a heretic could be a witness against a Christian, unless he could personally testify concerning an affair for which there were no Christian witnesses, or in a case of treason in which he personally participated.[75]

When a Moor appeared in court, he was required to swear an oath in the form prescribed by Alfonso X in the *Espéculo* (5.11.17). Standing with his hands raised and facing the south, the Moor swore his oath at the door of the mosque in the presence of a court official. Confessing that there was no God but God, the omniscient Creator, he swore by the truth revealed to Muḥammad, God's prophet and messenger; and should he lie, he called down upon himself the penalty of eternal separation from God and Muḥammad and exclusion from paradise.[76]

As a practical example of Muslim oath-taking, one can mention the assistance given in 1263 by former Muslim residents of Écija to the Christian authorities who wished to mark off the boundaries of the municipal district. "The Moors swore by their *alquabla* that they would tell the truth in this matter." The word *alquabla* or *al-ḳibla* referred to the direction of Mecca,

---

[75] FSepúlveda, arts. 40–41, 42a, 68–70, pp. 74–75, 89; *PMH Leges*, 1:310; 2:20, 30; *CODOM*, 3:57–58, no. 40; Ladero Quesada, "Mudejares," p. 280.

[76] The text of the oath was repeated in the assembly of Jerez (1268), art. 47, *CLC*, 1:84; in the *Leyes nuevas*, art. 29, given to Burgos by Alfonso X; and in the *Ordenamiento de las Tafurerías*, art. 41, *Opúsculos legales*, 2:196, 230–31; *Partidas*, 3.11.21.

toward which Muslims were accustomed to turn when they prayed or took part in other solemn ceremonies.⁷⁷

Monetary penalties were imposed for crimes such as homicide, physical injuries of various sorts, rape, and robbery committed by Moors against Christians or vice versa. The life and the body of a Christian were usually valued more highly than those of a Muslim. The *fuero* of Nájera in 1076 fixed the fine for killing a Moor at twelve and a half *solidi*, half the cost of a cow and equal to that of an ass, while the *fuero* of Zorita (art. 243) required half the fine that one would pay if a Christian were wounded or killed. On the other hand, the *fuero* of Béjar ranked the death of a Moor with that of a Christian. If a Moor killed a Christian, he was subject to whatever fines the Christian wished to impose and his body was placed at the disposal of the victim's heirs.⁷⁸

The *Leyes del estilo*, compiled in the late thirteenth to early fourteenth century for use in the Castilian royal court, stipulated that the fine for killing a Moor should be in accordance with local custom, but should not be as great as the fine for killing a Christian. If no sum were specified, then the penalty would be death or expulsion from the realm as determined by the king (art. 84). If the dead body of one of the king's Moors were found within the municipal boundaries, the town government would have to pay a homicide fine of one thousand *maravedís* to the Crown. If the body were that of a free Moor be-

---

⁷⁷ María Josefa Sanz Fuentes, "Repartimiento de Écija," *HID* 3 (1976): 543: "E otrosy los moros juraron por su alquabla que dirian verdad sobre este fecho." A. J. Wensinck, "Kıbla," in *Shorter Encyclopedia of Islam*, eds. H. A. R. Gibb and J. H. Kramers (Leiden–Ithaca, 1974), pp. 260–61.

⁷⁸ FNájera, in Muñoz y Romero, *Colección de Fueros*, p. 290; FBéjar, arts. 313–15, 398, pp. 85, 93; FZorita, arts. 243–46, p. 145; FSepúlveda, arts. 40–43, pp. 74–76. See also FAlba de Tormes, arts. 89–90, pp. 323–24; FLedesma, arts. 29–30, p. 221; FSalamanca, arts. 60–61, 109–10, pp. 102, 119–20; FMadrid, art. 68, p. 59; FBaeza, arts. 243–45, pp. 104–5; FÚbeda, tit. 26, pp. 299–300; FCoria, arts. 120–21, 123, pp. 45–46; FUsagre, arts. 128, 130, 132–33, pp. 49–50; FAlarcón, arts. 229–30, 296, pp. 218, 245; FAlcaraz, arts. 4.19–21, 4.92, pp. 218, 246; Customs of Castello-Bom, Castel-Rodrigo, Castello Melhor, *PMH Leges*, 1:759, 864, 910; González, *Repoblación*, 2:132, 137.

longing to the *aljama*, this fine would not be exacted unless required by royal charter (art. 103).[79]

Tributes

The Mudejars were required to pay a variety of tributes to the Crown.[80] Most common was an annual capitation tax (*pecho de los moros, alfitra, alfitrán*) payable by everyone. Afonso I of Portugal in 1170 set the amount at one *maravedí* for the Moors of Lisbon, Almada, Palmela, and Alcácer, but they also owed one-tenth of their produce and were required to work in the royal vineyards. When Afonso III received the surrender of Faro in 1249, he assured the Moors who remained that they would be obliged to pay only the tributes owed to the previous Moorish kings.[81] In 1260 Alfonso X fixed the tax at one *maravedí* for Moorish sharecroppers, shopkeepers, and craftsmen in Alicante, but at one-half for those who made their living from the sea.[82] Andalusian documentation indicates that, besides the capitation tax, the Moors paid the Crown a tax on land (*almarjal*), and one-tenth of the harvest (*diezmo*). In 1254 the king granted the tenth owed by the Moors of the diocese of Córdoba to the cathedral chapter. The Moors may also have owed regular labor services. Alfonso X, for example, required the Moorish craftsmen of Córdoba to work on the cathedral two days a year.[83] On occasion, he also levied an extraordinary tax

---

[79] *Leyes del estilo*, in *Opúsculos legales*, 2:274, 280–81.

[80] Alfonso VIII, to encourage Moors to settle in Deza, required them to pay one-fifth of the harvest each year and two *mencales* in March for *fonsadera*, but otherwise they were exempt from tribute (González, *Alfonso VIII*, 3:637, no. 947).

[81] *PMH Leges*, 1:396; 2:98–100; Leite de Vasconcellos, *Etnográfia portuguesa*, 4:306–9, 319, 322, 328.

[82] *CODOM*, 3:74–75, no. 55. The Moors of Seville in 1253 owed "el pepion que daban por su cabeza cada dia en mi alfandega." González Jiménez, *En torno*, p. 70.

[83] González Jiménez, *En torno*, pp. 70–72; *MHE*, 1:33–36, I, no. 18.

upon the Moorish and Jewish communities, as, for example, the *oncenas* (eleventh) imposed in 1252.[84]

In the cortes of Seville in 1252 (art. 41), Alfonso X declared that no one was authorized to exempt the Moors from taxation, but from time to time he ceded Moorish tributes owed to the Crown to the municipalities. In 1254, for example, he granted five hundred *maravedís* from their annual tribute payable at Michaelmas to Córdoba for the repair of the city walls. Two years later he gave the tenth owed by the Moors of Alicante to the town council; in 1261 for the maintenance of the walls he gave the town the poll tax of one *maravedí* payable by the Moors at Martinmas. A similar concession was made to Orihuela in 1274. Sancho IV in 1285 allowed the military order of Santiago to retain the tributes owed by the Mudejars settled on its domains. Four years later he gave one-tenth of the tribute of the Moors and Jews to the see of Cartagena.[85]

The Crown's total income from Mudejar tributes is unknown, though there are some indications of amounts paid by specific places. Sancho IV's accounts for the half-year from December 1293 to June 1294 reveal the following sums: Seville, 8000 *maravedís*; Córdoba, Constantina, and other Andalusian towns, 5000; Madrid, 1300; Burgos, 1092; Coria, 569; León, 480; Santa Olalla, 423; and Almoguera 414. The Moors in the diocese of Palencia owed 5692 *maravedís*, and those in the dioceses of Ávila and Segovia taken together, 6705. The accounts for the year ending in November 1294 show that the Moors of Seville paid a tribute of 5500 *maravedís*, those of Córdoba 2000, and those of Constantina 1150, but these were the only towns on the Andalusian frontier for which an amount was recorded. The total reported for Córdoba may not have included the 500 *maravedís* from the tribute payable by the *aljama* at

---

[84] Fernández y González, *Estado social y político*, p. 333, no. 27; *MHE*, 1:4–5, no. 3 (January 20, 1253).

[85] Ballesteros, "Las Cortes de 1252," p. 141; *CODOM*, 3:35, 57, 74–78, 148, nos. 23, 39, 55, 59–60, 135; *MHE*, 1:25–26, no. 14; Fernández y González, *Estado social y político*, p. 339, no. 31; Gaibrois, *Historia*, 3:lxii–lxiii, clxx–clxxi, cxcviii, nos. 95, 279, 313; Carlé, *Concejo medieval*, pp. 59–60; Ladero Quesada, "Mudejares," p. 283.

Michaelmas that Alfonso X promised to the city in 1254. Given this and other alienations, the royal revenue from the Mudejar tribute was apparently not very great. In any case, the figures suggest the relative size of the Moorish communities in different regions. Amounts are also given for the combined Jewish and Moorish communities of the archdiocese of Toledo, the kingdom of León, and the dioceses of Plasencia and Cuenca, but there is no way of determining the relative contribution of each community. In all probability, most of that money was paid by the Jews. As the Moors generally paid a much smaller tribute than the Jews, it is likely that the Jewish population was much more numerous.[86]

Religious Freedom

Religious liberty was a right guaranteed to the Mudejars, though its practical exercise was clearly circumscribed and sometimes difficult. The *Siete Partidas* (7.25) described the Muslims as "a people who believe that Muḥammad was the Prophet and Messenger of God," but as his works did not reveal the great holiness characteristic of that state, "his religion (*ley*) was, as it were, an insult to God." Despite that, the law provided that "Moors should live among Christians in the same manner . . . as the Jews ought to do, observing their religion (*ley*) and not insulting ours." The law's stipulation, however, that they were not "to make their sacrifices publicly before men" suggests a certain ignorance of Muslim practice. The law did not permit the Moors to have mosques in Christian towns. Indeed, the mosques were declared to belong to the king who could give them to whomever he wished. Even though the Moors "do not have a good religion (*ley*)," while they lived

---

[86] López Dapena, *Cuentas y gastos*, pp. 197–99, 635–36; Gaibrois, *Historia*, 3:cccxcvi, no. 583; *MHE*, 1:25–26, no. 14; Fernández y González, pp. 339–40, no. 31; Miguel Ángel Ladero Quesada, "Las transformaciones de la fiscalidad regia castellano-leonesa en la segunda mitad del siglo XIII (1252–1312)," in *Historia de la hacienda española. Homenaje al Profesor García de Valdeavellano* (Madrid, 1982), p. 335; González, *Repartimiento*, 1:365.

among Christians they were assured of security in their property. Nevertheless, there was always a disparity between the rigors of the law and its execution.

In all of the principal cities the Mudejars were compelled to surrender the chief mosque to the Christians who then transformed it into a cathedral. Archbishop Rodrigo recorded that Alfonso VI assured the Moors of Toledo in 1085 that they might retain possession of the chief mosque, but during his absence, the newly installed Archbishop Bernard, abetted by Queen Constanza, seized the mosque. When the king discovered this, he was exceedingly angry but the Muslims dissuaded him from punishing the archbishop, lest they suffer later. Ladero Quesada thinks that this story is probably inaccurate, but Bernard F. Reilly suggests that after the failure of the king's initial policy of conciliation, he may have decided to deprive the Muslims of the mosque and left it to the queen and the archbishop to do so.[87]

In Córdoba, Jaén, and Seville, the principal mosque was similarly transformed. Alfonso X gave all the mosques in Seville, except three in the Jewish quarter (which were turned into synagogues), to the archbishopric.[88] The Mudejars of Murcia, nevertheless, retained their mosque next to the royal *alcazar* until James I of Aragón required them to surrender it after his conquest of the city in 1266. When they objected, he queried, "Do you think it proper that you should have the mosque at the gate of the *alcazar* and that I, when I am asleep, should have to hear in my head the cry, 'Allah lo Sabba o Allah?' " Some years later Sancho IV emphasized that the see of Cartagena was to have all the mosques in the diocese, as was the case in the archdiocese

[87] Jiménez de Rada, *De rebus Hispaniae*, bk. 6, chap. 24, pp. 137–38; Al-Maqqari, *The History of the Mohammedan Dynasties in Spain*, trans. Pascual de Gayangos, 2 vols. (London, 1840–1843), 1:264; Ladero Quesada, "Mudejares," p. 266; Reilly, *Kingdom of León-Castilla*, pp. 171, 182–83; González, *Repoblación*, 2:128–29, 137.

[88] Jiménez de Rada, *De rebus Hispaniae*, bk. 9, chap. 17, p. 206; *Chronique latine*, chap. 73, p. 149; *Primera crónica general*, 2:747, 767, chaps. 1071, 1125; *Chronica Adefonsi Imperatoris*, p. 125; González Jiménez et al., *Sevilla*, p. 84.

of Seville.⁸⁹ When Lisbon was taken in 1147 the principal mosque was transformed into a cathedral, but the Moors apparently later had two mosques, one larger than the other. There and in other places they seem also to have possessed cemeteries outside the city walls.⁹⁰ As the dispersal of the community in rural areas created obvious difficulties for formal worship, it is doubtful that there were mosques outside the towns.

The prohibition of public sacrifice and James I's objection to the call of the muezzin indicate that outward manifestations of the Islamic religion were forbidden. Moreover, the Mudejars were strictly enjoined not to insult the Christian religion in any way. In the cortes of Seville in 1252, Alfonso X declared that when priests carried the eucharist through the streets Jews and Moors had to give way and conceal themselves or fall to their knees until the procession had passed.⁹¹ Any Jew or Moor playing with dice, who spoke wrongly of God or the Virgin Mary or of other saints, would suffer the lash, and upon the third offense would have his tongue cut out. Forbidding Moors and Jews to spit on the cross or the altar, to deface paintings or images, or to throw stones at churches, Alfonso X explained that, just as the Moors prohibited Christians in their dominions to insult Muḥammad or his religion, it was only right that the Jews and the Moors "whom we permit to live in our realm, though they do not believe in our faith," should be punished in a similar manner (*Partidas* 7.28.56). Afonso III of Portugal similarly forbade Moors to do violence to churches.⁹²

Although the Mudejars were assured of security in their property, their right to acquire additional lands brought with it an unexpected financial burden, namely, the obligation to pay

---

⁸⁹ *Crònica de Jaume I*, 8:34, chap. 445. Charters of 1266–1267 indicate that the mosque of Murcia belonged to the see of Cartagena; *CODOM*, 2:29–31, nos. 32–34; Gaibrois, *Historia*, 3:lxv, no. 100 (December 14, 1285).

⁹⁰ David, *De expugnatione Lyxbonensi*, pp. 180–81; Leite de Vasconcellos, *Etnográfia portuguesa*, 4:338; González, *Repartimiento*, 1:365.

⁹¹ Vicente Argüello, "Memoria sobre las monedas de Alfonso el Sabio," *Memorias de la Real Academia de la Historia* 8 (1952): 33, no. 25.

⁹² *Ordenamiento de las Tafurerías*, art. 1, in *Opúsculos legales*, 2:216–17; *PMH Leges*, 1:329; 2:16 (Foro de Granda, prohibiting Moors to labor on Sunday); Ladero Quesada, "Mudejares," p. 292.

tithes on lands that had formerly belonged to Christians. However incongruous it may seem, the primary reason for this was economic rather than religious; the transfer of lands from Christian to Moorish hands ordinarily would mean a decrease in episcopal revenues from the tithe. Thus, the bishop of Ávila protested to Innocent III, who, in order to counteract this loss, declared in 1199 that Moors who acquired lands from Christians should continue to pay the tithe.[93] When the Mudejars of Palma, Castro, and Almodóvar tried to evade payment of the tithe in 1260 the king refused to exempt them. The bishop and chapter of Cartagena in 1271 demanded that Alicante pay the tithe on the tenth of the Moors which the king had earlier ceded to the town, but he objected.[94]

Aside from these impediments to the free exercise of their religion, the Mudejars were also effectively denied any possibility of propagating their faith by winning converts. The ban on any public display of religion and the restraints on sexual and social relations between Moors and Christians were intended to create obstacles to proselytization. The law, furthermore, made it extremely dangerous for anyone to convert to Islam (or Judaism). If perchance a Christian, losing "his sense and true understanding," committed "the very great treason" of becoming a Muslim, he would suffer the harshest penalties of the law. Not only would his property be confiscated, but if he remained in Christian territory, he would lose his life as well, as the law declared: "let him die for his error" (*Partidas* 7.25.5). The *Fuero Real* (4.1.1) put this more bluntly when it specified that an apostate should be burned to death. Should he return to the faith, he would endure the punishment of eternal infamy, banned from giving testimony, holding public office, making a will, receiving an inheritance, or concluding a contract of sale. Occasionally a person became a Muslim in order to do "some great service to the Christians that would redound to the great

---

[93] In 1177 Alfonso VIII required the Moors and Jews of Valladolid to pay a tithe to the bishopric of whatever lands they acquired there. González, *Alfonso VIII*, 2:472–73, no. 287; Demetrio Mansilla, *La documentación pontificia hasta Inocencio III (965–1216)* (Rome, 1955), p. 208, no. 193.

[94] González Jiménez, *En torno*, p. 72; *CODOM*, 3:35, 113, no. 103.

advantage of the realm." This may refer to someone who converted in order to spy on the king's Muslim enemies. Such a person would not be subject to the death penalty and if he returned to the faith, the penalties of infamy and confiscation would be removed and he would be restored to all the honors enjoyed by other Christians (*Partidas* 7.25.4–8).

The Mission to Islam

Hispanic Christians seem not to have made any concerted effort to convert the subject Moors. Expelled from cities or allowed to remain provided that they rendered loyal service to the Crown, the Mudejars were left undisturbed, for the most part, in their religious belief. Kings and bishops made no significant attempt to convert them. Royal policy did not see assimilation of the Muslims into Christian society as a primary goal. In its concern to maintain a settled population in territory acquired from the Muslims, the monarchy was willing to guarantee the subject people both the right to worship freely and to live according to their own laws. Uprooting the Muslims entirely or compelling them to become Christian at first did not seem to serve the needs of the Crown; only after the rebellion of 1264 did Alfonso X attempt to be rid of the Mudejars, but he did not require them to convert.

Some exceptional cases of conversion are recorded. Zaida, the daughter in-law of Al-Muʿtamid, king of Seville, became the concubine of Alfonso VI and apparently accepted Christianity. Abū-l-Qasim, the *alfaquí* of Toledo, converted when the city was taken in 1085.[95] In the *Cantigas de Santa Maria* Alfonso X attributed some conversions to the intercession of the Virgin Mary. In one instance a Moorish woman became a Christian when the Virgin brought her dead child back to life.

---

[95] Jiménez de Rada, *De rebus Hispaniae*, bk. 6, chap. 30, p. 143; Reilly, *Kingdom of León-Castilla*, pp. 234–35; Evariste Lévi-Provencal, "La Mora Zaida, femme d'Alphonse VI et leur fils l'Infant Don Sancho," *Islam d'Occident: Études d'histoire médiévale* (Paris, 1948), pp. 137–51; González, *Repoblación*, 2:127, n. 299.

A Moorish slave, possessed by a demon, was delivered by the Virgin and was baptized.[96]

More than likely when there was only a handful of Moors in a Christian community, as was probably the case in the northern parts of the peninsula, conversion or assimilation was inevitable, as the Moors opted to conform to the life-style of their neighbors. An eleventh-century text from the monastery of Sobrado suggests how this may have happened. The monks purchased several Moors, identified by their Arabic names and the Christian names they adopted after baptism and by their occupations (carpenters, ironworkers, textile workers, etc.). There is no indication whether they were compelled to be baptized, but they probably decided that their lives would be easier if they accepted Christianity.[97] Stipulations in the municipal *fueros* safeguarding an owner's right to inherit the property of a converted Moor who died without children, imply that some Moors were induced to become Christians by the promise of freedom.[98] Indeed, the Portuguese *foral* of Freixo (1152) declared that the "Moor or the slave who becomes a Christian and comes to Freixo will be free."[99] The names of many persons (Petrus Maurus, Melendus Maurus, Pelagius Maurus, etc.) in northern Portugal in the early thirteenth century indicate that they or their antecedents had converted, perhaps because of social pressures and the difficulty of maintaining religious practice without an organized community. Most of them were farmers cultivating their own land or tenants. Several of them were parish priests (e.g., Stephanus Maurus, Martinus Maurus). Juan Ordoñiz, "olim sarracenus et modo iam conversus ad fidem," who managed a vineyard for the dean of Oviedo in

[96] *Cantigas de Santa María*, 1:556–57, 615–19, nos. 167, 192.

[97] Eduardo de Hinojosa, *Documentos para la historia de las instituciones de León y de Castilla (Siglos X–XIII)* (Madrid, 1919), pp. 43–45, no. 28.

[98] FCuenca, art. 9.12, p. 254; FBéjar, art. 222, p. 72; FÚbeda, tit. 20.1, pp. 285–86; FAlarcón, art. 167, p. 177; FAlcaraz, art. 3.72, p. 177; González, *Repoblación*, 2:134–35.

[99] FFreixo, in *PMH Leges*, 1:378–81; FSepúlveda, art. 248, p. 149; FZorita, arts. 182–83, p. 115; FLedesma, art. 164, p. 245; FSalamanca, art. 241, p. 163; FMedinaceli, in Muñoz y Romero, *Colección de Fueros*, p. 445; FGuadalajara (1219), in González, *Fernando III*, 2:93, no. 75.

1256, was probably typical of others in Asturias-León who converted.[100] In the larger cities and towns where the numbers of Mudejars were more substantial and they were organized in *aljamas*, the possibility of maintaining their separate identity was greater.

The impetus for missionary activity among the Muslims came from outside the peninsula.[101] Northern Europeans, whose contacts with Muslims began to increase during the era of the Crusades, were astounded when they perceived the accommodation that Christians made to the dominant Muslim society. John of Gorze, the envoy of Otto the Great to the court of the caliph in the tenth century, and Hugh of St. Victor in the twelfth century, both castigated the Mozarabic Christians for failing to challenge the Muslims.[102] In the late eleventh century Abbot Hugh of Cluny, urged by Pope Gregory VII, sent his monk Anastasius to preach to the Muslims of Zaragoza, but without success.[103] In words reminiscent of Abbot Hugh, Pope Urban II in 1088 encouraged Archbishop Bernard of Toledo, himself a Frenchman, to "strive by word and example, God willing, to convert the infidels to the faith."[104] A generation

---

[100] Antonio Losa, "Os mouros de Entre Douro e Minho no século XIII," *Bracara Augusta* 16–17 (1964): 224–38, cites many examples from the *inquisitiones* of Afonso II and Afonso III published in *PMH*; Rúiz de la Peña, "Siervos moros," p. 149, n. 28.

[101] Robert I. Burns, "Christian-Muslim Confrontation: The Thirteenth Century Dream of Conversion," *Muslims, Christians and Jews in the Crusader Kingdom of Valencia: Societies in Symbiosis* (Cambridge, 1984), pp. 82–84; Benjamin Z. Kedar, *Crusade and Mission: European Approaches toward the Muslims* (Princeton, 1984), pp. 43–48.

[102] *Vita Joannis Gorziensis*, in *Patrologia Latina*, ed. J. P. Migne 222 vols. (Paris, 1844–1864), 137:298–310; Hugh of St. Victor to Archbishop Juan of Seville, about 1140, ibid., 176:1014.

[103] *Vita S. Anastasii*, in *Patrologia Latina*, ed. J. P. Migne, 222 vols. (Paris, 1844–1864), 149:429; D. M. Dunlop, "A Christian Mission to Muslim Spain in the Eleventh Century," *Al-Andalus* 17 (1952): 263–90; Allan Cutler, "Who Was the Monk of France and When Did He Write?" *Al-Andalus* 18 (1963): 149–69; Abdelmagid Turki, "La lettre du 'Moine de France' à 'Al-Muqtadir billāh, roi de Saragosse, et la réponse d'al-Bāyī, le faqih andalou. (Présentation, texte arabe, traduction)," *Al-Andalus* 31 (1966): 73–154.

[104] Mansilla, *Documentación*, pp. 43–45, 65, 121, nos. 27 (1088), 45 (Pas-

later, Peter the Venerable, abbot of Cluny, visited Spain in 1142/43 and employed the Englishman, Robert of Ketton, to translate the Koran into Latin, so that, having direct knowledge of Islamic doctrine, he would be able to refute it.[105]

Early in the thirteenth century St. Francis of Assisi planned to preach to the Almohad caliph in North Africa but fell ill before he was able to complete his journey. In his Rule he encouraged his friars to undertake missionary activity among the Infidels. Several friars preached briefly among the Spanish Muslims of Seville before continuing on to Morocco where they were executed in 1219.[106] As for the bishops, during the siege of Lisbon in 1147 Archbishop João of Braga suggested that some of the Moors might wish to "freely join the church of God," but the main thrust of his address to them was to exhort them to return to North Africa. Archbishop Rodrigo Jiménez de Rada of Toledo commissioned one of his canons,

---

chal II, 1101), 101 (Adrian IV, 1156); Marius Férotin, "Une lettre inédite de Saint Hugues, abbé de Cluny a Bernard d'Agen, archevêque de Tolède (1087)," *Bibliothèque de l'École des Chartes* 61 (1900): 339–45; idem, "Complément de la lettre de Saint Hugues," ibid. 63 (1902): 682–86.

[105] James Kritzeck, *Peter the Venerable and Islam* (Princeton, 1964). Chapter 30 of the Rule of the Military Order of Santiago, drawn up around 1175 by Cardinal Alberto de Morra (the future Pope Gregory VIII), admonished the knights that "quicquid contra eos [the Saracens] fecerint pro exaltatione nominis Christi faciatur, vel ut christianos ab eorum impugnatione defendant, vel ad culturam christianae fidei ualeant prouocare." The emphasis given to the defense of Christians against the Muslims in the prologue and elsewhere in the text probably represents the original intention of the knights, while the suggestion that they strive for the conversion of the pagans seems an afterthought perhaps added by the cardinal and repeated by Lucius III in his bull of 1184 confirming the order. There is no evidence that the knights actively sought to convert anyone. Enrique Gallego Blanco, *The Rule of the Spanish Military Order of St. James 1170–1493* (Leiden, 1971), prologue, chaps. 9–10, 30, pp. 82–84, 94–95, 110–11; Mansilla, *Documentación*, p. 149, no. 124. A thirteenth-century Castilian version of the Rule (chap. 34) called on the knights to "deffender la ecclesia de Dios" for the "acrescemiento de la fe de Dios," but said nothing of conversion. Derek W. Lomax, *La Orden de Santiago, 1170–1275* (Madrid, 1965), pp. 225–26.

[106] *The Rule of St. Francis*, chap. 12; Burns, "Christian-Muslim Confrontation," pp. 89–90; E. R. Daniel, *The Franciscan Concept of Mission in the High Middle Ages* (Lexington, 1975).

Mark of Toledo, to prepare a new version of the Koran in 1213, but otherwise neither Rodrigo nor his colleagues in Castile and Portugal seem to have troubled themselves unduly about the conversion of the Moors in Christian territory.[107]

The Dominican friars were quite active in missionary enterprise and enjoyed the support of King James I of Aragón, who admonished his son-in-law, Alfonso X, for not displaying greater zeal in this regard. The Castilian king did lend his support to the Dominican Arabic language school in Murcia and established a *studium generale* in Seville for Latin and Arabic studies, but as Burns points out, this was prompted by his intellectual interest in Arabic culture rather than his zeal for missions.[108]

With reference to religious conversion, Alfonso X in the cortes of Seville (1252) forbade any Moor to become a Jew or to advise anyone to convert to Judaism, or vice versa, but he said nothing of Moors converting to Christianity (art. 44). The *Partidas* (7.25.2), on the other hand, echoing the words of Pope Gregory the Great, counseled Christians "to labor by good words and suitable preaching to convert the Moors and cause them to believe in our faith and to lead them to it not by force nor by pressure . . . for (the Lord) is not pleased by service that men give him through fear, but with that that they do willingly and without any pressure." Infante Juan Manuel made the same point some years later, repeating a commonplace of Christian theology: "involuntary and forced services do not

---

[107] *Conquest of Lisbon*, pp. 117–19; Marie Thérèse d'Alverny, "Deux traductions latines du Coran au moyen âge," *Archives d'histoire doctrinale et litteraire du moyen âge*, 16 (1947–1948): 69–131. Concern for the Christians dwelling in Morocco, Seville, and other Saracen cities prompted Pope Celestine III in 1192 to authorize Archbishop Martín of Toledo to send bilingual priests to serve them. Pope Honorius III later commanded Archbishop Rodrigo to consecrate a bishop for the Christian community in Morocco. Neither of these actions concerned missionary efforts among the Mudejars of Spain or among the North African Muslims. Demetrio Mansilla, *Iglesia castellano-leonesa y Curia romana en los tiempos del rey San Fernando* (Madrid, 1945), pp. 74–76.

[108] *MHE*, 1:54–56, no. 25; Fernández y González, *Estado social y político*, pp. 344–45, no. 35; Burns, "Christian-Muslim Confrontation," p. 99.

please God... Jesus Christ never ordered that anyone should be killed or forced to accept his religion."[109]

While the *Partidas* (7.25.3) stressed that no one was to oppose any Moor who wished to become a convert, those who did convert found that their situation was not always a happy one. Christians were commanded to honor and show kindness to converts, refraining from calling them turncoats (tornadizos) or doing them any injury, for that would deter others from becoming Christians. The Portuguese customs imposed a fine of sixty *soldos* on anyone who called a convert a turncoat (*tornadizo*). The tenth canon of the Council of Peñafiel in 1302, assuring any Jew or Moor who became a Christian of continued possession of his property, revealed another difficulty facing converts, namely, attempts by relatives to deny their rights to family property or inheritance.[110]

The establishment of a Dominican house of studies at Murcia by St. Ramon de Penyafort was intended to train friars in the Arabic language so that they could undertake a mission among the Muslims. Though Ramon reported many conversions, the extent to which the mission was directed to the Mudejars of Murcia is uncertain.[111]

Nevertheless, a curious record of a dialogue between a young

---

[109] Ballesteros, "Las Cortes de 1252," p. 142; Juan Manuel, *Libro de los estados*, eds. R. B. Tate and I. R. MacPherson (New York, 1974), bk. 1, chap. 30, p. 45. I thank Benjamin Kedar for references to Gregory the Great, *MGH Epistolae*, 2:383; to Gratian, C.23, q.6, c.4.1: "Cum Deus aspernetur coacta servicia"; and to Ramon de Penyaforte, *Summa de casibus penitentie*, 1.4.2: "Coacta servicia non placent Deo."

[110] See Customs of Santarém and Beja, *PMH Leges*, 2:30, 61, 178; FZorita, arts. 182–83, p. 115; FLedesma, art. 164, p. 245; Leite de Vasconcellos, *Etnográfia portuguesa*, 4:339–40; José Sánchez Herrero, *Concilios provinciales y sínodos toledanos de los siglos XIV y XV* (Seville, 1976), p. 167, no. 1.

[111] Burns, "Christian-Muslim Confrontation," pp. 95–96. Jaume Riera i Sans, "La invenció literària de Sant Pere Pasqual," *Caplletra* 1 (1986): 45–60, has shown that St. Pedro Pascual, alleged bishop of Jaén and author of the *Impugnación sobre la seta de Mahoma* and the *Tratado del libre albedrío contra los fatalistas mahometanos*, is an imaginary figure who never existed. The works attributed to him and published by Armengol Valenzuela, *Obras de San Pedro Pascual*, 3 vols. (Rome, 1908), are extant only in fifteenth-century manuscripts which do not mention the name of any author.

52 CHAPTER 1

Muslim, Ibn Rashīq, a native of Murcia, and a Christian priest from Marrakech, who may have been a Dominican friar, suggests one possible approach that the missionaries adopted toward the adherents of Islam. Acting as one of two Muslim witnesses in support of a third Muslim who had to take an oath in a lawsuit with a Christian, Ibn Rashīq encountered a group of Christian priests, one of whom engaged him in conversation. Speaking in a reasonable tone and referring to Muḥammad with respect, the Christian focused the discussion on the question of the inimitability of the Koran, as expressed in the following passage: "If you doubt what we have revealed to our servant, produce one chapter comparable to this book" (*Koran*, 2.22). While the discussion was carried on in a courteous manner, Ibn Rashīq, after expressing the hope that God would restore Murcia to Islam and that He would free the people from the burdens of tribute and the snares of the enemy, expressed his disdain for his Christian interlocutors: "May God annihilate them to the last man." Evidently no one was converted as a result of this single encounter, which may have been typical of others between Christian and Muslim scholars. In the long run, each side must have gained a greater knowledge of the other.[112]

By the end of the thirteenth century Christian understanding of Islam was considerably better than it had been some centuries before. Sancho IV, for example, in his instructions to his son, revealed at least a superficial knowledge of Muḥammad's life and various aspects of Islamic doctrine and practice (viz., belief in one God, Muḥammad as God's messenger, observance of Friday, pilgrimage to Mecca, fast of Ramadan, prohibition of the use of pork and wine, description of paradise as a garden of pleasures, restriction to four legal wives but many concubines, and so forth).[113]

---

[112] Fernando de la Granja, "Una polémica religiosa en Murcia en tiempos de Alfonso el Sabio," *Al-Andalus* 31 (1966): 47–72; Burns, "Christian-Muslim Confrontation," p. 104. The translation of the Koranic text is from *The Koran*, trans. N. J. Dawood (Baltimore, 1959), p. 325; A. J. Arberry, *The Koran Interpreted* (New York, 1955), p. 32, renders it: "And if you are in doubt concerning that We have sent down on Our servant, then bring a sura like it."

[113] Agapito Rey, ed. *Castigos e documentos para bien vivir ordenados por el rey don Sancho IV* (Bloomington, 1952), chap. 11, pp. 128–33. On the knowledge

Though never once suggesting that the conversion of the Muslims was a royal responsibility, nor that of anyone else, Sancho IV did repeat two arguments from the Christian repertoire for debating Muslims. Contrasting Christian saints with Muslim holy men, one might ask how many miracles they performed after death. Or, interpreting the Koranic idea that Jesus was born when "the breath of God came upon Holy Mary" to mean that he was the Son of God, one could ask whether Jesus was not greater than Muḥammad who was born of sinful and mortal man. The king confidently believed that the Moor would have to agree that Jesus was preferable to Muḥammad and would have no answer when asked why he continued to adhere to the Islamic creed. Convinced that Muḥammad spread many lies, Sancho IV, after quoting in Arabic the phrase, "there is no God but God and Muḥammad is his messenger," concluded that he was in fact the messenger of the devil and that those who followed his teaching were in error. As their lives were displeasing to God, "when they die their souls are lost in hell ... because they do not belong to the flock of God's sheep." The majority of Christians more than likely would have agreed with Alfonso X, who, in the *Cantigas de Santa Maria*, described Muḥammad as "a false, vain, very crazy, and villainous dog," and with Sancho IV, who stated bluntly that "the Moor is nothing but a dog."[114]

Conclusions

In drawing all of this together, two principal conclusions seem evident. In the first place, the numbers of Mudejars apparently

---

of Islam in Christian Spain in the early Middle Ages, see Edward Colbert, *The Martyrs of Córdoba (850–859): A Study of the Sources* (Washington, 1962); and Kenneth Baxter Wolf, *Christian Martyrs in Muslim Spain* (Cambridge, 1988). For a more general view, see Norman Daniel, *Islam and the West: The Making of an Image* (Edinburgh, 1960).

[114] *Castigos e documentos*, chaps. 2–3, 11, pp. 45, 48, 128–33. Sancho IV quoted the Koranic words "arrohamen alla ygi yza men maryem," saying that they meant "that from the breath of God Jesus Christ came of Mary." This probably refers to sura 3; *Cantigas de Santa María*, 1:615–19, no. 192.

declined over the course of the twelfth and thirteenth centuries. As the reconquest advanced, Muslims elected to withdraw to the south. Aristocrats such as the family of Ibn Khaldūn opted to move to Granada and ultimately to North Africa. Even when they remained after the surrender of towns and castles, the pressures of living in a dominant Christian society caused many eventually to seek the comfort of Muslim territory. An old man among the Moors evacuating Gibraltar in 1309 revealed the plight of his fellows when he queried Fernando IV:

> My lord, why do you drive me hence? When your greatgrandfather King Fernando took Seville he drove me out and I went to live at Jerez, but when your grandfather Alfonso took Jerez he drove me out and I went to live at Tarifa, thinking that I was in a safe place. Your father King Sancho came and took Tarifa and drove me out and I went to live at Gibraltar, thinking that I would not be in any safer place in the whole land of the Moors . . . but now I see that I cannot remain in any of these places, so I will go beyond the sea and settle in a place where I can live in safety and end my days.[115]

The Mudejar population of Andalusia suffered a precipitous decline when Alfonso X ordered their expulsion following their revolt in 1264. While some historians have argued that evidences of Moorish traits in Andalusian art, food, dress, and other aspects of life are themselves testimony to the existence of a substantial Mudejar population in Andalusia, both González Jiménez and Ladero Quesada have rejected this. Emphasizing the steady decline of the Mudejars, they suggest that one must look for other explanations of Moorish influences, such as continual social, commercial, and military interaction along the Granadan frontier.[116]

In Murcia, the Mudejars were quite numerous even after the revolt of 1264, but apparently attrition also occurred there. Elsewhere in Castile and Portugal Mudejar remnants were scat-

---

[115] *Crónica de Fernando IV*, chap. 17, in *BAE*, 66:163.

[116] González Jiménez, *En torno*, pp. 77–78; Ladero Quesada, "Mudejares," pp. 290, 296.

tered, in a somewhat isolated and depressed state, lacking in numbers, leaders, and strength.

Given their dependent condition, it is not surprising that the Mudejars did not produce a significant body of literature, nor do they seem to have been employed by Alfonso X among the translators in his court.[117] A measure of their assimilation to the dominant Christian culture is the existence of several treatises, primarily concerning Muslim law and practice, written in the Castilian language but using Arabic characters. The principal examples of this so-called *aljamiado* literature date, however, from the fifteenth and sixteenth centuries and thus lie beyond the scope of this essay.[118]

The second principal conclusion is that no persistent effort to convert the Mudejars seems to have been undertaken. Some sporadic missionary efforts were made among the independent Muslim communities of Granada and Morocco. Surely some parish priests must have endeavored to convert individual Mudejars, but records of their success have not come to light. The bishops seem to have followed the lead of the monarch, allowing the Moors to continue in the observance of their religion without attempting to preach the gospel to them in any sustained manner.

In a society in which each group was distinguished by the privileges it possessed, there was nothing incongruous about the continued existence of the Mudejars as a body privileged to have their own law and to follow a religion apart from that of the dominant Christian community. This was indeed a practical solution to the need for manpower. So long as the Mudejars

---

[117] Evelyn Procter, *Alfonso X of Castile: Patron of Literature and Learning* (Oxford, 1951), pp. 122–25, pointed out that the translators fell into three groups: Jews, Spaniards, and Italians. "Maestre Bernardo el arábico," who assisted in the translation of the *Libro de la açafeha*, may have been a convert from Islam. González, *Repoblación*, 2:131, n. 310, noted that the astronomers Aben Raphel and Alquibicio worked on the *Libro de las Tablas*. John E. Keller, *Alfonso X el Sabio* (New York, 1967), pp. 134–52.

[118] Eduardo de Saavedra, *Discurso leído ante la Real Academia Española* (Madrid, 1878); Anwar G. Chejne, *Muslim Spain: Its Culture and History* (Minneapolis, 1974), pp. 375–96.

were willing to obey the Christian king and to pay tribute to him, they could be tolerated and given privileges.

The alternatives were wholesale expulsion and consequent economic loss, or execution, or mass conversion. As we have seen, Alfonso X did resort to wholesale expulsion in Andalusia after suppressing the Mudejar uprising. If he and his nephew, Juan Manuel, took seriously the notion that God did not wish forced service, then mass conversion was out of the question. By the very nature of things, the Mudejars would have to be converted one by one as a consequence of dialogue and persuasion. That would also leave the possibility that some would never be persuaded.

In the later Middle Ages, as the notion of the state grew stronger, the anomaly of the Mudejar situation (and also of the Jews, who were more numerous) became more apparent. When every effort was being directed toward the buttressing of royal authority, the achievement of juridical unity, and the subordination of all men in equal measure to the Crown, the presence of the Mudejars (and Jews) seemed increasingly odd. If kings chafed against canon law and the privileged status of the clergy and insisted that all the men in their kingdoms, including the clergy, were fully subject to royal law, they would certainly find the distinctive status of the Mudejars unacceptable.

The common term used to refer to different faiths was *ley* ("law"), a word that emphasized the inextricable intermingling of religion and law and the consequent influence that one's religious belief had over the totality of one's life and actions. Thus, if any change were to be made in the status of the Mudejars, it would affect both religion and law, as indeed it did. Conversion then meant not only the abandonment of Islamic theological ideas and religious beliefs, but also the abandonment of an entire legal system and the acceptance of both Christian doctrine and the civil law of the Christian community.

In the atmosphere of the late Middle Ages and the early modern era, as the state began to embrace the whole of the lives of its citizens, a plurality of religions and legal systems could not be maintained, as the Jews learned at the close of the fifteenth century and the Mudejars discovered in the sixteenth and seventeenth centuries.

2

MUSLIMS IN THE THIRTEENTH-CENTURY REALMS OF ARAGON: INTERACTION AND REACTION

Robert I. Burns, S.J.

EUROPEAN MEDITERRANEAN SOCIETIES in the high Middle Ages were frontier societies.[1] They lived in conjunction to, and interacted with, their Muslim neighbors. European and Islamic cultures interpenetrated each other in a number of ways, from interchange of slave populations and commercial guest-communities to military and technological influences. A third society was present at every

---

[1] Much of this chapter is based on my books, where detailed bibliography is available on the Realms of Aragon, its various Muslim communities, and the wider background. See especially *Islam under the Crusaders: Colonial Survival in the Thirteenth-Century Kingdom of Valencia* (Princeton, 1973); and *Muslims, Christians, and Jews in the Crusader Kingdom of Valencia: Societies in Symbiosis* (Cambridge, Eng., 1984, 1986). See also my *Crusader Kingdom of Valencia: Reconstruction of a Thirteenth-Century Frontier*, 2 vols. (Cambridge, Mass., 1967); *Medieval Colonialism: Postcrusade Exploitation of Islamic Valencia* (Princeton, 1975); *Moors and Crusaders in Mediterranean Spain* (London, 1978); *Jaume I i els valencians del segle XIII* (Valencia, 1981); *Society and Documentation in Crusader Valencia* (Princeton, 1985); and *The Worlds of Alfonso the Learned and James the Conqueror: Intellect and Force in the Middle Ages* (Princeton, 1985). An annotated and indexed bibliography on the Muslims of these realms, though touching only tangentially on those of Catalonia and Aragon (see below), is Míkel de Epalza's *Moros y moriscos en el Levante peninsula (Sharq al-Andalus): introducción bibliográfica* (Alicante, 1983), continued in the issues of *Sharq al-Andalus: estudios árabes*, 1 (1984) to date. Thematic and bibliographic essays on all aspects of Mudejar history and culture are in the continuing series of congresses at Teruel, *Simposio internacional de mudejarismo*, 1 (1981) through

level of this interchange and integration: the Jewish communities within both Islam and Christendom, many of whose members moved as well between the two. At a more profound level both European and Islamic cultures had much in common from their Hellenistic and Judaic inheritance.

In both Islamic and European worlds a significant mode of interaction was the formal incorporation of whole native but alien communities, permanently resident with their own sociopolitical and legal structures within the larger or dominant society. Christian and Jewish mini-societies thus lived as native to their locales within Islamic societies, while Muslim and Jewish mini-societies lived within Christian societies. Each such community, even as it interacted with the dominant society, shrank from taint of assimilation to the other; and none could allow the other to share its own structure and daily life. The ethnicity in each case was religious, coloring all aspects of individual and community expression. To accommodate was to assimilate, to lose something of the self. In order to preserve identity, one had to become an accomplice in one's own exclusion. Subject

---

3 (1986) to date. Three new journals include Mudejar materials among their wider Hispano-Arabist range: *Awrāq, Al-Qanṭara* and *Sharq al-Andalus*. For Valencia, see also the works of Barceló Torres, Bramon, Ferrer i Mallol, Guichard, and Ruzafa García below in n. 6 and of Epalza in nn. 8 and 19. Only two works attempt to cover the Realms of Aragon as a unit, and then only for the fourteenth-century Mudejars. John Boswell, *The Royal Treasure: Muslim Communities under the Crown of Aragon in the Fourteenth Century* (New Haven, 1977), centers on the decade of the wars with Castile (1356–1366), excluding the Balearics, but has much archival information on the century's full trajectory. M. T. Ferrer i Mallol, *Es sarraïns de la corona catalano-aragonesa en el segle XIV: segregació i discriminació* (Barcelona, 1987), focuses on the growing restrictions over internal and external mobility, on the increasing segregation in residence and in social and sexual interaction, and on the curbing of intrusive public expressions of worship such as the muezzin, with rich archival detail and 157 new documents. For background, see too L. A. McMillin, "Portrait of the Enemy: 'Saracens' in the Catalan Grand Chronicles," and C. M. Davis, "The Mudejars of the Crown of Aragon in the Early Documents of Jaume the Conqueror, 1218–1227," both in *Sharq al-Andalus* 4 (1987): 49–57, 123–29, respectively. Leonard P. Harvey's forthcoming volume, *Islamic Spain, 1250 to 1500* (Chicago, 1990) is also worth of note.

communities perforce assimilated to a degree, and to a degree had to redefine themselves in bastard forms. So intense and universal a grip did one's culture exert, that even a conquered Muslim's conversion and thus removal into the Christians' sphere, for example, did not always mitigate the popular repugnance and hostility toward him as stranger.

This situation was not static but varied with time and place, both in its larger structure and in the myriad variables which shaped each individual expression of that evolving structure. The interaction of the three societies lends special fascination to the thirteenth-century western Mediterranean world of diffused city-states and region-states, a world affluent and maniacally energetic. We might approach this vast subject from any number of aspects: the conscious structures by which each society accommodated the others; or the actual relations, public and private, of each with the others; or the active contexts defining the possible variations, such as the context of political alliances, or of theological and popular attitudes, or of warfare, scholarship, or trade; or, finally, of the homely details of daily life within the subject society. Here we shall examine a relatively little-known Mediterranean Christian country—or rather congeries of linked countries, or (in its widest expansion) a maritime empire.

Our focus is on its subject Muslims, in relation to and interaction with their Christian conquerors. Contemporary Christians called them by the misnomer "Saracens" in Latin, and "Moors" in Romance. Today's term, "Mudejars," found at least from the fifteenth century among the Castilians, apparently echoed the Arabic *al-mudajjan* for "allowed-to-remain," in the sense of thirteenth- and fourteenth-century Muslim chroniclers in the West who spoke of the *ahl al-dajn*, a tributary-allied Muslim group under treaty agreement. These Mudejar populations fared variously in the several regions we are about to examine, so that an overview of their situation is advisable before concentrating on the most unusual of the component realms, the mixed society of the kingdom of Valencia.

The Realms: Catalonia, Aragon, Balearics, Valencia

The Crown or Realms of Aragon formed a loose assemblage of autonomous principalities and feudal entities, bonded together only by a common dynasty.[2] Its core was two sovereign states. The rural and stockraising upland, the kingdom of Aragon, adjoined and resembled Castile. Its Aragonese language, fractious barons, feudal parliament, rural economy, strange calendar, and warrior people set it apart from its adjoining sister-state of Catalonia. Mediterranean Catalonia had its own language, institutions, urban character, affluence, cross-cultural commerce, and merchant people. It was a typical component of that commune-cum-count world which rimmed the western Mediterranean from the Ebro to the Tiber, and which assumed cognate political forms as diverse as the autonomies of Marseilles, Venice, Genoa, and Dubrovnik. Catalonia had few magnates (some thirty), while its multifarious knights and esquires participated enthusiastically in commerce even as its merchant notables adopted a chivalric and noble style. Not a warrior but a money society would relate to the Muslims here, a society where the producers and consumers of culture were these mixed merchant-investor classes. The Catalan count Jaume (and Arago-

---

[2] For a general introduction, see T. N. Bisson, *The Medieval Crown of Aragon: A Short History* (Oxford, 1986); and the alternating Dufourcq chapters in *Histoire économique et social de l'Espagne chrétienne au moyen âge* (Paris, 1976), much improved in its translation as *Historia económica y social de la España cristiana en la edad media* (Barcelona, 1983) with an extra bibliography of 2600 items, each tied into a text segment. See too the Arago-Catalan sections of standard histories on medieval Spain, esp. Joseph F. O'Callaghan's *History of Medieval Spain* (Ithaca, 1975); Jocelyn Hillgarth's *Spanish Kingdoms 1250–1516*, 2 vols. (Oxford, 1976–1978); and Angus MacKay's briefer *Spain in the Middle Ages: From Frontier to Empire, 1000–1500* (New York, 1977). For the thirteenth century, see my *Worlds of Alfonso and James*, chaps. 1, 2, 6, and 8. Comprehensive detailed studies as well as bibliographical essays are in the monumental *Jaime I y su época*, which is the *X Congreso de historia de la Corona de Aragón*, 3 vols. to date (Zaragoza, 1979–); for the reign of James I's son and successor, see the *XI Congreso* as *La società mediterranea all'epoca del Vespro*, 2 vols. (Palermo, 1983). On the historiography of King James himself, Ernest Belenguer, *Jaume I a través de la història*, 2 vols. (Valencia, 1984).

nese king Jaime) was also lord of the great commercial city-state of Montpellier, and held a variety of feudal claims and protectorates stretching over Occitan southern France. James the Conqueror organized his conquests from Muslims as a kingdom of Majorca or the Balearic islands (1229) and a kingdom of Valencia (by 1245). Confounding all his titles into one, he proudly declared himself in 1241 "king from the Rhone to Valencia," a claim which concealed his dwindling control in southern France. By the thirteenth century the action of a common dynasty had generated throughout the component realms any number of unifying interactions, patterns, and expectations.

In each of James' two major Iberian holdings, at his accession, interaction with Muslims was very different. Urbanized Catalonia held only several thousand Mudejars in residence, located in communities mostly in the border regions of Lérida (inland from Barcelona, on the frontier with Aragon) and Tortosa (at Catalonia's southern coastal tip). Muslim slaves were common everywhere, as elsewhere around Mediterranean Europe, and Muslim merchants were prominent at the great port of Barcelona. A major fonduk or quarter for foreign Muslims was a feature of the port, with its institutions, mosques, baths, and services for the flow of merchants. A tiny community of domestic Mudejars seems to have congregated there; Teresa Vinyoles i Vidal locates this at the seashore, between the gates of Fra Menors and of Sant Daniel. The situation at Lérida was typical of the Catalan Mudejar model. These border conquests had come as the last phase of a conquering advance throughout the eleventh century and into the twelfth, during which the Catalans had "systematically evacuated" the resident Muslims (in the phrase of Rodrigo Pita Mercé), replacing them with a steady flow of Christians from the Pyrenean valleys and Catalonia. For the later conquest of the Lérida region, however, the Catalans had offered surrender constitutions, so that the Muslims stayed on from 1150 until after 1610—over four hundred years as Mudejars and at the end as a pseudo-convert Morisco remnant.

The treaty privileges set up the Leridan Muslim communities

as public entities, with their own juridical personality within the Christian state. The Muslims kept a suburb of Lérida as their urban headquarters and privileged enclave, retained their civil and criminal legal system and personnel with Muslim magistrates, assessed and collected taxes within the community, and continued to own and buy farms (though now under Christian tax-lords). Their religious *qāḍī* stayed on as the community's head, with a Muslim *qā'id* as crown delegate or representative (his powers swallowed up by the king's bailiff in the late thirteenth century). Not one *amīn* but two served as active liaisons between the Christian and Mudejar administrations, their role growing by such action into a measure of leadership and even dominance within the *aljama* (a word designating each community as well as its council). These Muslims clung devoutly to their religion, resisting the fiercely conversionist movements which began just before mid-thirteenth century; but their mosques here were not allowed minarets or muezzins. Despite erosion of their elites by emigration, they maintained an active stratum of intellectuals or subintellectuals (functionaries, theologians, and the like) who constituted a guiding establishment or *'ulamaā'*, of which remnants visibly remained even in the seventeenth century.

Most Leridan Mudejars were illiterate farmers who dominated the green belts of the region, along with a valued minority of artisans such as leatherworkers, ceramicists, carpenters, tailors, and sculptors. Besides a stratum of rich Mudejars, even the ordinary farmers as a whole were reasonably affluent. Marriage came early; couples usually stayed monogamous except for a rare exception among the rich, and produced families larger than those of the Christians. These Mudejars seemed to the Christians a happy lot, expressing themselves in many feasts, an exuberant folklore, native music, and dancing. By the end of the thirteenth century enough Mudejars had so assimilated as to be indistinguishable frequently from Lérida's Christians, alarming the bishop and king (and probably the Muslim leaders) and provoking general legislation. Pita Mercé sees the Mudejars' privileged condition in Lérida as strongest during the immediately postconquest century and a half, a "relative liberty" of movement, of public expression of religion, of distribution throughout the crafts and economic works, and of cultural and personal expression. Then came a century of progressive restriction in all those aspects, beginning with legislation for special dress and haircut; and finally, from 1492 to 1610, an era of persecution and forced conversions. The barons and landlords valued their work ethic and the income it brought, and they tried to protect this investment against church and townsmen. This picture owes more to the surviving later documentation, from mid-thirteenth century on in an increasingly rich flow through the fourteenth and fifteenth centuries.

Most Catalan regions had no such experience of Mudejars. Floods of Catalan settlers had truly appropriated the lands conquered from Muslims. As late as 1229 a general council of the Catalan dioceses was much more preoccupied with Albigenses and Jews among their Christian populations than with the few Muslims. Only the Lérida and Tortosa regions, taken just before 1150, afforded a moderate experience of permanent Muslim communities. The twelfth- and especially the thirteenth-century Catalan context was a dizzying rise in affluence and international trade, in which Catalans were more likely to meet a Muslim merchant, or trade to a North African port, or enter the pirate expeditions so popular with both sides. In short, the busy world of urbanized Catalonia both marginalized the few Muslim *aljamas* and encountered the Muslims elsewhere as fellow merchants, town slaves, and enemy seamen. The framework by which Catalans related to their fewer *aljamas* copied the same peninsular tradition as that of upland Aragon—a suburb *morería*, largely peasant-tenants, and pacts specifying the full range of legal, religious, institutional, and economic autonomy. The relative liberty of these centuries, soon to be encroached upon and progressively diminished, may owe something to benign neglect by the expanding and confident Catalans. Later, when the major conquests by the Catalan peoples finally took place, they happened on a massive scale over a mere decade or two, expanding the Realms marvelously and corralling through Majorca and Valencia the circle trade with North Africa, leading to a contest with Genoa for dominance of the whole western Mediterranean. Thus a different kind of Catalan, in differing domestic and international circumstances, was to confront the very different species of Mudejar society in thirteenth-century Valencia.[3]

In contrast to Catalonia, the upland kingdom of Aragon had long been (to borrow Elena Lourie's classic phrase) "a society organized for war." Its barons and small-town militias had greatly enlarged that kingdom by pushing back Islamic power

[3] For Catalonia, see Pere Balañá i Abadía, *Els musulmans a Catalunya (713–1153), una aproximació bibliogràfica*, 502 titles (very few on Mudejars) as "Suplemento bibliográfico" no. 2, to *Sharq al-Andalus* 3 (1986). See also Pascual Ortega, "De mudéjares a moriscos; algunas reflexiones en torno a las relaciones sociales de producción y la conflictividad religiosa: el caso de la Ribera d'Ebre (Tarragona)," *Miscel·lània de textos medievales* 4 (1988): 319–33. On Lérida, see the small volume by Rodrigo Pita Mercé, *Lérida morisca* (Lerida, 1977), esp. chaps. 1–2, 7, 13–14; see also idem, *Lérida árabe*, 1 vol. to date (Lérida, 1974); and Josep Lladonosa i Pujol, *Història de Lleida*, 2 vols. (Lérida, 1972–1974), 1, pt. 2. On Fraga, see Rodrigo Pita Mercé, *Fraga musulmana* (Huesca, 1954). On Tortosa, see J. M. Font Rius, "La comarca de Tortosa a raíz de la reconquista cristiana (1148), notas sobre su fisonomía político-social," *Cuadernos de historia de España* 19 (1953): 104–28; and idem, "La carta de seguridad de Ramón Berenguer IV a las morerías de Ascó y Ribera del Ebro (siglo XII)," *Homenaje a Don José María Lacarra de Miguel*, 5 vols. (Zaragoza, 1977), 1:261–83. Both are now in Font Rius's collected *Estudis sobre els drets i institucions locals en la Catalunya medieval* (Barcelona, 1985), pp. 75–92, 561–76. On Morisco remnants, see Carmel Biarnés i Biarnés, *Apunts d'història d'Ascó: els moriscos a Catalunya; documents inèdits* (Ascó, 1981). Among the very few articles on Barcelona, see David Romano, "Musulmanes residentes y emigrantes en la Barcelona de los siglos XIV–XV," *Al-Andalus* 41 (1976): 48–87. For the Occitan regions, there is only the very disappointing *Islam et chrétiens du Midi (XIIe–XIVes.)*, Cahiers de Fanjeaux 18 (Toulouse, 1983); for what can be salvaged from this symposium, see my review article in *Catholic Historical Review* 70 (1984): 90–93. Charles E. Dufourcq has explored the relations of the Catalans (including Catalan-speaking Valencia and the Balearic islands) with Islamic North Africa in his monumental *L'Espagne catalane et le Maghrib aux XIIIe et XIVe siècles, de la bataille de Las Navas de Tolosa (1212) a l'avènement du sultan mérinide Abou l-Hasan (1313)* (Paris, 1966), see esp. pp. 68–88 on Catalan contacts with Muslims, and pt. 1 in general for the period to 1275. On the Catalan experience and several images of the Muslim, see Michel Zimmerman, "L'Image du monde musulman et son utilisation en Catalogne du IXe au XIIe siècle," in *Minorités et marginaux en France méridionale et dans la péninsule ibérique*, ed. Pierre Tucoo-Chala (Paris, 1986), pp. 471–95.

in the eleventh and twelfth centuries. Mudejars there numbered perhaps some 100,000 by the thirteenth century. After the catastrophic losses of the Black Death and the Castilian wars, John Boswell estimates them at about some 70,000—30 percent of Aragon's total population of 230,000 in 1365. The relation of the Aragonese to their Muslims was paradoxical. Aragon had conquered south progressively in a chronic state of raiding brawls against Islam, taking key points regularly—Huesca in 1096, Naval in 1099, Tarazona and Zaragoza in 1118, Tudela in 1119, Calatayud in 1120, Daroca in 1142, Alcañiz in 1157, and Teruel in 1170. Despite this bellicose roll-call, the underpopulated Aragonese valued their Muslim tenants highly and treated them relatively generously. Their basic attitude is reflected in the folk-saying, "No Moor, no money" ("Quien no tiene moro, no tiene oro"). For four centuries most revenues in Aragon would come from Muslim tenants. Unlike Muslim slaves, these "Moors of Peace" enjoyed their several traditional surrender pacts or constitutions, which guaranteed administrative autonomy, an Islamic legal system, a religious establishment, and basic tax-cum-rent arrangements.

Like most Aragonese Christians, the Mudejars were country people. Even as late as the fifteenth century, Aragon was to have only ten towns of more than two thousand inhabitants. Any urban Muslims remaining after each early conquest were removed to a suburb outside the main walls. The numerous Mudejars were characteristically skilled farmers on intensively cultivated and irrigated lands, grouped onto large estates owned by barons, military orders, municipalities, church corporations, or even the Crown. Though there were hired and contract-lease farmers, most of these Muslims in effect owned their farms, in that the landlord could not remove them and conversely they could will, sell, or lease their property and move away. Paying a traditional share of crops as tax or perhaps rent, they seem at once proprietors and share-tenants. Not all the Mudejars were farmers. Muslim craftsmen, dye-masters, boatmen on the Ebro River, leatherworkers, and providers of many kinds of service shared their hamlets and urban quarters. Construction was largely in Mudejar hands; the legacy of Mudejar architecture is a boast of Aragonese towns today, its remnants a major tourist attraction. Geographically the communities clustered mostly in a belt along the Ebro River which halved Aragon. This extramural peasant society, Islamic descendants of indigenous peoples, slowly but progressively assimilated to their Christian masters—in names, costume, and eventually language. Still, each *aljama* preserved its institutions, customs, mosque activities, schools, and many elements of its former way of life. The contextual conditions of such preservation, of course, amounted at a deeper level to distortion and cultural recrystallization—a survival society.[4]

[4] J. M. Lacarra, "Introducción al estudio de los mudéjares aragoneses," *Aragón en la edad media* 2 (1979): 7–22. Maria Luisa Ledesma sums up his conclusions in her "Mudéjares," in *Gran enciclopedia aragonesa*, 13 vols. (Zaragoza, 1980–1983), 9:2376–78, with Lacarra's map of Mudejar distribution; her booklet *Los mudéjares en Aragón* (Zaragoza, 1979) covers the same material. See also idem, "La población mudéjar en la vega baja de Jalón," *Miscelánea ofrecida al Ilmo. Sr. D. José María Lacarra y de Miguel* (Zaragoza, 1968), pp. 335–51; and idem, "Notas sobre los mudéjares del valle de Huerva (siglos XII al XV)," *Aragón en la edad media* 3 (1980): 7–27. See also M. J. Viguera, *Aragón musulmán* (Zaragoza, 1981), esp. chap. 5. Lacarra's great collection, "Documentos para la reconquista y repoblación del valle del Ebro," *Estudios de edad media de la Corona de Aragón* 2 (1946), 3 (1947), and 5 (1952), also in book form, 2 vols. (Zaragoza, 1982–1985), are only very partially exploited by J. C. Liauzu, "Un aspect de la reconquête de la vallée de l'Ebre aux XIe et XIIIe siècles: l'agriculture irriguée et l'héritage de l'Islam," *Hespéris-Tamuda* 5 (1964): 5–13; and idem, "La condition des musulmans dans l'Aragon chrétien aux XIe et XIIe siècles," ibid. 9 (1968): 185–200. More penetrating and satisfactory is W. C. Stalls, "Aragonese *Exarici* in the Twelfth Century: Their Status and Conditions of Landholding," *Sharq al-Andalus* 4 (1987): 131–44. The posthumous publication of Francisco Macho y Ortega's doctoral dissertation, including transcription of many documents, deserves note: "Condición social de los mudéjares aragoneses (siglo XV)," *Memorias de la Facultad de filosofía y letras de la Universidad de Zaragoza* 1 (1922–1923): 137–319, and "Documentos relativos a la condición social y jurídica de los mudéjares aragoneses," *Revista de ciencias jurídicas y sociales* 5 (1922): 143–60, 444–64. The dissertation of Donald F. Thayer, "The Mudejars of Aragon during the Twelfth and Thirteenth Centuries" (Ann Arbor [photocopy], 1973), draws heavily on the more available Catalan data but offers useful detail. Against Lacarra, he argues that the majority of Aragonese Muslims had long fled by this time, only 20 percent remaining. See also the studies on Mudejars of Teruel and other Aragonese localities in *III Simposio* (Teruel, 1984), esp. the thematic-bibliographical essay

If Catalonia and Aragon had very different experiences in the pre-thirteenth-century reconquest, and relations differently qualified with their internal Muslims, their thirteenth-century conquests of Majorca and Valencia represented a wider extreme from either experience. Newly Christian Majorca seems to have lost the larger part of its Muslims to flight and expulsion; Charles Dufourcq estimates that only twenty thousand remained behind. Numerous slaves and free Muslims do appear in Christian Majorca's documents, but functioning public communities or *aljamas* are absent. Ricardo Soto Company, therefore, characterizes these scattered, unprivileged individuals as a "decapitated" or acephalous society. A few of the rural populations do seem to have originated as arranged surrenders by odd bands—not negotiated and privileged but mere tenant agreements as with the rural Muslims later in farms just around Valencia city. The island soon became a major slave mart of the western Mediterranean, thus further obscuring our view of native versus imported Muslims. Rural Muslims predominated, both as free men and as severely restricted slaves, or more exactly in general slavery but with various exceptions and contract situations. Despite provocation, their numbers and depressed condition precluded revolt. Majorca's smaller neighbor, Minorca, was an even more special case: fighting to the bitter end, its population was entirely enslaved.[5]

---

by Mercedes García Arenal, pp. 175–86. For the fourteenth century, see Boswell and Ferrer i Mallol, above, n. 1. The situation in neighboring Navarre, in some ways cognate, is introduced by Mercedes García Arenal and Beatrice Leroy, *Moros y judíos en Navarra en la baja edad media* (Madrid, 1984) with thorough bibliographical information and documentary appendix. The more complete treatment of Akio Ozaki is available in Japanese articles and privately circulated typescripts—with Spanish publication promised, the first of which is "El régimen tributario y la vida económica de los mudéjares de Navarra," *Príncipe de Viana* 47 (1986): 437–84, and *Anuario de estudios medievales* 16 (1986): 319–68.

[5] As an introduction to the murky history of Majorca's postconquest Muslims, see Ricardo Soto Company, "La población musulmana de Mallorca bajo el dominio cristiano (1240–1276)," *Fontes rerum balearium* (Palma, 1978–1980), 2:65–80; 3:549–564, to be continued; idem, "Sobre mudèixars a Mallorca fins a finals del segle XIII," *Estudis de prehistòria, d'història de Mayurqa i d'història de Mallorca dedicats a Guillem Rosselló i Bordoy* (Palma de Mallorca,

The Aragonese had experience of subject Muslim communities for a longer time and on a wider scale than the Catalans in the era before the Valencian crusade. The Catalans, however, brought to the Valencian situation a more practical commercial attitude toward Muslims abroad and at home, a wider horizon of Islamic contacts, and eventually a larger body of Christian settlers. The two experiences converged in Valencia, where the local Mudejar population would for a generation remain larger than that of all the other realms together. To explore the interacting Mudejar-Christian world of the thirteenth century, then, we must turn not to the partly assimilated Mudejar peasant society of ruralized Aragon, nor to the relatively isolated border societies marginal to urban-commercial Catalonia, nor even to the reduced and enslaved Mudejar society of the Balearics, but rather to Valencia.[6]

1982), pp. 195–221; and idem, "El primer tràfic esclavista a Mallorca," *L'Avenç* 35 (1981): 60–65. See also Alvaro Santamaría Arández's chapter in *Historia de Mallorca*, ed. J. Mascaró Pasarius, 10 vols. (Palma, 1978), 3:14–15; and Elena Lourie, "Free Moslems in the Balearics under Christian rule in the Thirteenth Century," *Speculum* 45 (1970): 624–49. A number of indirectly pertinent papers presented at the *V Jornades d'estudis històrics locals* at Palma de Mallorca in 1985 have appeared with the alternate title *Les illes orientals d'al-Andalus i les seves relacions amb Sharq al-Andalus, Magrib i Europa cristiana (ss. VIII–XIII)*, ed. Guillem Rosselló-Bordoy (Palma, 1987). See also Guillem Rosselló-Bordoy and J. Sastre Moll, "El mudejarismo en Mallorca en la época de Ramon Llull," *Bolletí de la Societat arqueològica luliana* 39 (1982): 257–63, from account books ca. 1310. For the fourteenth century, see N. E. Gais, "Aperçu sur la population musulmane de Majorque au XIV^c siècle," *Revue d'histoire et de civilisation du Maghreb* 9 (1970): 19–30. Francisco Franco Sánchez has a *Bibliografía sobre temas árabes de las Baleares* of 740 titles, including Mudejar entries, as "Suplemento bibliográfico" no. 3 to *Sharq al-Andalus* 3 (1986).

[6] Besides my own books above in n. 1, see also M. C. Barceló Torres, *Minorías islámicas en el país valenciano: historia y dialecto* (Valencia, 1984), which particularly studies the language and appends 270 Arabic local documents for the period 1366–1595; M. T. Ferrer i Mallol, *La frontera amb Islam en el segle XIV: cristians i sarraïns al país valencià* (Barcelona, 1988), including 238 documents; idem, *Les aljames sarraïnes de la governació d'Oriola en el segle XIV* (Barcelona, 1988), with 137 documents; Dolors Bramon, *Contra moros i jueus: formació i estratègia d'unes descriminacions al país valencià* (Valencia, 1981), which follows the whole trajectory of Mudejar-Christian interaction here in a penetrating analytical discussion; Clifford R. Backman, "Mudejars in the Criminal Laws of

Four reasons particularly recommend this. First, Valencia's Muslims vastly outnumbered the crusader settlers, so that a mere colonial overgrid had to conciliate and dominate the native population. Not only security and tradition dictated this policy, but the profit motive itself. This is a maximum Mudejarism, worth very special study. Second, the Muslims of Valencia represented a highly advanced community admired throughout Islam as an affluent "paradise," its preconquest cities serving as the major commercial entrepot for the rest of Islamic Spain. Third, the turbulent thirteenth century, with its explosive growth for the Realms of Aragon and its deadly crisis for Islam in West and East, allows us to watch a full generation or two in the very act of acculturative transference from a free Islamic society to a subject Mudejar subspecies. Finally, the accident of the conquerors' acquiring Valencian Játiva's paper mills, and consequently of the Crown's elaborating its unusual archival registers, has furnished us with a unique wealth of pro-

---

the *Furs de Valencia*," *Sharq al-Andalus* 4 (1987): 93–99. For the fourteenth century, see Boswell and Ferrer i Mallol as above in n. 1. See also Mark D. Meyerson, "The War Against Islam and the Muslims at Home: The Mudejar Predicament in the Kingdom of Valencia during the Reign of Fernando 'El Católico," *Sharq al-Andalus* 3 (1986): 103–13; and idem, *Between Convivencia and Crusade: The Muslim Minority in the Kingdom of Valencia During the Reign of Fernando el Católico* (Berkeley–Los Angeles, in press); The survey of Pierre Guichard recapitulates his several articles: "La repoblación y la condición de los musulmanes," in *Nuestra historia*, eds. Manuel Mas Santacreu et al., 7 vols. (Valencia, 1980), 3:44–82. My bibliographical "Mudejar History Today: New Directions," *Viator* 7 (1977): 127–43, and thematic "Los mudéjares de Valencia: temas y metodologia" (*I Simposio de mudejarismo* [1981]: 453–497), must now be supplemented by Manuel Ruzafa García, "Los mudéjares valencianos en el siglo XV: una perspectiva bibliográfica," which includes graphs illustrating the remarkable proliferation of Islamic-Mudejar publications since the 1950s (*III Simposio* [1986]: 291–303). Of special note are the pioneering archeological explorations in the Eslida region by Karl W. Butzer and a team of Spanish and American colleagues; see "Medieval Muslim Communities of the Sierra de Espadán, Kingdom of Valencia," *Viator* 17 (1986): 339–420, and its preliminary version "Una alquería islámica medieval de la Sierra de Espadán," *Boletín de la Sociedad castellonense de cultura* 61 (1985): 306–65. Among recent local studies, see esp. Joaquín Navarro Reig, "los mudéjares contestanos en el siglo XIII," *Anales de la universidad de Alicante, historia medieval* 6 (1987): 175–206.

saic information on the subject society. This surviving documentation illumines especially the Crown's lands, which included almost all cities and their agricultural districts; beyond them great sweeps of rural regions supported a system of jurisdictional lords, secular far more than ecclesiastical. The Crown retained ultimate control and legal jurisdiction over all Mudejars, however, even as it delegated economic and much legal responsibility to these "feudal" or rather manorial-rental petty lords in the hinterlands. In terms of mingling and interaction, both types of Mudejar may be considered together.

James the Conqueror, count of Barcelona and (less impressively) king of upland Aragon, had battled and maneuvered from 1232 to 1245 in a formally declared papal crusade to subdue the Almohad province he was to call the "kingdom" of Valencia. His many surrender agreements with each conquered community had a common core of privileges as a kind of constitution; he granted these partly from pragmatism, mostly from traditional practice in his own (as he notes) and other Spanish kingdoms, but fundamentally because their provisions were necessary if he or any other Mediterranean ruler were to accommodate any considerable alien body within a unitary society formally established as Christian. Moderns tend to see the process as a cynical economic and military necessity, with a religious gloss; James the Crusader obviously saw it as a splendidly religious extension of Christendom's frame, with profit as a proper added benefit. Mudejarism is commonly assimilated today to the *dhimma* provisions for Infidels within Islam, simply as adapted; the pre-Islamic Sasanian model for the *dhimma* institution reveals rather an immemorial impulse of Mediterranean empires, not at all alien even to the early West in the form of Jewish communities and Arian barbarian garrisons. An imperial tradition then, a service to Christendom and God, a military practicality, and an economic expedient—the tangle of motives and pressures is more human than the single motivation we are tempted to supply. King James was not so different from rich men of today who present buildings to their universities in an unabashed welter of motives: philanthropic altruism, family tradition, vanity in their name memorialized, status within their peer group, advertisement perhaps for their corporation, and (as the trigger) a very substantial tax write-off. As Mudejarism continued through the centuries, newer motives and pressures reshaped it. We tend to explain that evolution by the increasing irrelevance of the original single motive, a constant trajectory downward. The process seems rather to have been cyclical, as Mark Meyerson notes below, a copying and recrystallization of basic Mudejarism in Valencia.

What strikes us first about these survivalist communities is their basic structure. The public documents in King James' archives naturally focus on the component elements—the taxes owed, the Islamic officials to be dealt with, the parallel legal system, the military obligations, the arrangements for mosques and Islamic religious organization, and the distinct contexts of baronage-landlords versus the Crown's agents. Naturally enough, such recurrent themes receive the most attention from historians; we are forced to see the conquered through those aspects which most implicated the conquerors. Just below this level of vision, however, one can discern other elements: the community military leaders coopted as Mudejar lords; the Muslim craftsmen constituting the country's paper industry; the coordinating elite and patrician families; the activities of *aljama* councils; the farmers and the irrigation communities; the trades, the problem of language; the public baths; piracy and slaving; the internationally wandering sheep industry; literary elements; physical boundaries of every kind from farm to region; and a general populace whose acts of public-private worship continuously punctuated each working day and enlivened the town streets and rural roads. Below this level again, a surviving random charter can reveal a barber, a shipowner, a pilgrim, a crossbow instructor, a criminal, or a great landowner. On each level the shared experiences and borrowed mechanisms of the two societies can be explored.

These topics in turn occasion interpretation and conjecture. From exiguous references, or from Romance toponymy, can we discern the preconquest rural mode of production, or the relative weight of Berber and non-Berber demographics? From archeological rummaging can we know something about the early lord's grip (in Aragonese or opposed Catalan pattern) on his castle and tenants, and by implication something of the previously free farmer's reaction to having a European-type landlord? Indeed, can we ferret out the various kinds of preconquest farmers, perhaps mostly share-farmers, so as even to approach this problem with any confidence? Interpretation here, as on many points, involves macrohistorical or microhistorical analogies, and reflects as well each historian's idiosyncratic limitations and capacities.[7]

Going one level deeper, we reach a problem of meaning: Was the conqueror "tolerant" or "intolerant," and were the conquered reasonably well off or abominably mistreated or hopelessly divorced from their necessary core of identity? This question is bedeviled by semantic traps and confused by the imposition of modern value systems and of purely modern possibilities. The novice especially is fatally attracted to a premature plunge into its murky depths. Neither side would have accepted our modern Enlightenment idea of tolerance; we cannot solve dilemmas of the past with conceptual tools based on experiences available only to the present. A parallel and perhaps false problem is the meaning of the total trajectory of Mudejar experience; here the observer disdains the historical experiences, different both in space and time, supplanting the multiple realities with an abstract single situation everywhere, a philosophico-juridical condition rather than an evolving human reality. Though the Mudejar field has always tempted Spanish historians to generalizations, we are only now beginning to get the basic local and generational groundwork studies which might one day make such grand syntheses possible. The overwhelming mass of documentation still sits in the archives, awaiting the painful piecemeal labor of transcription and contextual interpretation. What we can see clearly is an Islamic subculture, wounded and reconstituted, a proud survivalist community, a transition and transformation. Míkel de Epalza

[7] For an introduction to these problems, see my *Muslims, Christians, and Jews*, pp. 31–36 ("Castles in Valencia"), pp. 39–51 ("Mudejar Farmers: Constructing Models"), and pp. 54–60 (motivation, influence of *dhimma*).

argues that such separate *aljamas*, loosely linked by their common identities, constitute a unique form of Islamic society.[8]

Interchange: Structure, Demography, Religion, and Language

The two communities, Christian-European and Islamic-Maghribian, met in the crusade generation in Valencia at a moment critical for each. Their confrontation in massed array at the battle of Las Navas de Tolosa in 1212 had dissolved the Almohad Empire uniting western Islam, and had shattered Spanish Islam (Al-Andalus) into political fragments. The ensuing civil wars, intrigues, assassinations, petty-state building, wars-within-wars, and general turmoil had both demoralized the Muslims and invited Christian invasion. In fact, King James marched into Valencia to support one side of an Islamic civil war, itself a complex of factions enmeshed in wider Islamic war. Conversely, James' Christians had reached a critical point. The battle of Muret in 1213 had begun a long process of retreat from southern France, constant if indirect conflict with the advancing Franks of St. Louis IX and Charles of Anjou there, and an ever-enlarging horizon on the maritime and Muslim fronts. Each society in crusader Valencia, Islamic and Christian, also constituted a local situation within its much wider cosmos. To understand their meshing, one must have some appreciation of the stage each cosmos had arrived at. A generation or two be-

[8] Míkel de Epalza, "Historia medieval de la península: tres culturas o tres religiones," *I Congreso internacional "Encuentro de las tres culturas"* (Toledo, 1983), pp. 99–104; idem, "Les morisques, vus à partir des communautés mudéjares précédentes," in *Les morisques et leur temps* (Paris, 1984), pp. 29–41. On the mutual incomprehension, or rather the contradictory contextual perceptions, see also idem, "Attitudes politiques de Tunis dans le conflit entre Aragonais et Français en Sicile autour de 1282," *XI Congreso de historia*, 2:579–98, especially the Maghribian view of the Christians' "reconquest" (pp. 582–87) and of "tribute" to a Christian state (pp. 588–90). See also Burns, "The Mudejars of Medieval Valencia: A Unique Community of Islam," *Islam: Continuity and Change*, ed. Thomas Michel (Rome, 1987), pp. 23–33 (also in *Salaam* [New Delhi] 8 [1987]: 189–98).

fore King James' Crusade, a thoroughly Islamicized and Arabized Valencia, aggressively Malikite-Sunnite in reaction to the Fatimid Shiite threat, had been radically revised in its institutions and character by Berber Almohad governance. On the Christian side, during the century before the Valencian crusade, Aragon and Catalonia had learned to live in union, each supplying its special strengths, while the Realms rose to world-power status—a progress the Mongol advance in the East, so destructive to Islamic power, would accelerate.

If the Muslims and Christians in Valencia each had their own wider cosmos and world vision, both peoples claimed the local area as peculiarly their own. The Mudejars would not perceive themselves as marginal or doomed, nor would the Christians acknowledge themselves to be invaders; each was at home, begrudging the alien. All these self-perceptions, local and wider, conditioned the interaction between the two societies. They dictated a chain of serious Mudejar revolts during each decade, for example, with Granadan-North African support, culminating in a great counter-crusade in 1276. And they drew King James away from consolidating his Valencian conquest to disperse his energies into southern France, Italian affairs, and crusades projected first to Byzantium and later to the Holy Land. The larger context allows us to see, indeed, that the very ending of the Valencian crusade in 1245, trumpeted by King James and Pope Gregory IX, was no triumph but a truce forced upon both parties by events in Maghribian Islam and in Frank-threatened Provence. The consequent "revolt" was therefore a natural resumption of hostilities after those external factors changed. Each society in Valencia affected the other, therefore, not only on the local or regional level but also as its higher and international levels; and both societies in their interaction were influenced by the external context.[9]

[9] For the dynamic between James' Provençal policy, his declaration of victory in Valencia, and Al-Azraq's revolt, see my *Muslims, Christians, and Jews*, chap. 10; idem, "The Loss of Provence—King James' Raid to Kidnap Its Heiress (1245): Documenting a 'Legend,' " in *XII Congreso de historia de la Corona de Aragón*, 3 vols. (Montpellier, 1987–1988), 195–231; idem, "The Crusade against al-Azraq: A Thirteenth-Century Mudejar Revolt in International Per-

At the most local level, the basic structure of Valencian Mudejar communities can be examined in the half-dozen surviving surrender constitutions, cast in the form of *cartas pueblas* or settlement charters. Other Valencian documentation reveals these central provisions as virtually universal. In the rare instances where a long siege ended in barely negotiated surrender, either in a crusade or a subsequent revolt, only the religious and bare administrative privileges were given. Thus the Muslims at first had to abandon Valencia city, while rural proprietors in its district had to hold their farms as mere share-tenants at the pleasure of the Christian owners. Christian settlement was heavier in such lightly privileged places, and the Muslim rural populations diminished there more swiftly.

The demographic balance in the kingdom of Valencia was never static. At first the Crusaders who remained amounted to little more than oases in a Sahara of Muslims. Settlement increased with painful slowness; some of its patterns and displacements can be discerned in the kingdom's *Repartiment* or book of land distribution. A quarter-century after the crusade had ended, however, King James still complained that only thirty thousand settlers (individuals or households?) had arrived, whereas one hundred thousand were essential to keep the kingdom safe from recovery by the Muslim masses. Mudejar numbers also fluctuated. Valencia city and Burriana, in resisting to the end, lost their whole urban populations to exile. Elsewhere the affluent or mobile drifted away progressively to Granada or North Africa. Each revolt displaced some population, especially notables. Dufourcq suggests that perhaps "20 percent" of those Muslims remaining by 1270 would have departed by 1300. On the other hand, the king and barons and

spective," *American Historical Review* 93 (1988): 80–106; idem, "A Lost Crusade: Unpublished Bulls of Innocent IV on al-Azraq's Revolt in 13th-Century Spain," *Catholic Historical Review* 74 (1988): 440–49; and idem (with Paul Chevedden), "Al-Azraq's Surrender Treaty with Jaume I and Prince Alfonso in 1245: Arabic Text and Valencian Context," *Der Islam* 66 (1989): 1–37. An example of radical external change affecting Valencian options can be seen in A. R. Lewis, "The Catalan Failure in Acculturation in Frankish Greece and the Islamic World During the Fourteenth Century," *Viator* 11 (1980): 361–69.

church labored to bring in Muslim settlers and to stanch the outflow, so as to maintain and increase a population so valuable economically.

The pattern of displacement is still being debated, as is its pace. The considerable data is susceptible of various interpretations and mapping. As late as 1337 a report to Rome by the metropolitan of the Catalan dioceses reckoned that Valencia's Mudejars could muster fifty thousand warriors. The same report quotes the bishop of Valencia at the beginning of the fourteenth century as having complained that mosques outnumbered churches in his diocese, while Muslims constituted "half or over half" of his jurisdiction. Realizing that the diocese was not the whole kingdom of Valencia, that the bishop's complaint probably referred to the most central part of the diocese where Christian church services were needed, and that the metropolitan was retailing hearsay in an offhand way, it is clear that the Mudejars everywhere seemed an oppressive presence. Even with the multiple expulsions, mob attacks, and flight during the thirteenth century, most of the Muslims apparently remained in place. Only in the fourteenth century would the decrease become a public problem and then a crisis, met by ineffective efforts to restrict emigration and mobility. As Boswell notes, it was not only the impact of the Black Death but more importantly the steady emigration throughout the fourteenth century, and mostly the disastrous flight during the last half of that century, which depopulated the Realms' *aljamas*. If Mudejars still constituted two-thirds of Valencia's population at the end of the fourteenth century, they may well have outnumbered Christians during the thirteenth century by four or five to one. Many generations later, by the mid-fifteenth century, M. C. Barceló Torres estimates, it is "very possible" that Mudejars numbered only one-third as many as the Christian population of Valencia. Henri Lapeyre reckons Valencian Muslims by 1600 specifically as 31,000 households against 65,000 Christians, to a total of 96,000.[10]

---

[10] Burns, *Islam*, pp. 72–81; Barceló Torres *Minorías islámicas*, pp. 64–67. For Boswell and Ferrer i Mallol, see below, n. 18. See Henri Lapeyre, *Géographie*

In this situation, each culture insidiously acculturated the other. No community of native Mozarabic Christians was available during the crusade generation to mediate that flow, though a large Jewish population had a role. The Muslim now inhabited a humiliating level of inferiority, traumatic in the light of Koranic destiny and superiority. The colonial authorities, however few and far between their groupings, had commandeered a network of mosques to serve as parish churches in every corner of the kingdom (even where Christians had not yet settled), had begun a Gothic cathedral and a number of Gothic churches, and were changing the urban landscape by introducing more plazas and other building projects. The Mudejar had to cope with a Western bureaucracy, new regulations and fees, jostling Christians at markets and public gatherings, the spectacle of more enterprising or opportunistic colleagues affecting a Romance surname or European mode of dress, and Christians coopting his public baths on an alternating schedule. The *aljama* itself, as a form of conciliar government, was a novelty imposed by Christian needs; and the tax-gatherer (*amīn*) was assuming undue importance in it as liaison between the two cultures. Conversely, the Europeans planted themselves in an exotic ambience, lived in towns embarrassingly "Moorish" with tangled street patterns, were surrounded by Muslim servants, slaves, mobs, retainer-bands, and rural farmers, and had

---

de l'Espagne morisque (Paris, 1959), p. 30, and the elaborate statistical study on pp. 16–91. Over these later centuries the distribution pattern radically shifted, of course, some areas remaining dominantly Muslim, others becoming relatively free or variously mixed. As much as the demographic balance, these distribution patterns dictated the nature of cultural interchange. Tulio Halperín Donghi maps his demographic estimates in *Un conflicto nacional: moriscos y cristianos viejos en Valencia* (Valencia, [1955–1957] 1980), pp. 284–286; app. A–C. Salvador de Moxó sums up current scholarship on the advancing Christian settlement in *Repoblación y sociedad en la España medieval* (Madrid, 1979), pt. 2, chap. 5 (Aragon), chap. 6 (Catalonia), chap. 7 (Balearics and Valencia). See also Dufourcq, *Histoire économique*, p. 169; my "Immigrants from Islam: The Crusaders' Use of Muslims as Settlers in Thirteenth-Century Spain," *American Historical Review* 74 (1975): 22–42; and the crown document listing Valencian *aljamas*, transcribed in my "Rehearsal for the Sicilian War: Pere el Gran and the Mudejar Countercrusade in the Kingdom of Valencia, 1276–1278," *XI Congreso* (1982), 2:259–87.

begun that selective borrowing in language, manners, and dress that other Christian societies would see as differentiating the Valencian Christian. The two peoples did not exactly "live together" harmoniously, as Américo Castro's famous term *convivencia* might suggest, but rather live symbiotically—recoiling but constantly impinging, each resigned to needing the other, each attracted to aspects of the other, but each repelled by that wholly Other.

To explore Valencian interchange, it will help to focus on specific situations. Conversion constitutes one such arena, affecting both the faith-community betrayed and the community into which the convert immigrates. Some Christians in Valencia became Muslims, but this was rare. Such conversion was a capital offense, with confiscation of property the penalty; in both Islam and Christendom apostasy was equated with treason. A Muslim convert to Christianity, by the same laws, could never reverse his decision without also falling under the death penalty. Religious assimilation to the colonial masters, on the other hand, brought obvious rewards; but a convert's life was not entirely happy. His former Muslim colleagues and family shrank from him, slanging and abusing him so that both King James and King Peter had to pass general decrees against molestation. The Muslim community also resented the loss of real estate which formed part of its patrimony, and the diminution of community control; it fought the laws introduced to transfer such property to the newly positioned owner, until eventually the convert was allowed only lifetime usufruct. Local Christian landlords and tax authorities resisted conversion of Mudejars even more stubbornly. Profits from neo-Christians were considerably less than those from Mudejars, once the church tithes and firstfruits had been deducted from the gross. As King James put it when arguing for explusion of rebellious Mudejars from Valencia: "I know your income will go down because you don't gain as much from Christians as from Saracens." This was an old story; Pope Innocent III had complained to the Catalan clergy in 1206 that "very many" Mudejars wanted baptism but were foiled by greedy lords. Just before the close of the Valencian crusade, James faced the problem of abrogating any "statute or agreement or even rooted custom" forbidding conversion.

Slaves so frequently sought baptism to gain freedom that churchmen passed their own laws requiring a testing period. Even the Jewish communities of the new kingdom suffered from slaves' conversions; "very many Jews" in the slave business, one charter tells us, sought redress from the Crown. The Valencian *Furs* freed slaves who converted with their lord's consent; due to popular outcry the code soon reversed itself and kept the convert in slavery. (This sequence parallels the experience of the converted Muslim slaves on Majorca and in the crusader Holy Land.) As a final deterrent to conversion, even the Christian population rebuffed converts. Ramon Lull scolded his Catalan readers for not welcoming but disdaining these new brothers. During the anti-Muslim riots that shook the Valencian kingdom from end to end in 1275, converts suffered along with Mudejars, revealing the strong ethnic prejudice underlying the religious bias. The Muslim, whether Mudejar or, after conversion to Christianity, still seemed alien. In terms of assimilation, it is instructive to contrast the acculturated Catalan and Aragonese Muslims with their brothers in Valencia, where even the converts would revert on occasion to their distinctive previous clothing. At the end of the thirteenth century, when Lérida's Mudejars frequently showed no distinction in dress or behavior from Christians, to the distress of the local bishop and the king, the converts in Valencia resumed "Moorish dress" at marriage feasts of their Mudejar friends, putting aside for the occasion their "Christian dress," also to the distress of the Crown.

Against all odds, many Valencian Mudejars did convert. Individual converts turn up at random in the Valencian records from before 1240 on. During the very siege of Valencia city, as a significant claim to ecclesiastical jurisdiction, churchmen elaborately baptized two Muslims under the beleaguered walls. The most celebrated convert, of course, was the ex-*wālī* of Valencia, the Almohad prince of the blood Abū Zayd, his reception hailed by the pope. At times a whole community of converts took joint action and thus left a record of its existence, as at Valencia city in 1275, Almusafes and neighboring towns in 1276, and Murviedro in 1281. In 1280 the Crown appointed the Dominican Arabist Joan de Puigventós to the office of visiting and supporting converted Muslims throughout the kingdom of Valencia; royal officials were ordered to gather the converts at each locality. At the turn of the century, the Crown even chartered a guild or brotherhood of converts.

The most powerful drive for proselytizing the Mudejars came from the new mendicant orders. Flocking to this promising frontier, Franciscans and Dominicans launched a sustained conversionist movement, intruding into the *aljamas*, with forced attendance by the Mudejars and at first with threatening Christian mobs in tow. The Franciscans favored a direct and confrontational approach, while the Dominicans (and some Franciscans, including the third-order layman Ramon Lull) put their hopes on rational argumentation, especially from shared metaphysical premises. The celebrated Arabic schools of the Dominicans in Valencia were at Valencia and Játiva, each centering on an agreed zone of activity divided by the Júcar River. For this rationalist labor in King James' conquests, Ramon Martí's polemical *Pugio fidei* against Moors and Jews, his elaborate *Vocabulista* of Arabic/Latin, and Thomas Aquinas's most famous work, the *Contra gentiles*, were constructed.

The Dominicans reported substantial success to Rome, starting with conversion of "almost all" the Muslim intellectuals hired to help staff these schools. Raymond of Penyafort, who gave up the generalate of the order to lead the conversionist movement in James' realms against Mudejars and Jews, extravagantly claimed ten thousand converts here and in the Castilian conquests. His successor Humbert de Romans in 1256 was likewise enthusiastic about progress. Penyafort's contemporary biographer also records his subject's success. Unfortunately for these hopes, as Dominique Urvoy has demonstrated, Almohad collapse on the eve of the crusade had triggered a Malikite religious revival, with a decisive turn from metaphysics to Sufi mysticism, thus blunting the entire rationalistic methodology.

What resulted from all approaches was a modest but significant body of converts, enough to rouse mendicant enthusiasm and Muslim anxiety. The reactive effect of this frontal assault doubtless fortified the Islamic communities, since the majority stood firm in their faith and the movement itself seems to have diminished with the closing of the schools after the turn of the century. As a form of interaction between the two peoples, conversionism had several faces—a passage for many into the conqueror's community, a reactive consolidation of orthodoxy among the great majority of Mudejars, "race" or ethnic prejudice among the settlers culminating in overt attack even against converts, a considerable problem in secular and ecclesiastical legal circles, and (as evidenced by the wedding-guest converts who resumed their "Moorish dress") even a rickety bridge between the two religious groups. Slaves and lords, bishops and popes, the Crown and mendicants and Jews all maneuvered and pondered the repercussions. The conversionist movement was Europe-wide at the time, with missioners off in chiliastic frenzy to Mongolia, Morocco, and a dozen other ethnic areas from Lithuania to Ethiopia and India, so that a dynamic of mutual causality might also be drawn between those wider events and the highly conversionist Valencian frontier.[11]

[11] On converts and conversionism in Valencia, see my "Christian-Islamic Confrontation in the West: The Thirteenth-Century Dream of Conversion," *American Historical Review* 76 (1971): 1386–1434, revised but lacking much of the footnote information in my *Muslims, Christians, and Jews*, chap. 3; idem, "Journey from Islam: Incipient Cultural Transition in the Conquered Kingdom of Valencia (1240–1280)," *Speculum* 35 (1960): 337–56; and idem, "The Missionary Syndrome: Crusader and Pacific Northwest Religious Expansionism," *Comparative Studies in Society and History* 30 (1988): 271–85. For the wider background, see Benjamin Z. Kedar, *Crusade and Mission: European Approaches toward the Muslims* (Princeton, 1984); Robert Chazan, *Daggers of Faith: Thirteenth-Century Christian Missionizing and Jewish Response* (Berkeley, 1989); and Jeremy Cohen, *The Friars and the Jews: The Evolution of Medieval Anti-Judaism* (New York, 1982). On Cohen, however, see also my "Anti-Semitism and Anti-Judaism in Christian History," *Catholic Historical Review* 70 (1984): 90–93. Missionary theory and approaches to infidel peoples are covered by James Muldoon, *Popes, Lawyers, and Infidels: The Church and the Non-Christian World, 1250–1550* (Philadelphia, 1979), esp. pp. 36–37 on the twenty target-peoples around 1250. For the convert Abū Zayd, see Emilio Molina López, *Ceyt Abu Ceyt: novedades y rectificaciones* (Almería, 1977); M. C.

The conquerors' systematic assimilative assault on the Mudejar population's inmost identity, its religion, had minimal success, though its interactive consequences must have been profound and lasting. Less basic, but still the most vital boundary-maintaining mechanism of any society after its religion is its language. No radical communal change was likely as long as this soul and color of Islamic life persisted, with its baggage of concepts, angles of vision, values, emotions, hopes, supports, and mental structures. Unlike the Mudejars of Aragon proper, Valencia's Mudejars clung to their language. Even in the late fourteenth century, Boswell notes, the Crown's translation problem in the north was to find a Mudejar literate in Arabic, while in Valencia it was to locate a Mudejar (or else an Arabist Jew or Christian) literate in Romance.

Recent detailed studies demonstrate that Valencia's Muslims were not bilingual on the eve of the crusade, despite a contrary assumption by linguists and historians. A number of individuals in the Mudejar camp had some practical grasp of Romance, just as some Christians could function with Arabic. Opportunism, administrative needs, missionary imperatives, and general coexistence of the two peoples increased the numbers in each camp, and especially provided interpreters. Much later, in fifteenth- and sixteenth-century Valencia, Arabic fragments introduced into sermons or literary productions indicate an evolution toward more general Christian acquaintance with elements of the alien language. Fourteenth-century Valencian Mudejars remained stubbornly unilingual. The natural increase of those few who could function in Romance seems to have

---

Barceló Torres, "El sayyid Abū Zayd: príncipe musulmán, señor cristiano," *Awrāq* 3 (1980): 101–9; Burns, *Islam*, pp. 301–4 and index under "Abū Zayd"; and idem, "Príncipe almohade y converso mudéjar: nueva documentación sobre Abū Zayd," *Sharq al-Andalus* 4 (1987): 109–22. On fourteenth-century minimal conversion, see Boswell, *Treasure*, pp. 378–81, and Ferrer i Mallol, *Sarraïns*, chap. 4 (the episodes on dress at Lérida and Valencia, in 1293 and 1304, respectively, are in the documentary app., docs. 1 and 4). By 1371 the Valencia city Muslim quarter was almost wholly inhabited by descendants of converts and other Christians—eighty households as against some sixteen of Muslims (ibid., p. 309, doc. 99).

slowed or reversed as successive conflicts increasingly ruralized the communities and drove them back upon themselves.

M. C. Barceló Torres has published an exhaustive study of this persistence of Arabic through succeeding centuries. She provides a technical analysis of its grammar and rhetoric, based on a collection of 270 documents from 1366 to 1595. Barceló Torres shows how Arabic maintained near-universal dominance among these Mudejars in later centuries, both as a public and a private language, not only in oral form but as a literate vehicle of culture. She rightly insists that Arabic was an official language of the Realms in Valencia. Its schools were protected by treaty constitutions, and tax receipts were accepted in Arabic by Christian treasury officials. Muslim public scribes functioned throughout Valencia, their contracts or documents roughly equivalent to the Christian instruments. The entire *dhimma*-type organization fostered the public survival of Arabic: continuance of an Islamic legal system, elections and internal administration, mosque services and sermons, and a mass solidarity of sheer numbers. As for Arabic's private continuance, Barceló Torres finds that "the immense majority" of Valencia's Mudejars in the next centuries spoke Arabic, and that literacy even among the ordinary folk seems to have been relatively high. Conversely, those Muslims with some grasp of Romance as a second language spoke it poorly and could not write it. Few Christians knew Arabic even during the later centuries of fully evolved contact, while the Muslim masses were accessible only in that language. Thus the Mudejars were locked into a conceptual, emotional, and linguistic system which excluded the colonial society and maximized the influence of their own religious leaders. The language barrier (a sacred language in a sense that neither Latin nor Hebrew claimed) was the primary practical factor alienating Mudejars and Valencian Christians. For four centuries, it remained the shield of Islam.[12]

---

[12] See Barceló Torres, *Minorías islámicas*, pp. 121, 136–51, and on the Valencian dialect, pp. 161–205; and idem, "La llengua àrab al país valencià (segles VIII al XVI)," *Arguments* (Valencia) 4 (1979): 123–49. See also Dolors Bramon, "Una llengua, dues llengües, tres llengües," *Raons d'identitat del país valencià ("pels i senyals")* (Valencia, 1977), pp. 17–47. For the thirteenth century,

The linguistic framework for reaction or confrontation between the two peoples raises several related questions. First, did these Muslims take Romance names (or an additional Romance name) and at what pace? Through most of the century such name-substitution was relatively rare in Valencia. It seems an "increasingly common phenomenon" as the fourteenth century wore on, Boswell notes; this may be less a sign of increasing interaction between the two separate populations than a byproduct of the Mudejars' lower morale and loss of nerve as Christian dominance came to seem both permanent and more oppressive. Second, though one can understand why Catalan had minimal influence on Valencian Arabic, why did Arabic not impinge on Catalan the way it was affecting Castilian (most of Castilian's Arabisms entered the language in the thirteenth century)? The wary hostility between these two Valencian peoples in close proximity may account for some of this. After all, Castile brutally swept the Mudejar population onto isolated estates, while Castilian elites patronized Arabic fashions and culture.

More significant, however, is the mature level of crusade Catalan (where Castilian was still groping toward its developed forms); Catalan was also more a single language then, as the chronicler Ramon Muntaner recorded, with minimal dialect differences. To this may be added the contrasting pattern of Muslim-Christian contact already established. The urbanized Catalan peoples formed part of an advanced Mediterranean European complex, with only a limited reconquest memory, while ruralized Castile had long reacted with the Muslims along its advancing frontier and had now burst upon an Islamic culture

---

see my "The Language Barrier: Bilingualism and Interchange," chap. 7 of *Muslims, Christians, and Jews*. Linguistic context and contending positions are discussed in Antoni Ferrando Francès, "Les interrelacions lingüístiques en la València doscentista: comentaris a les aportacions de Robert I. Burns," *Afers* 7 (1988–1989): 214–29. Ana Labarta has a dozen articles on Valencian Morisco dialect and writings, in *Awrāq, Al-Qanṭara, Dynamis*, and other journals. See also Boswell, *Treasure*, pp. 94, 203, 382–84; Joan Fuster, *Poetes, moriscos, i capellans* (Valencia, 1962), pt. 2. For the wider scene, see Federico Corriente, *A Grammatical Sketch of the Spanish-Arabic Dialect Bundle* (Madrid, 1977).

decidedly more advanced than its own. Finally, the topic of Arabic influence on Valencian has not been well investigated and may yet yield surprises. Even the Arabic loan-words are difficult to find in lexicons, because Catalan often drops the revealing article *al*; such words, however, are abundant. María Jesús Rubiera notes that Catalan Arabisms especially concern agriculture and the crafts. The evolution of Valencian as a Romance form distinct from Catalan doubtless owes much to the original frontier experience, in which an Islamic environment played a role along with the merely linguistic.[13]

Interaction: Daily Life and Mentality

Valencia's Mudejars, unlike those in some other regions, kept their military role. The men retained their weapons, practiced military games or exercises, and manufactured arms. Mudejar militia contingents were drafted into the royal armies in times of crisis, and were valued for naval service, though never as officers in authority over Christians. They routinely garrisoned local defenses and helped keep them in repair. In the late 1270s

[13] On Arabic impact on Catalan, see J. M. Nadal and Modest Prats, *Història de la llengua catalana*, 1 vol. to date (Barcelona, 1982), chap. 5, pt. 6, "Els arabismes del català"; and Joan Coromines, "Mots catalans d'origen aràbic," in his *Entre dos llenguatges*, 3 vols. (Barcelona, 1976–1977), 3:68–177. See also Manuel Sanchis Guarner, *La llengua dels valencians*, pp. 105–34, who stresses instead a Mozarabic substratum; idem, *Aproximació a la història de la llengua catalana* (Barcelona, 1980), pp. 128–35; V. L. Simó Santonja, *Valenciano o catalan?* (Valencia, 1975), pp. 212–17, who argues for a strong borrowing from and by the Valencian Mudejars (but see Barceló Torres, *Minorías islámicas*, pp. 131–33); idem, "Precisiones sobre algunos arabismos en valenciano y otros nuevos," *Estudis en memòria del professor Manuel Sanchis Guarner: estudis de llengua i literatura catalanes* (Valencia, 1984), pp. 25–28; and Míkel de Epalza, "Relacions de la cultura àrab i la cultura valenciana," *La cultura valenciana ahir i avui*, ed. Rafael Alemany (Alicante, 1986), pp. 65–76. Among the excellent studies by Míkel de Epalza, Joan Solà, Antoni Ferrando, and others in *Las lenguas prevalencianas* (Alicante, 1986), see esp. M. J. Rubiera, "Elementos árabes del valenciano," pp. 93–96. Boswell, *Treasure*, p. 381 (quote). Muntaner, *Crònica*, ed. Ferran Soldevila, *Les quatre grans cròniques* (Barcelona, 1971), c. 29.

the Crown sent the Jew Samuel b. Manasseh, of its Arabic chancery, from *aljama* to Valencian *aljama* to draft well-trained contingents of lancers and crossbowmen from each. At the French invasion of 1285, the Valencian *aljamas* sent six hundred Mudejar troops to the defense of Gerona, where their fearlessness and marksman skills made them legendary. The cardinal-legate behind that French crusade against the Realms of Aragon excoriated the king "who joined himself with Saracens" against Christendom, and who otherwise "could not stand alone." His comment points up the mutual influence of Muslim and Christian: a public role and esteem for Mudejars in the Realms, and a much improved army for the Christians of the Realms.

Particularly notable as a hybrid expression of mutual adaptation were the *almogàvers*, irregulars or special-forces sections of the royal army, drafted from the border ruffians of both peoples. Bernat Desclot describes these feared fighters as mixed "Catalans and Aragonese and Saracens"; their etymology in Arabic *al-mughāwir* underlines their non-European origins. An example of Valencian local defense was the obligation laid upon the Mudejars of the Vall de Uxó by their surrender constitution that "they must defend all my land" but were "not to go to places of war." At a more exalted level were the military aristocrats who survived the crusade as local leaders for the Crown (but who rapidly disappeared in the wake of several decades of rebellion). King James was angry when such military enclaves proved reluctant to aid him against Mudejar rebels. Mudejar retainers formed small private armies for Valencian nobles. In 1281 such a body drove off a Christian troop sent to rescue a Muslim slave woman, initiating a legal turmoil. Eventually these troops of retainers and tenants became a conservative force in league with Valencia's Christian aristocracy against the towns and Christian farmers. The Mudejar as Muslim warrior must have lent a certain dignity to his community in that bellicose era. He also represented a fairly generalized interaction, which would continue through subsequent centuries, notably when in 1347 the Crown drafted Mudejars to help put down rebellious Christian nobles in Valencia. During the war against

Castile in the 1360s, Boswell notes, "whole populations of Valencian Muslims were commandeered by the king to defend fortresses in endangered areas."[14]

Common patterns of life could draw Mudejar and Christian together in these early decades. Valencia was a hydraulic community, for example, its several *huertas* crisscrossed with irrigation networks pumping precious water from springs and rivers of unequal flow. This delicate mechanism, which King James extended considerably, required cooperation and skill on the part of both peoples; they constituted a water community practicing a difficult technical art. Due to stiff resistance and consequent forced surrender during the crusade, ownership of the irrigated regions of Valencia city and Castellón (then Burriana) passed to Christians. This doomed the Mudejars there to eventual displacement, so that virtually all would disappear over the next century. Even there, however, the first generations of Christian proprietors badly needed their Mudejar tenants. And meanwhile the acculturative diffusion of terms, techniques, and processes went forward both formally and nonformally.

A curious hybrid artifact from the postconquest water community is the Water Court or Tribunal, which still meets weekly at Valencia city's cathedral door, where black-robed farmers solemnly judge irrigation disputes. Though most Valencians and tourists believe they are witnessing an Islamic survival, this is a medieval colonial adaptation of the previous unipersonal jurisdictions in the *huerta* and of consultative sessions with those same persons as experts. Thomas Glick has analyzed the evolution of this hybrid, from nonjudicial consultation by

[14] Burns, *Islam*, chaps. 12 and 13, esp. "Muslims in the Christian Armies," pp. 288–99. See Boswell, *Treasure*, chap. 4, for the subsequent century. See also Burns, *Muslims, Christians, and Jews*, pp. 24–36, on Mudejar "lords"; and for the Crevillente lord, Pierre Guichard, "Un seigneur musulman dans l'Espagne chrétienne: le 'ra'ïs' de Crevillente," *Mélanges de la Casa de Velázquez* 9 (1973): 283–334. On the Mudejar retainers as leagued with conservative lords, see Ricardo García Cárcel, *Las germanías de Valencia* (Barcelona, 1975), pp. 208–16 (anti-Mudejar "paroxysm"); and cf. his earlier study with Eduard Císcar Pallarés, *Moriscos i agermanats* (Valencia, 1974). Desclot, Crònica, in Soldevila, *Cròniques*, caps. 79 (*almogàvers*), 136 (cardinal).

88 CHAPTER 2

persons who otherwise enjoyed their several subjurisdictions, down to the ad hoc jury-like decision visible in the early fifteenth century, to the formal and permanent tribunal now immemorially established. This represents a long dialogue between municipal authorities, Islamic relics, and the needs of a mixed rural community. Some such dialogue must have occurred in various other contexts of rural life. Whatever their type of economic base, most Mudejar proprietors or tenants related also to a local Christian power—a landlord for some, the Crown or a municipality for others, or for others again an ecclesiastical corporation. Military orders had their Mudejar tenants, as did the bishops and the eleemosynary and monastic institutions. For the Muslim, this shift from Islamic state control to a private arena also meant regular contact between each society in the rural-economic context.[15]

An unexpected interaction between the two peoples, subtly but profoundly altering an important aspect for both, centered on paper. Islamic paper manufactured at Játiva had been famous around the Mediterranean for its quality and quantity. The Realms of Aragon produced no paper, and the little they imported had not displaced parchment in governmental records. For over five years after the final conquest of Valencia's southernmost border, Játiva's domestic-type manufacturing continued in Muslim hands unchanged. Imposition of direct crown control there came in the 1250s, with removal of its Mudejar dynasty and administration to Montesa castle. Some time during the next twenty years, the Crown forced power technology into the conservative craft, attempting to mass produce with a central labor force in a water-powered mill. The resultant uproar roused the entire community and forced the king in 1287 to withdraw his plan and cease his building.

Water mills soon arrived nevertheless; and even from the late 1250s the royal chancery had begun its practice, then unknown

[15] Thomas F. Glick, *Irrigation and Society in Medieval Valencia* (Cambridge, Mass., 1970), pp. 65–68, 230–32 and *passim*. See also Glick's sensible discussion of socio-cultural interaction in general, though applied to an earlier period in Spain, in *Islamic and Christian Spain: Comparative Perspectives on Social and Cultural Formation* (Princeton, 1979), chap. 9.

in Western governments, of making official copies en masse on paper of outgoing documents of every kind. This occasioned a cheapening of the product, with successive efforts in this century and the next to reform the situation. King James, and his son after him, drew substantial profits from the burgeoning craft; they closely regulated it as a royal monopoly centered at Játiva alone, with detailed regulations as to its warehousing at Valencia city, its measurements, and its wholesaling. Stealing paper pulp became a serious crime. By this mechanization the Crown profoundly modified the most important industry of the Valencian Mudejars. It increased the community's output and affluence, and brought the craftsmen into close (and at times bellicose) cooperation with royal officials. On the Christian side, it transformed the nature and quantity of recordkeeping and marks a turning point in the history of government, bureaucracy, and the Western psyche—the "Paper Revolution."[16]

Aside from the practical business of taxes or the urgent business of Christian polemics and conversionism, the intellectual elites of both societies had little to say to each other. Some have conjectured that this silence evidences a sudden and total flight of Islamic elites. We must be careful here. Evidence does show a loss of many of the more mobile affluent people, especially in the rare case of brutal conquest as at Valencia city. Unlike the Christian takeovers at places such as Murcia or Majorca, however, Valencian Islam was gobbled up whole, a society wounded but at first intact. Progressive revolts and expulsions eroded the administrative elites, with those they patronized; but Muslims remained the great majority throughout this century. Ample evidence demonstrates a reasonable stratum of affluent and even wealthy Mudejars among them, in town and country, who certainly supported the usual intellectual or subintellectual strata. Islamic society did not have only a single

[16] Much misunderstanding and false claims cloud this whole story—from nonexistent paper mills in twelfth-century Catalonia to nonexistent water-powered paper mills in Islam's Maghrib. I have thoroughly disentangled these many problems in my *Society and Documentation*, chaps. 23–28, including power technology, techniques, marketing, and crown control.

rootless class of intelligentsia and the creative, anyway, to move en masse: it wove these into its fabric at many levels and in various modes. The *faqīh* class is abundantly evident in postcrusade Valencia, as is a lively Koranic legal system. And the mosque schools here remained unusually good.

If truly distinguished names seem absent, that norm for testing a culture must itself be examined. First, precrusade Valencia had not sparkled with scientific or literary productions, because the Almohad era had discouraged the cultural elements. The Crusaders thus inherited an intellectual-creative scene dispirited internally. More to the point, our rich documentation for reconstructing Valencia's Mudejars comes almost exclusively from Christian sources, and mostly from pragmatic government documents. Chancery personnel had little occasion for, or interest in, recording any aspect of Mudejar cultural life. On the Arabic side, external Islamic communities rather wrote off the humiliated Mudejars, even the Hispanophile Ibn Khaldūn professing a disdain for these now invisible brethren. Politically the Islamic powers still mourned and acted upon their lost brothers; but the easy cultural links had snapped and travel interchange was less facile. Nor did James the Conqueror or Peter the Great become patrons of Islamic culture after the style of their contemporary, Alfonso the Learned of Castile, in deliberately translating and assimilating Islamic arts and sciences. Finally, wholesale destruction of Arabic records and books much later sealed from the historians' sight any such view of Valencia's early Mudejar community.

One field of learning not only lies open to examination but provides an instructive lesson in Mudejar-Christian interaction. Medicine, in its research and instructional side particularly, developed into a cross-cultural confrontation. Luis García Ballester, who has studied the phenomenon throughout Spain from the thirteenth to the sixteenth century, sees Valencian Mudejar medicine as enjoying "a brilliant and fugitive moment of splendor which persisted during the first fifty to seventy-five years following the conquest." Not a static moment but a dynamic evolution, it involved three main elements, each represented by a distinguished Valencian. The first individual is Arnau de Vilanova, representing García's "frontier medicine," the fruitful convergence of Islamic, Judaic, and Christian traditions inescapably mixed. Born during the Valencian crusade, Arnau took up residence at Valencia city some time after the conquest; his daughter later became a nun there. He mastered Arabic, and in his enthusiasm for Islamic medicine translated a series of its important works into Latin, including a treatise by the Valencian Abū Ṣalt Umaiya. In the early 1280s Arnau studied Hebrew and the Talmud at Barcelona. His seventy scientific works made him the first great figure of Western medicine, and its pioneer also in pharmaceutical advance. His positions as professor at the University of Montpellier and as physician-regular to three kings of Aragon and three popes, gave him a Europe-wide forum. Michael McVaugh sees him as "the principal figure in Montpellier's fusion of the western empirical tradition with the systematic medical philosophy of the Greeks and Arabs." To García he represents the Valencian mix of the three peoples in its earliest stage, and the gift of Islam within that promising context.

A counter-movement is represented by Andreu Albalat, bishop of Valencia from shortly after the crusade in 1248 up to the death-year of King James in 1276. Dominican, royal counselor, papal legate, and brother to the metropolitan for the Realms, Andreu fostered by his patronage of medical studies the scholastic medical mode as against the Judeo-Arabic. Reactive and hostile to the Muslim presence, vigorously "Christianizing" Valencia during thirty years by such expedients as eight synods and a Gothic cathedral, Andreu brought Italian medical influence boldly into Valencia and the Realms. García sees the two instructional models as encapsulating the two opposed mentalities: the domestic model of Judeo-Arabic medicine proclaimed by the *Furs* law code of Valencia, and the European scholastic (or here rather Italian) model with its centralized University of Valencia.

The third figure caught up in this tension is the distinguished Valencian Mudejar, Muḥammad al-Shafra al-Qirbilyanī, born and raised in Crevillente near Elche during the last third of the century; when Crevillente's Mudejar lordship or enclave was directly absorbed by the Crown in 1318, Muḥammad emigrated to Granada. Ironically, he had undertaken his medical and surgical studies under the Christian Mestre Bernat, whose views he espoused vigorously against what he saw as Mudejar and Christian decadence of the profession. In Muḥammad we see the triumph of the colonial elite over the pure native traditions, the alien tradition internalized. Medical licensing, by a board de facto Christian and by examinations in Latin books, soon tightened the Christians' psychological control. An effort from 1359 to restrict Christian access to men and women Muslim doctors (the women were licensed as regular physicans explicitly to treat men and women) proved ineffectual but signaled the coming decline. Having become physicians in the Christian manner, "at the cost of cultural disintegration," they were caught in rising intolerance in the Realms from the late fourteenth century onward, and dwindled in numbers as the Mudejars became increasingly ruralized. Direct promulgation of Arabic medical literature continued, but mostly within the Jewish communities. Mudejar medical learning passed from scientific to folk medicine.

During that thirteenth-century "brilliant moment of splendor" in the medical field, one influential component has been neglected. Jews trained after the Arabic-domestic model of the *ḥakīm* were prominent at court and as liaisons between Muslims and Christians. Like their Mudejar counterparts, they were at once savants and physicians, repositories of many levels of ancient Greco-Arabic wisdom. Such physicians had an exalted status far beyond that of any modern doctor, and their circulation in the contacts and administration of the Realms must be entered into our cross-cultural reckoning.[17]

[17] Luis García Ballester, *La minoría musulmana y morisca*, vol. 1 of his projected *Historia social de la medicina en la España de los siglos XIII al XVI* (Madrid, 1976), quotations from pp. 12, 18, 29, materials largely from chap. 1, pp. 15–65. Michael McVaugh, who is editing Vilanova's *Opera medica omnia*, 2 vols. to date (Granada, 1975–), does the entry "Arnald of Villanova" in the *Dictionary of Scientific Biography* (New York, 1970–), 1:289–91 (quotation) and in the *Dictionary of the Middle Ages*, ed. J. R. Strayer, 13 vols. (New York, 1982–1989), 1:537–38. See also "Autumn of the Creative Class," in my *Islam*, pp.

Unlike the medical drama, other sciences had no intercommunity social impact, so that Christian records convey no similar information. Játiva's historian and traveler 'Abd Allāh b. Aḥmad who died in 1323, or Cocentaina's thirteenth-century Mudejar mathematician and astronomer Abū 'l-Hassam 'Alī b. Abialī, or the later sage al-Shāṭibī ("the Jativan") hint at less-documented glories. Barceló Torres has also discovered a continuing scholarship, preservative if not particularly creative, in the centuries following the thirteenth. Arabic books were common and scholars visited Granada and Cairo to study. The school category included higher learning, and there are further names of Valencian Mudejar scholars in the sciences, grammar, theology, and law. Still, the positive intellectual-creative mixing in Valencia is not to be found in scholarship, art, and formal letters; there the acculturative impact on both people was more reactive and hostile. The pervasive and significant influence must be sought at the subintellectual levels, so subtle that only long-term consequences can reveal it, in folklore, peculiarly Valencian aspects of daily life, loan-words, entertainment, stories, attitudes, and expectations—the Valencian *mentalité*. Here too the reactive must be studied as well the positive.

Mudejar life was not all of a piece in Valencia. Urban craftsmen, merchant entrepreneurs and shipowners, professional soldiers and retainers, stockmen on the international sheepwalks, skilled hydraulic farmers and ordinary dry-farmers, Albufera lagoon fishermen, tax farmers and *waqf* managers, Koranic scholars, and other occupational groups and levels of affluence appear in the king's registers, each group having little in common with the other in its own daily rounds. The "Moors of the Mountains" in the far south, in their special tax-collectory, could be contrasted with those of other geographic areas of Valencia, an unusually variegated country with a complex political

---

413–20. On the *ḥakīm*, see my *Muslims, Christians, and Jews*, pp. 157–59; and idem, *Society and Documentation*, pp. 127–31. See too Antoni Cardoner i Planas, *Historia de la medicina a la Corona de Aragón* (Barcelona, 1973), esp. pp. 35–54; Barceló Torres, *Minorías islámicas*, pp. 139–40. Al-Shafra is remembered and honored in Alicante, with "Premios al-Shafra" awarded to local authors.

background. And the mere passage of time, as immigration increased by new patterns and ever-wider distribution, and as administrative Christian power and ecclesiastical presence consolidated, meant an ever-evolving balance between the two peoples. The century has a unity of its own, nevertheless, distinct from the more punitive and even catastrophic fourteenth century.

The Black Death in 1348 altered the population pattern and balance, while extrinsic crises and opportunities brought essential changes to the Realms and to their Mudejar communities, ranging from the constitutional and economic to the psychological. This era is being extensively studied as a period of imperial expansion and domestic change. Boswell has particularly investigated its Mudejars, underlining the crucial loss of their population and affluence due to the war between Aragon and Castile in the 1360s, bringing "far-reaching" changes in Mudejar life-style, loss of "huge amounts of property" by Muslims, an increased pace of enslavement, "a considerable decrease in personal mobility," "staggering proportions" of defection by Valencian communities and individuals to the Castilian invaders, and a continuing severe decline of population. Ferrer i Mallol is exploring a wider trajectory in that century, with a steady leakage of Mudejar population, punctuated by exoduses during the 1296–1304 Castilian war, the Granadan invasions of 1302 and 1331/32, and the civil wars in 1336 and 1347. She finds a truly troublesome diminution of Mudejar population at least from 1345, aggravated by the Black Death and the Castilian wars, then decreasing more drastically while authorities variously tried to stem the flow, until major legislation was introduced in 1403 to immobilize the Mudejars. Just as the profile of the Realms and of Europe itself underwent major changes, so too did Mudejar life. In the Valencian kingdom, despite all changes, the demographic weight of Islam remained heavy, while interaction continued in new and old patterns. In the late fourteenth century, two-thirds of Valencia's population remained Muslim, compared to one-third for Aragon and a negligible 3 percent for Catalonia. Even at the end of four centuries under Christian rule, one-third of Valencia's final mixed population would be Moriscos.

Even the catastrophic fourteenth century, however, is not always what it seems. The famous decree in 1311 by the ecumenical Council of Vienne, prohibiting the call of the muezzin in Christian lands, illustrates the complexity. Ferrer i Mallol has studied the decree in Valencia. Technicalities delayed its promulgation in Christendom until 1316; several years of papal pressure thereafter finally moved James II to apply this novelty. He had conferences of Mudejars called in several Valencian regions, six representatives from each important *aljama*. There his officials explained how the king could not refuse the council's order, but they strongly reassured the *aljamas* that no other religious privilege would change. The Valencian barons resisted on a large scale on nonroyal lands. A church council of the Realms in 1330 complained of this noncompliance, and decreed excommunication on recalcitrant landlords. Pope John XXII rebuked King Alfonso and ordered compliance. In 1338 King Pere the Ceremonious moderated the Vienne decree itself, but almost immediately had to reverse himself. Some *aljamas* were arranging individual compromises with the Crown; in 1357 Játiva agreed to have the muezzin call from ground level. In 1360 the Tortosa synod again forbade muezzins, but depopulation from the Castilian wars forced the king to guarantee muezzins to various communities to hold their loyalty. In 1371 the Valencian *corts* demanded full prohibition; the king refused, and also recommended the trumpet call as not covered by Vienne. Trumpets sounding above the church bells then infuriated the townspeople. As prince, Martí was severe on the matter of muezzins in his Valencian holdings in the 1380s but was soon making exceptions. As king he tried severity again in 1403; his successor also tried in 1417. In short, even this major setback for Mudejar religious expression was not so simple a matter as historians suppose.

The thesis of a continual decline, either from the thirteenth century or after the Black Death, down to the final expulsion in the seventeenth century, is traditional and remains popular. Jacqueline Guiral-Hadziiossif challenges the traditional "image of the Valencian Muslim serf" confined largely to farming by the fifteenth century. Most rural Mudejars continued to have a mixed agricultural-artisan life, a continuum with the Mudejar artisans of the towns. A considerable percentage of town Muslims continued the maritime commerce of their predecessors; "among the [Mudejar] crowd of individual small-merchants" in the Africa–Granada trade were great mercantile houses with branches abroad. Mudejar merchants traded also to Italy, Languedoc, and the Atlantic. Whatever their disabilities, Mudejars were "well integrated into the economic life" of the kingdom, without discrimination. Guiral-Hadziiossif detects "the first signs of a popular and generalized hostility" only from the mid-fifteenth century—a startlingly different conclusion from that of Ferrer i Mallol for the previous century.

Mark Meyerson's research on Valencia's Mudejars in the last quarter of the fifteenth century challenges the traditional view even more strongly and in far greater detail. He finds a Muslim society still remarkably stable, prosperous enough (with a class of growing affluence plus an underclass immobilized by poverty), not under the pressures of their colleagues in Castile but protected by the Crown and sought after by the landowners, without the rebellions of the thirteenth and fourteenth centuries. Meyerson discounts the "ideological antagonism"; it was a permanent given, a component taking varying forms as stresses and circumstances dictated, but manageable as new coping mechanisms emerged. He sees rather a major difference between the economic-social situation of the Mudejars in the thirteenth or fifteenth century and the situation in the fourteenth and sixteenth centuries. Late fifteenth-century Muslims were more integrated with the Christian society in its economic functioning, less a counter-society than an adaptive, resilient community. In short, traditional Mudejarism had survived all blows, recovered well, and was fixed firmly in place in Valencia. For Meyerson the tragedy of the expulsion here has other roots and meanings.[18]

[18] Boswell, *Treasure*, pp. 236–39, 287, 385–87, 391–94. Ferrer i Mallol, *Sarraïns*, chaps. 8, 9; on muezzins, pp. 88–94. A thorough orientation for

Other terms of interaction and influence between the two peoples in thirteenth-century Valencia suggest themselves. The Islamic *muḥtasib* or public inspector became the Christian *mostassaf* as elsewhere in Spain, with the Christian form of that institution then reciprocally reinforcing the preexistent Mudejar office! Information on Valencia's *mostassaf* invites exploration of how this region's unique Mudejarism shaped that yo-yo interchange locally. Another functionary prominent in either society, with a similarly long history in Islamic and Christian Spain, was the *shīʿa* and his Latinate counterpart the *exea*. He represented the civil authority and bereaved families of his homeland, traveling abroad to negotiate the unending series of ransoms for his coreligionists. In Valencia the Christian *exea* was no longer the primitive merchant-rescuer but a crown appointee of distinction. Joan de Cámera held the post for southern Valencia until 1273, when King James appointed first Guillem d'Antist and then Eximeno Pérez de Isco, responsible for the convoys of ransomed Christians coming in and of ransomed Muslims going out. Four years later we see the Crown settling two foreign brothers, ʿAlī and Muḥammad "Abcocon" (Abū Qaqūn?), at Valencia city, accepting them as coming in the office of counterpart *shīʿa*. They could arrange to ransom and convoy Muslims to Islamic lands and Christians into the Realms. The two offices thus overlapped, each supplementing the other. Both men and their staffs enjoyed a profitable monopoly, ransoming the affluent. More visible to the general populace, and doubtless more significant as go-betweens and mediators of cultural elements, were the caritative ransomer orders, the Trinitarians and Mercedarians, who had convents and halfway houses in Valencia; in this formative generation, their ransom preaching, alms collecting, and travels into Islamic

---

fourteenth-century Spain is *La investigación de la historia hispánica del siglo XIV: problemas y cuestiones* (Madrid, 1973), with extensive bibliographical-thematic articles on Aragon, Catalonia, Majorca, Murcia, and related topics. On demographics, see also above, n. 10 and text; for Meyerson, see n. 6. See also Jacqueline Guiral-Hadziiossif, *Valence, port méditerranéen au XVe siècle (1410–1525)* (Paris, 1986), pp. 337–48.

lands contributed toward defining relations between the two societies in Valencia.

A significant peculiarity too is the absence of Mudejar architecture in so uniquely Mudejaresque a land as Valencia. Where Aragon's much less dominant Mudejar presence invited a creative proliferation of this hybrid, Valencian Christians systematically avoided it. This seems a classic illustration of reactive acculturation, of retreat into mediocre replications of European Gothic in thirteenth-century Valencia to reinforce identity and separatism. Minor influences, such as carpentry in a Valencian church or decorative elements affecting the earliest portion of the Romanesque-Gothic cathedral, are so rare as to emphasize the universal lack. More ambiguous is the Islamic-Mudejar ceramics tradition. It has long been fashionable to root the celebrated plates and pots of Valencia, especially of Paterna and Manises, in precrusade and postcrusade Muslim industry. A Mudejar pottery craft was indeed protected at Játiva in the mid-thirteenth century, and the *Furs* code gave tax relief throughout Valencia to all makers of pots, pitchers, tiles, "and any other product of earth or glass." We do not find the craft at Paterna and Manises until the early fourteenth century, however, by our present fragmentary evidence. Then the first ceramicists there were Mudejars; Christians soon joined them, and the two art traditions seem to converge.

The very taxes paid by Mudejars and Christians offer to our view convergences and analogies. Even an element so small and obscure as the tax or service called *sofra* (Arabic *sukhra*) opens a fresh view on the variety of interchanges. Epalza has clarified the nature of this original Islamic work or community service; its resiting in the alien Christian-Mudejar society reoriented and expanded it, assimilating it eventually to European labor services for a landlord. Its name and function retained some vestige of its origins, however—a hybrid in the early generation of Valencian Mudejars and a link with the Islamic past.

A final example of neglected elements through which to explore interchange is the autobiography of King James the Conqueror, largely the product of his Valencian experiences. The only autobiography of a Western ruler, structured in a bizarre conception-to-burial format, relentlessly focusing only on the godly military "Deeds" of its title, and alien to the ecclesiastical culture of its time, this strange book resembles the autobiographical-biographical genre of rulers' deed then dominant in Islam. At the same time it receives that alien genre into a confessional-biographical European tradition, producing a hybrid whose influence on Valencian and the wider Catalan literate mentality was decisive. Unlike the schizophrenic productions of the Majorcan Franciscan Anselm Turmeda in the following century, who as a convert to Islam and noted holy man became the only European notable as a classic author both in Arabic and a European language, King James instead absorbed and inculturated to produce a synthesis of *mentalités* at this one level.[19]

[19] On the *muhtasib-mostassaf*, see Pedro Chalmeta's extensive *El "señor del zoco" en España: edades media y moderna, contribución al estudio de la historia del mercado* (Madrid, 1973), pt. 2, chaps. 4–5. On the *shī'a-exea*, see J. W. Brodman, *Ransoming Captives in Crusader Spain: The Order of Merced on the Christian-Islamic Frontier* (Philadelphia, 1986), pp. 7–9, 111; M. T. Ferrer i Mallol, "La redempció de captius a la corona catalano-aragonesa (segle XIV)," *Anuario de estudios medievales* 15 (1985): 237–97, esp. pt. 5; and idem, "Els redemptors de captius: mostalafs, eixees o alfaquecs (segles XII-XIII)," *Homenatge al Prof. Frederic Udina* (Barcelona, forthcoming). The *Il Simposio de mudejarismo* is devoted entirely to the topic of some three to four dozen studies, while substantial portions of both the first and the recent third symposia (twenty-five papers in the latter) also explore it. See, e.g., Asunción Alejos Morán, "Carpintería mudéjar en una iglesia valenciana," *II Simposio*, pp. 261–69. As an introduction, see also G. M. Borras Gualis, *Arte mudéjar aragonés* (Zaragoza, 1978); and Basilio Pavón Maldonado, *Tudela, ciudad medieval: arte islámico y mudéjar* (Madrid, 1978). On ceramics, see Burns, *Islam*, p. 93, adding to the bibliography there Andrés Bazzana et al., *La cerámica islámica en la ciudaad de Valencia*, 1 vol. to date (Valencia, 1983–), pp. 13–21; and P. López Elum, "La conquista cristiana de Mallorca y Valencia, y su repercusión en el ámbito de la cerámica," *V Jornades d'estudis*, pp. 241–46. On *sofra*, see "Sofra as Link and Rupture," in my *Muslims, Christians, and Jews*, pp. 67–71, which advances and deepens my previous more detailed contribution on the subject as against Pierre Guichard's "Le problème de la sofra dans le royaume de Valence au XIIIe siècle," *Awrāq* 2 (1979): 64–71. See esp. the pioneering study of Valencia's Islamic *sukhra* by Míkel de Epalza and M. J. Rubiera, "La *sofra* (*sujra*) en el Sharq al-Andalus antes de la conquista catalano-aragonesa," *Sharq al-Andalus* 3 (1986): 33–37. See Pedro López Elum, "Carácter plurifuncional de la sofra," *Anuario de estudios medievales* 17 (1987): 193–206, who merely reframes the data without

Valencian Versus Sicilian Mudejarism

It may be helpful to compare, however briefly, the Valencian model of Mudejar-Christian relations with that of Norman/ Hohenstaufen Sicily which faced Valencia across the western Mediterranean. The respective models are broadly comparable, though two factors complicate the process: (1) Sicilian documentation is meagre compared with the Valencian riches, despite the fine old collections of S. Cusa and Michele Amari; and (2) Sicilian Mudejarism went through its death-throes during the half-century before the Valencian form emerged. The fragmented community observed by Ibn Jubayr in Sicily in 1185, with its high functionaries at the Norman court, its mosques, schools, markets, tomb-shrines, and autonomous quarters, was already in a state of decline, apprehension, emigration, and conversionist pressure. In the next decade, anarchy and revolt transformed the situation into a precarious one. Final confrontation came under Frederick II Hohenstaufen, who vigorously put down the various Muslim rebels and expelled the Muslim remnants to far-away reservations like Lucera, until he had "ended all vestige of the Muslim presence" in Sicily. The small Luceran colony survived another generation, pressured by the new Angevin rulers, and in 1300 was dispersed and enslaved by Charles II of Anjou. Valencian Mudejars during the thirteenth century, from the 1230s through the long reign of James the Conqueror and his son Peter the Great, experienced their period of greatest strength. Despite rebellions, James and his barons and prelates worked actively to sustain their numbers in town and country, and encouraged immigration of outside Muslims on a considerable scale. Thus a fairer comparison might take Sicily's twelfth-century communities with Valencia's thirteenth-century ones, or Sicily's last generation with those of Renaissance Valencia, despite the clumsy chronological-contextual cross-over.

---

having followed the evolution of the dispute. On King James' autobiography in its Islamic setting, see my *Jaume I i els valencians*, pp. 7–14; and idem, "The King's Autobiography: The Islamic Connection," in *Muslims, Christians, and Jews*, app. 1.

Within the thirteenth-century frame, however, we note any number of similarities or analogous situations. A preoccupation with conversion affected both lands, for example; and even Ramon Lull, the major spokesman for the conversionist movement in the Realms of Aragon, held a conversionist commission from Charles II of Anjou in 1294 at Lucera in Apulia. Both Sicilian and Valencian Muslims served in the respective royal armies as contingents; and both manufactured valued weapons for the Christian armies. In both places the Arabic language survived, though in unequal degree, as a boundary-maintaining mechanism. Both kings distrusted their Muslim populations, and both became involved in serious wars of repression against their rebels. Conversely, King James did not imitate Frederick of Sicily and Alfonso el Sabio of Castile in encouraging Islamic learning, art, and manners; instead he labored to transform the architectural and symbolic appearances of conquered Valencia after European models.

James' Catalan administrators and settlers had little previous experience of such interior colonies of Muslims, while the more backward or ruralized Aragonese had a limited, largely structural rural experience. This circumstance made the maximum Mudejarism of Valencia, a sea of Muslims around islands of Christians, more akin to conditions in earliest than in late Norman Sicily. At the prosaic structural level, we find in both countries organization by *aljamas*, each with its *qā'īd*, *qāḍī*, and council of sheiks, and the expected taxes, ubiquitous institution of slavery, and proud craftsmen. An intriguing similarity in the initial structure of both populations was the stratum of aristocratic families. By the phenomenon Epalza calls "eminential" government in Islamic lands, basic power had always remained with such families under very loose control by a central government. During internal crises and external threat, these families provided leaders, often taking over the local castles and forts. Both in Valencia and Sicily the Christian rulers appropriated these leaders as a kind of Mudejar feudalism or as clients and functionaries. Henri Bresc believes that a key to the easy control of Sicily's Muslims was betrayal by these families: the conquerors coopted and even converted them, so that few natural leaders remained available to Sicily's rebellious communities.

'Azīz Aḥmad suggests that the difference between Spain and Sicily in the treatment of Muslim populations was Spanish intolerance over against Norman tolerance and commingling. Bresc has attempted a more penetrating analysis in his brief paper on the problem of acculturation in Sicily and Valencia. He finds that Sicily's destruction of its Muslims was brutal and swift, without the long period of relative self-possession by Valencia's Muslims through the fourteenth century. This Latinization he attributes especially to massive Christian immigration, successful conversion tactics (especially via the Greek clergy and strategic monasteries), and the deterioration of Arabic as the common language until by 1250 the remaining Muslims generally used Romance language and names. (Aḥmad sees language as more enduring, and makes a case for its survival at least in a formal sense.)[20]

Similar comparisons between the countries and their regions throughout the Iberian peninsula might be fruitful. The Mudejar situation was differently experienced in the several realms of Castile and in Portugal. Across time, the Mudejar complex evolved, as its Christian and Muslim contexts underwent change in all component elements. To interpret any Mudejar experience, even the "same" experience of one region in different generations, one must insert it into those contexts—for instance, the local, the structural, and the immediate as well as the wider European and Islamic, and the personal. A substratum of identity and continuity does need to be discerned and appreciated, over geographical-human spaces as over time; the Morisco is the Mudejar writ large, as Epalza insists, the experience of the one not alien to the other. Paradoxically, however, the Mudejars of any given Iberian time and place differ in striking ways from those of another. As with any other society or individual, the Mudejars suffered history.

[20] 'Azīz Ahmad, *A History of Islamic Sicily* (Edinburgh, 1975), pp. 68 (tolerant), 86 ("all vestige"), 105 (language survives), 106 (Lull). Henri Bresc, "La feudalizzazione in Sicilia dal vassallaggio al potere baronale," in *Storia della Sicilia*, ed. Rosario Romeo, 10 vols. (Naples, 1977–1981), 3:505–8; and idem, "Mudéjars des pays de la Couronne d'Aragon et Sarrasins de la Sicile normand," *X Congreso, Corona de Aragón*, 3:51–60.

3

THE END OF MUSLIM SICILY

David S. H. Abulafia

THE KINGDOM OF SICILY has long been characterized as an island of tolerance; the harmonious coexistence of Greek and Latin, Jew and Muslim is said to be symbolized by the unashamed mixing of Byzantine, Romanesque, and Arabic styles in King Roger II's *Cappella Palatina*, or by Frederick II's correspondence with Muslim scholars and his patronage of Jewish translators.[1] Yet this is only to speak of the royal court, and of the kingdom without its mainland half. There, despite some settlement in the late Byzantine period, few Muslims could be found until Frederick II emptied the island of Sicily of its Muslim rebels, resettling them at Lucera in Apulia from the 1220s on. In any case, the fact that he had a Muslim rebellion on his hands is revealing; for the *convivencia* of Christian and Muslim on the island had broken down decades before his birth. Repeated outbreaks of violence in Palermo, in 1160/61, for instance, prove how fragile the peace between communities was already under the Norman kings. At first sight, then, the harmony attributed to the royal court seems far removed from a grimmer social reality beyond the palace walls. Yet the royal court is itself an indicator of the fundamental changes that were taking place in the religious and ethnic composition of Sicily between about 1100 and 1300: the Christianization of the island under the dual influence of

---

[1] See, e.g., D. C. Douglas, *The Norman Fate, 1100–1154* (London, 1976), pp. 146–49, for an extreme statement of a positive view. Ernst Kitzinger has tended to argue that the Palatine Chapel speaks for the symbiosis of Latin (even Norman-French), Greek, and Arab. See, e.g., idem, *The Art of Byzantium and the Medieval West* (Bloomington, 1976), pp. 290–313.

the Greek and Latin Churches; the arrival of large contingents of emigré mainlanders from Campania, Apulia, Liguria, Tuscany, and even from beyond the Alps; and the creation of a Romance language in Sicily, a young offshoot of mainland Italian dialects, first clearly revealed in a school of Sicilian court poets whose lack of inspiration is compensated by their influence on greater successors in Tuscany. In identifying these phenomena, it is possible also to identify the hand of the royal court, which did much to mold the new, Latinized Sicily of the thirteenth century. Perhaps a quarter of a million Muslims had lived on the island at the time of the Norman conquest, consisting of more than half the population (the rest largely Greek, with some Jews); about twenty thousand Saracens were deported to Lucera; and, even though a few lingered on in Sicily and its dependent islands, this 90 percent reduction in a century and a half raises the question of where most of the Muslims went and who came in their stead.

The transformation of Sicily can be approached from another direction—its economic relations with its Mediterranean neighbors and the effect these relations had on the composition and commercial function of the Sicilian cities. For just as the island itself was Latinized, so too were its trade routes. From the early twelfth century the Genoese, Pisans, and Venetians were able to establish trading bases in Palermo and Messina, partly to service their longer trade routes to Syria and Africa and partly to gain access to the grain, cotton, and other raw materials of the island.[2] One of the purposes of the Genoese-Sicilian treaty of 1156 was to assure the safety of Christian shipping bound through Messina for the Levant; but another purpose was to guarantee access to wheat, skins, and raw cotton produced on the island itself.[3] All this did not mean that

---

[2] David Abulafia, *The Two Italies: Economic Relations between the Norman Kingdom of Sicily and the Northern Communes* (Cambridge, England, 1977), pp. 90–8.

[3] Henri Bresc, *Un monde méditerranéen. Économie et société en Sicile, 1300–1450*, 2 vols. (Rome–Palermo, 1986), p. 16, sees cotton and even silk as the prime interest of the northern Italians in the twelfth century, giving way by about 1200 to wheat. This would fit well with studies of the western Sicilian

END OF MUSLIM SICILY   105

the northern Italians at once became the dominant commercial force on the island; but over a period of two hundred years they effected a gradual switch in Sicily's prime trading relations, away from North Africa and the Muslim world toward northern Italy and the Christian West. The trade between Sicily and North Africa, once in the hands of Muslims and Jews (as the Cairo Genizah texts make plain) now fell largely into the hands of merchants of Latin descent, many of whom were not even permanently domiciled in Sicily: Tuscan wine merchants furnished Tunis with its alcohol by 1300, but also carried many items that were not prohibited to Muslims.[4] Lines of communication linked Palermo to Champagne and Flanders.[5] And, whereas in the late twelfth century the majority of Palermo's merchants were still Muslim, by the late thirteenth century they were mainly Latin, and that probably means, in large measure, immigrants or descendants of recent immigrants.[6] A unique commercial contract from around 1160, drawn up in Arabic between Sicilian Muslims and a Latin named William, indicates that as early as the mid-twelfth century a Western merchant was providing loans to the Arabs of the island; the document speaks for the transition from Muslim and Jewish domination of the trade routes to Christian, even northern Italian, ascendancy.[7]

---

estates referred to *below*. The treaty of 1156 mentions both cotton and wheat, and it would be dangerous to hazard a guess as to their relative importance. But between the Norman conquest and the reign of Frederick II primary foodstuffs either gained a lead or increased an existing lead.

[4] David Abulafia, "A Tyrrhenian Triangle: Tuscany, Sicily, Tunis, 1276–1300," in *Studi di storia economica toscana nel Medioevo e nel Rinascimento in memoria di Federigo Melis*, ed. C. Violante (Pisa, 1987), pp. 53–75.

[5] Abulafia, *Two Italies*, pp. 95, 183, 263–64.

[6] Ibn Jubayr, *The Travels of Ibn Jubayr*, trans. R. J. C. Broadhurst (London, 1952), p. 348, says of the Muslims of Palermo: "In their own suburbs they live apart from the Christians. The markets are full of them, and they are the merchants of the place." Ibn Jubayr also says that the Muslims of Palermo maintained many mosques, but clearly some had been appropriated by the Christians, such as the Friday mosque that became the site of the cathedral or the mosque that is supposed to have formed the core of the buildings of the monastery of San Giovanni degli Eremiti.

[7] S. Cusa, *I diplomi greci e arabi di Sicilia*, 2 vols. (Palermo, 1860–1862), 2:502–4, 719; inaccurate translation in G. Trovato, *Sopravvivenze arabe in Si-*

So too in Messina. There, in the mid-thirteenth century, a Catalan settlement took root several decades before the Aragonese conquest of Sicily in 1282.[8] Boccaccio's story of the pot of basil portrays a group of Sangimignanesi resident in Messina;[9] and other, real, Tuscans are revealed in a document of 1239, describing the property of the daughter of a Lucchese merchant resident in the port. She owned a half-share in a warehouse in the new part of Messina; this property was surrounded by the possessions of an Amalfitan and of a citizen of Ravello, and it bordered on the street or quarter of the Pisans.[10] Over the generations, the inhabitants of the Sicilian cities lost their affiliations of origin, intermarried, and created a reasonably homogeneous, but primarily Latin, society. The Greek citizens of these towns played an insignificant role in their long-distance trade by 1300. There were very few Greeks involved in the

---

cilia: documenti arabo-siculi del periodo normanno (Monreale, 1949), pp. 73–76. The document appears to involve Muslims from Cefalù and Corleone and to speak of a sea voyage from Cefalù or another point to Messina and then back to Palermo. The money mentioned is perhaps Genoese. See David Abulafia, "The Crown and the Economy under Roger II and His Successors," *Dumbarton Oaks Papers* 37 (1983): 10, nn. 81–82, repr. in David Abulafia, *Italy, Sicily and the Mediterranean, 1100–1400* (London, 1987), chap. 1. Another Sicilian Muslim with business ties to the Latins in 1162 was "Caitus Bulcassem" (Qāʿid Abu'l-Qāsim), surely a member of the Ḥammūdid dynasty that dominated the Sicilian Muslim community in the twelfth century, and maybe even the "leader and Lord" of the Muslims interviewed by Ibn Jubayr in 1185 (Abulafia, *Two Italies*, pp. 247–49; *Travels of Ibn Jubayr*, pp. 358–59). If the identification is correct, he was one of the wealthiest Muslims on the island, and a very rare example of a Muslim businessman who sent agents to Genoa. His Genoese contact, Solomon of Salerno, was himself a subject of the king of Sicily, domiciled in Genoa.

[8] Carme Batlle, "Les relacions entre Barcelona i Sicília a la segona meitat del segle XIII," in *La società mediterranea all'epoca del Vespro: VII Centenario del Vespro Siciliano/XI Congresso della Corona d'Aragona, 1982, 2: Communicazioni* (Palermo, 1983), pp. 147–62; David Abulafia, "The Merchants of Messina: Levant Trade and Domestic Economy," *Papers of the British School at Rome* 54 (1986): 196–212.

[9] Giovanni Boccaccio *Decameron*, ed. Vittore Branca (Turin, 1984), pp. 526–32 (Giornata 4, Novella 5).

[10] L. R. Ménager, ed., *Les actes latins de S. Maria di Messina (1103–1250)* (Palermo, 1963), pp. 150–58.

trade of Messina with Cyprus around 1300, even though their knowledge of their ancestral language should have been an advantage. Instead we find such names as Pietro del fu Vitale "the Genoese," a citizen of Messina; or Oberto Manayra of Savona, a resident at Marsala; or Benvenuto of Pistoia, an inhabitant of Agrigento—the last two cities ancient centers of Muslim settlement.[11]

Nor were the new settlers all from the great trading centers of northern and southern Italy or, later, Catalonia. Naples, Amalfi, Gaeta, Florence, Pisa, Milan, and Barcelona are all represented, but so too are Assisi, Orvieto, Turin, and countless small inland settlements. A Bolognese appears resident at Cefalù as early as 1188; Piedmont and Liguria dispatched a substantial number of settlers, beginning at the end of the eleventh century with the colonization of parts of central and eastern Sicily. The special links between the family of Roger II's mother and Liguria help explain this phenomenon, for Adelaide was an Aleramico, a member of a great feudal family in the hinterland behind Savona, and not surprisingly the earliest settlers include such individuals as Obbertus of Savona or Gualterius de Garrexio, whose name refers to a small town near Savona.[12] Some small towns in those areas still preserve local dialects apparently of northwest Italian origin; Aidone, Nicosia, and Novara di Sicilia seem to be cases in point.[13] But the stream of immigrants from Piedmont was renewed in the fourteenth century, when the area round Corleone was resettled; this stream, if not continuous, never dried up completely, nor did it consist entirely of men of commerce. Under Frederick II Ghibelline refugees from Piacenza, Brescia, and elsewhere were reported, and even if the tales about them are unreliable, the

[11] Abulafia, "Merchants of Messina," p. 206.

[12] L. Villari, "Note sui comuni lombardi di Sicilia," *Archivio storico messinese* 58/9 (1957–1959): 155–62; C. A. Garufi, "Gli Aleramici e i Normanni in Sicilia e nelle Puglie," *Centenario della nascita di Michele Amari*, 2 vols. (Palermo, 1910), 1:47–83.

[13] Abulafia, "Crown and the Economy," pp. 11–13; G. Tropea, "Effetti di simbiosi linguistica nelle parlate gallo-italiche di Aidone, Nicosia e Novara di Sicilia," *Bollettino dell'Atlante linguistico italiano* 13/14 (1966): 3–5.

memory of such immigration may reveal an awareness of the transformations taking place in the Sicilian countryside around this time.[14]

The immigrants came to a lightly populated island; and, though many settled in towns, the Sicilian rulers eagerly encouraged the cultivation of unused or abandoned lands. Unfortunately, one effect of the presence of these "Lombardi" was the destruction of neighboring peasant communities. In the 1160s the Lombardi, under their leader Roger Sclavus, launched a series of pogroms among the Muslims, forcing them to flee westward to safer areas, where the population was still predominantly Arab. At times there was also new Muslim settlement in Sicily, particularly during the famines that struck North Africa in the middle of the twelfth century; but the Norman kings of Sicily, as rulers also of Mahdia and Tripoli on the African coast, encouraged these newcomers to return to their place of origin. The intention was to foster the economic recovery of Norman Africa, but there may also have been an awareness that further Muslim immigration would be violently opposed by the Greeks of Palermo and by the Latins and Greeks of eastern Sicily.[15] In any case, some of the African settlers in Sicily were Christians who had good reason to escape the persecutions of the Almohads.[16] By 1200 the Muslims were already concentrated mainly in the west of the island and on the high ground to the south and east of Palermo. As their num-

[14] Abulafia, "Crown and the economy," p. 12; H. Bresc, "La formazione del popolo siciliano," in *Tre Millenni di storia linguistica della Sicilia: Atti del Convegno della Società Italiana di Glottologia, Palermo, 1983* (Pisa, n.d.), pp. 243–66.

[15] David Abulafia, "The Norman Kingdom of Africa and the Norman Expeditions to Majorca and the Muslim Mediterranean," in *Anglo-Norman Studies 7: Proceedings of the Battle Conference, 1984*, ed. R. Allen Brown (Woodbridge, 1985), pp. 36–37, repr. in David Abulafia, *Italy, Sicily and the Mediterranean, 1100–1400* (London, 1987), chap. 12.

[16] Roger II appears to have encouraged Christian settlement in North Africa also. See Abulafia, "Norman Kingdom of Africa," p. 38. There is a late reflection of this in Joachim of Fiore's *Expositio in Apocalypsim*, pars iv, distinctio iv, in *Crusade and Mission: European Approaches toward the Muslims*, ed. Benjamin Z. Kedar (Princeton, 1984), p. 221.

bers declined so did the agricultural skills that they had brought with them from Africa. On the Monreale estates around 1200 specialized cultivation and crafts gave way to a more monotonous concentration on production of wheat. No doubt the interests of landlords in part accounted for this; but it is likely that skills were evaporating as the Muslim population declined in numbers.[17]

Yet the transformation of Sicily into a Christian island was also, paradoxically, the work of those whose culture was under threat. The Muslims either left the island for Africa or, later, Lucera; or they were slaughtered; or they converted—not necessarily *were* converted, but occasionally converted of their own accord. On the Monreale estates in western Sicily, around 1180, a new Christian generation of peasants emerges, with sons with names such as Philippos succeeding fathers with what are obviously Muslim names—Aḥmad, even Muḥammad.[18] Monreale is one area, however, where pressure to convert was probably strong; these lands also became a focus of opposition by Muslim rebels. Among the Muslim elite of Palermo a similar transition also occurs: ʿAbd ar-Raḥmān, "Slave of the Merciful," a prominent civil servant, possibly becomes Christodoulos. At any rate, the Spanish Muslim visitor Ibn Jubayr insists that William II made extensive use of Muslims at court "who all, or nearly all, concealing their faith, yet hold firm to the Muslim divine law"—a point which confirms the refusal of the king to tolerate outward expressions of Islam at what was a decidedly Christian court.[19] In the country, though probably

[17] On this process, see the valuable article of H. Bercher, A. Courteaux, and J. Mouton, "Une abbaye latine dans la société musulmane: Monreale au XIIᵉ siècle," *Annales: Économies, Sociétés, Civilisations* 34 (1979): 525–47.

[18] These remarks are based mainly on a paper by Jeremy Johns at the symposium of the Society for the Promotion of Byzantine Studies, Oxford, 1984. See the tables and map in Bresc, "Formazione," indicating Muslim arrivals from as far as Persia and India in the Norman period—movement across vast spaces on a scale entirely typical of the medieval Muslim world.

[19] H. Bresc, "Mudejars des pays de la couronne d'Aragon et Sarrasins de la Sicile normande: le problème de l'acculturation," in *X Congreso de Historia de la Corona de Aragon, Zaragoza, 1979* (Saragossa, n.d.), p. 55; Kedar, *Crusade and Mission*, pp. 50–52; *Travels of Ibn Jubayr*, p. 340.

not at court, conversion to Greek orthodoxy seems more common than conversion to Roman Catholicism, and this may reflect the long-standing presence of Greek monks and priests in the Sicilian countryside. The Greek Church had long been more visible to the Sicilian peasantry, Christian or Muslim, than the Norman-dominated Latin Church. But it is important not to read too much into the evidence of personal names, either. As late as the mid-thirteenth century, Latin landlords sometimes gave their children Arabic or Greek names if they lived among Greek or Arabic speakers.[20] And, though the Norman rulers clearly encouraged conversion to Christianity, they offered few inducements to the peasants such as a lessening of their obligations; whether Muslims or Christians, their legal status remained much the same. In fact, Ibn Jubayr attributed unhealthy motives to the converts from Islam. He recounts how, "should a man show anger to his son or his wife, or a woman to her daughter, the one who is the object of displeasure may perversely throw himself into a church, and there be baptised and turn Christian. Then there will be for the father no way of approaching his son, or the mother her daughter." Some fathers escaped this threat by offering their pubescent daughters to visiting Muslims, who could take them abroad away from the temptation of apostasy.[21] The reference to conversions by Muslim women is particularly interesting; but the impetus to conversion came not only from the individual. It was said that if Ibn Ḥammūd, leader of the Muslims of Sicily, were to change faith, so would the entire Muslim community on the island.

Pressure to convert clearly came in waves. A revealing remark by Archbishop Romuald of Salerno indicates that Roger II became more enthusiastic about converting Jews and Muslims at the end of his life; secular matters occupied him less, and he made generous gifts to the new Christians.[22] Since, as has been

---

[20] Bresc, "Formazione," p. 249.

[21] *Travels of Ibn Jubayr*, pp. 359–60.

[22] Romuald of Salerno, *Rerum italicarum scriptores* ser. 2, 7:1 in *Chronicon*, ed. C. A. Garufi, p. 236: "Circa finem autem vite sue secularibus negociis ali-

seen, the peasantry did not apparently gain in economic status by conversion, and since Romuald's view is that of a courtier close to the king, it is quite likely that the primary emphasis lay on the conversion of Muslim and Jewish notables. Hence, indeed, his ire at the apostate Admiral Philip of Mahdia, who was executed at the end of Roger's reign. Roger had already made plain, in the *Assises* of Ariano, his detestation of those who abandoned the Catholic faith.[23]

At the royal court, then, the high Muslim officials were expected to pay more than mere lip service to Christianity, as early as Roger II's time. The Granadan pilgrim Ibn Jubayr described how the Muslim courtiers of William II were shielded by the hand of Allāh, so they could invisibly prostrate themselves in prayer at the prescribed times, even when the king was looking on:

> Another singular circumstance concerning these pages is that when in the presence of their Lord and the hour for prayer is at hand they will leave the chamber one by one that they might make their prayers. They sometimes do so in a place where the eye of the king might follow them, but Almighty and Glorious God conceals them. Thus they continue to labour in their purpose, covertly advising the Muslims in their unending struggle for the faith.[24]

Maybe King William had few illusions about what was going on; yet the assumption that Muslim pages would accept Christianity suggests a formalized hostility to Islam at court, and only the very greatest, notably Ibn Ḥammūd, managed to resist pressure to convert. It is impossible to say how long this community of Muslim *marranos* lasted; there survives nothing from

---

quantulum postpositis et ommissis, Judeos et Saracenos ad fidem Christi convertere modis laborabat, et conversis dona plurima et necessaria conferebat."

[23] Abulafia, "Norman Kingdom of Africa," p. 42, n. 84. On him and other courtiers of Muslim origin, see Dietlind Schack, *"Die Araber im Reich Rogers II."* (Inaugural-Dissertation, phil.-Fak., Free University of Berlin, 1969), pp. 142–50. Schack notes the words of the *assises*: "Apostantes a fide catholica penitus execramus, ultionibus insequimur, bonis omnibus spoliamus" (p. 149).

[24] *Travels Ibn Jubayr*, p. 343.

late medieval Sicily to compare with the later Qur'āns of the Valencian Moriscos. Such Muslims as appear in Sicily in the documentation of the fourteenth and fifteenth centuries were rare visitors from abroad, very few of whom managed to settle, or slaves. Evidence from personal names in modern Sicily suggests many Christianized descendants of Jews and Muslims still live on the island, but it is impossible to say whether a family such as Buscetta has Jewish, Muslim, or Christian Mozarabic antecedents.

Sicilian Islam was already under severe criticism from the Muslims of the twelfth-century Maghrib. The Sicilian Muslims were said to be lax in observance; but even to live under Christian rule was undesirable.[25] North African sages could hardly view with equanimity the presence of Muslims in the armies and navies of the Norman kings during the attack on Alexandria in 1174, or, later, with Frederick II during his crusade. The elite left; townspeople found their mosques converted into cathedrals and monasteries, notably in Palermo; in the countryside the structure of leadership disintegrated. This possibly helps explain the switch in cultivation away from specialized crops to the wheat that the Latin landlords, with an eye on the international or at least Sicilian urban food market, would tend to prefer. The disappearance of the Muslim aristocracy had particularly dire effects on the Muslims throughout Sicily. The Muslim traveler Ibn Jubayr recorded the demoralization of leading Sicilian coreligionists in his diary of 1184/85. He met the "leader and Lord of the Muslim community in this island," the *Qā'id* Abu'l-Qāsim ibn Ḥammūd, who was visiting Trapani and who was still feeling the effects of confiscation of part of his wealth and of gossip about his links with the Almohads. He had again been appointed to a post in the government, but was evidently aware that the king's favor was entirely conditioned on his good conduct; it was hardly an example of royal indifference to the religious tastes of the king's courtiers. In-

---

[25] For disapproval of trade with Christian-ruled Sicily in the verdicts of Islamic judges in North Africa, see H. R. Idris, *La Berbérie orientale sous les Zirides, X^e–XIIe siècles*, 2 vols. (Paris–Algiers, 1962), 2:666, where a *fatwa* of Al-Mazari is cited stating that Muslims may not go to lands conquered by the Infidel, however urgent their needs (e.g., to buy grain in times of famine).

deed he said to Ibn Jubayr, "I have wished to be sold [as a slave], I and my family, that perhaps the sale would free us from the state we are in and lead us to our dwelling in Muslim lands."[26] Hyperbole, perhaps, for Ibn Jubayr recalled seeing the magnificent palaces of Ibn Ḥammūd's relatives in Palermo, and later Frederick II was to grant the Genoese the palace of "Gaetus Bulcasim" in Trapani; but the Muslims of Sicily were fully aware that their future held no guarantees of prosperity.[27] And at Messina the civil servant ʿAbd al-Māssīh told Ibn Jubayr: "You can boldly display your faith in Islam. . . . But we must conceal our faith and, fearful of our lives, must adhere to the worship of God and the discharge of our religious duties in secret."[28]

A decade later the Muslims of western Sicily rose in open rebellion; their defiant leader Ibn ʿAbbād had even minted his own coins not long before 1220, probably at his stronghold of Entella. The last rebels were not flushed out until the 1240s.[29] It has been suggested that Islam survived in secret in the Sicilian countryside, just as it clearly did briefly at court, but the many Muslims who appear on the island from the 1280s on seem to be imported slaves, of whom more shortly.[30] Interestingly, the years around 1200 saw the appearance in Sicily of Islamic styles of pottery, made perhaps with royal encouragement. The so-called Gela ware, colored in yellow, green, and brown, was developed from twelfth-century Muslim Sicilian models, using a form of glazing as yet hardly known in Latin Europe. The origin of the potters, however, is uncertain.[31]

[26] *Travels of Ibn Jubayr*, pp. 358–59.

[27] The grant of the "domum que fuit Gaeti Bulcasimi" dates to 1200, a time when Frederick himself had no say in the government of Sicily (Abulafia, *Two Italies*, p. 250, n. 66).

[28] *Travels of Ibn Jubayr*, p. 342.

[29] On the coins, see F. D'Angelo, "La monetazione di Muhammad ibn 'Abbad emiro ribelle a Federico II di Sicilia," *Studi Magrebini* 7 (1975): 149–53. For other interesting perspectives, see Jeremy Johns, "Monte Guastanella: un insediamento musulmano nell'Agrigentino," *Sicilia Archeologica*, 16:33–51.

[30] See Bresc, "Mudejars," pp. 56–57; and for later slaves, see Verlinden's works mentioned below.

[31] David Abulafia, "The Pisan *bacini* and the Medieval Mediterranean Economy: A Historian's Viewpoint," *Papers in Italian Archaeology 4: The Cambridge*

What also survived was the Arabic language, but only in the most remote parts of the kingdom, particularly in the offshore territories of Malta and Pantelleria, where an unusual degree of cultural autonomy persisted.[32] Pantelleria acquired a special status in the thirteenth century as a Hohenstaufen-Hafsid condominium; here at least a Muslim population was able to survive relatively undisturbed. In essence, the island's Muslims possessed a special statute of autonomy, subject to Sicilian overlordship and the payment of half the revenues to the Hafsids.[33] The case of the decline of Islam on Malta is not typical of the rest of the *Regno*, but it is reasonably well documented for the reign of Frederick II.[34] Before then, the Maltese islands had experienced a Norman invasion in 1090 and a more definitive conquest in 1127, though at the end of the twelfth and start of the thirteenth centuries their rulers were Genoese counts whose loyalty to the Sicilian kings was spasmodic.[35] In

---

Conference, pt. 4, *Classical and Medieval Archæology*, British Archæological Reports, International Series 246, eds. C. Malone and S. Stoddart (Oxford, 1985), p. 293, repr. in David Abulafia, *Italy, Sicily and the Mediterranean, 1100–1400* (London, 1987), chap. 13.

[32] See A. T. Luttrell, "Approaches to Medieval Malta," in *Medieval Malta: Studies on Malta before the Knights*, ed. A. T. Luttrell (London, 1975), and other articles in the same volume. The only general history of Malta in the Middle Ages is A. Vella, *Storija ta'Malta* (Valletta, 1974), vol. 1, which is primarily concerned with political history and is written in Maltese.

[33] R. Brunschvig *La Berbérie orientale sous les Hafsides des origines à la fin du XVe siècle*, 2 vols. (Paris, 1940–1947), 1:26; R. Brunschvig, "Note sur un traité conclu entre Tunis et l'empereur Frédéric II," *Revue tunisienne* (1932): 153–60, dates the agreement concerning Pantelleria to 1221; see also H. Bresc, "Pantelleria entre l'Islam et la Chrétienté," *Cahiers de Tunisie* 19 (1971): 105–27. In the late thirteenth century Leon de Lucera was governor of the island. Was he a Christian as Bresc (*Monde méditerranéen*, 2:622–23) assumes? Muslims remained responsible for the exercise of justice on the island at this time, and were still to be found there in the fifteenth century. By 1444 there were forty-three Jews on the island, active in cotton production, a presence which Bresc sees as a late example of a process visible in Sicily proper in the thirteenth century—the use of skilled Jewish agriculturalists and artisans to replace lost Arab manpower.

[34] For what follows, see Luttrell, "Approaches," pp. 34–40.

[35] David Abulafia, "Henry, Count of Malta and His Mediterranean Activities, 1203–1230," in Luttrell, *Medieval Malta*, pp. 104–25.

1175 Bishop Burchard of Strassburg said of Malta that it was "a Sarracenis inhabitata, et est sub dominio regis Sicilie."[36] Contrary to the wishful thinking of the island's modern inhabitants, it is hard to prove continuity in Christian observance on Malta through the Middle Ages. For Luttrell, "Malta was never really Norman;" it was after the Genoese counts were relieved of the island around 1222 that the archipelago became integrated into the rest of the *Regno*.[37] The Muslim majority on Malta was not immune from the treatment that had been meted out to the Muslims of Sicily proper. Frederick II's Admiral of the Fleet, Henry, Count of Malta, of Genoese origin, participated alongside his master in the siege of Celano, in the Abruzzi. When Celano fell and was razed, its refugee population (all Christian) was gathered together by Henricus de Morra, chief justiciar of the Sicilian kingdom. The *Celanenses* arrived in Sicily, where the emperor decided they should be sent on to settle Malta.[38] Ibn Khaldūn believed that Frederick included the Maltese Muslims among the Saracens sent to settle Lucera in Apulia, a statement which would date the expulsion from Malta to approximately the same period as the settlement by the *Celanenses*.[39] Evidence that a Muslim of Maltese descent once lived at Lucera may be provided by a reference in 1301 to a certain *Dallesium Maltesium* in the now-lost archives of the Angevin kings of Naples.[40] The remote island was also used as a prison for exiles, a medieval equivalent of the modern prison on Asinara. It has even been suggested that the use of the term *malta* to mean a prison, in the works of Dante and his contemporaries, originated during this period.[41] For Frederick Malta

[36] Luttrell, "Approaches," p. 32, citing *MGH*. SS. 21, 236.

[37] Ibid., pp. 32, 34.

[38] *Rerum italicarum scriptores*, in *Ryccardi de sancto Germano notarii Chronica*, ed. C. A. Garufi, ser. 2, 7:2 (Bologna, 1938), pp. 112–13, but only in one version of the text.

[39] M. Amari, *Biblioteca arabo-sicula, versione italiana*, 2 vols. (Turin–Rome, 1880–1881), 2:212–13. Ibn Khaldun says Frederick himself went to Malta to expel the Muslims; this is a misconception.

[40] Luttrell, "Approaches," p. 37, n. 214.

[41] Ibid., p. 36, n. 206.

was a favorite source of falcons, while northern Italian merchants had an interest in its cotton.[42]

Around 1241 Frederick II received a report on conditions on Malta, at a time when he was working hard to maximize his revenues to help pay for his Italian wars. He learned that Malta had its own distinctive customs, but also that there were still plenty of Muslims on both Malta and Gozo. The existence of a majority of Christians may of course conceal a high rate of conversion from Islam to Christianity, though at least some of the Christians were likely *Celanenses*. The following statistics of the number of families on the two islands were offered to Frederick:

Christians: 1250 (Malta, 1047 [emended by Luttrell from 47]; Gozo, 203)
Muslims: 836 (Malta, 681; Gozo, 155)
Jews: 33 (Malta, 25; Gozo, 8).[43]

Apparently separate were eighty-four North African *servi*, possibly from Jerba, but also apparently Muslims. Yet the majority of Maltese Muslims were not newcomers who arrived after the expulsion of the old population to Lucera, but were *villani curie sarraceni* who paid the Crown one-quarter of what they produced, in kind, and who were apparently established peasant families whose obligations were defined by long usage.[44] Thus it is likely that here at least the deportations to Lu-

---

[42] Abulafia, "Henry, Count of Malta," p. 106; idem, *Frederick II: A Medieval Emperor* (London, 1988), pp. 267, 337.

[43] E. Winkelmann, *Acta imperii inedita saeculi XIII*, 2 vols. (Innsbruck, 1880–1885), 1:713–15; for the emendation by Luttrell of xlvii into mxlvii, see his "Approaches," pp. 38–40.

[44] Conversion from Islam might not have been enough to shake off the status of a *servus curie sarracenus*, a title that could as much be determined by descent as by religion. The exact process of change is invisible. Henri Bresc, "The Secrezia and the Royal Patrimony in Malta, 1240–1450," in Luttrell, *Medieval Malta*, p. 131, notes that the *servi* and *ancille* documented around 1241 were still seen in 1271 and were only granted complete liberty around 1372; he sees the incorporation of Malta into the royal demesne as part of a wider process of the creation of large *latifundia* which concentrated on the production of wheat. Cf. Bercher et al., "Une abbaye latine," pp. 536–37. But in fact he also shows

END OF MUSLIM SICILY 117

cera did not signal the end of Islam; nor, certainly, did they signal the end of a distinctively arabicized culture, which enveloped also the Christians of the islands, whether they were converted Muslims or new settlers, and which was characterized by the survival of Arabic speech.[45] In the late fifteenth century the Jews of Malta appear to have used a form of Arabic that was more or less identical to that of the island's Christians. It was, of course, written in Hebrew characters, just as the Christians adopted at some stage the Latin alphabet when writing Maltese Arabic.[46]

The use of Arabic did, however, continue in Sicily—not generally, but as the *koiné* of the Jews. There are noticeable differences between the economic and cultural standing of the Jews of Sicily and those of Spain. Among the Sicilian Jews, Arabic remained an everyday language until their expulsion at the end

---

that cotton was a particularly important local product in the late fourteenth and fifteenth centuries, and it is probable that cotton cultivation continued uninterrupted from Norman to Aragonese times. See Bresc, "*Secrezia*," pp. 131–32. The year 1271 or a little earlier may also mark the virtual extinction of Islam in Malta, since a document of Charles I of Anjou mentions the possessions of the "quondam Sarracenorum de ipsis insulis ejectorum" (Bresc, *Monde méditerranéen*, 2:625). Malta had been a bone of contention in the struggle between Hohenstaufen and Angevins, with Genoese and Pisan interests also at work on the island. In 1267 Conradin of Hohenstaufen offered Malta to the Pisans in return for naval aid, but Manfred had already negotiated in 1257 with the heirs of Henry, count of Malta, for a return of much of Malta to the Genoese (see Luttrell, "Approaches," p. 40). Charles' joint crusade to Tunis with Louis IX in 1270 also highlighted the importance of the island. It may thus have seemed that the Maltese archipelago was strategically too valuable, and the inhabitants too untrustworthy, to permit the continued existence of a Muslim enclave there.

[45] The earliest document in Maltese is the fifteenth-century *cantilena* or lament of Pietro Caxaro. See Luttrell, "Approaches," pp. 66–67, for the text and translation. See also G. Wettinger and M. Fsadni, *Peter Caxaro's Cantilena: A Poem in Medieval Maltese* (Malta, 1968); Bresc, *Monde méditerranéen*, 2:626.

[46] G. Wettinger, *The Jews of Malta in the Late Middle Ages* (Valletta, 1984) is based on both Latin and Judeo-Arabic documents of late fifteenth-century Malta, and analyzes the material from both a historical and a linguistic perspective. The author's transcriptions into the Latin alphabet and his translations into Maltese are an object lesson to those who preserve a touching belief in the Punic rather than Arabic origins of the island's language.

of the fifteenth century, though in the late fifteenth century it was used more in the compilation of documents (in Hebrew characters) than in daily speech.[47] They gave their children Arabic as well as Hebrew names; yet they do not seem to have been socially or economically isolated from their Christian neighbors, at least in the smaller towns, until the mid-fourteenth century. Rabbi Abraham Abulafia, a Spanish Jew who traveled in Sicily, Greece, and the Holy Land in the late thirteenth century, mentioned the use of Arabic and Italian among the Jews, implying that Italian was the language of intercourse with Christians, while Arabic was the language of the Jewish community. There is an obvious comparison to be made with the later use of Castilian (*Ladino*) among the Jews of the Ottoman world as an archaic language confined to the Jews themselves:

> Note that the Jews who live among the Ishmaelites speak Arabic like them; those who live among the Greeks speak Greek; those who inhabit Italy speak Italian, the Germans [*Ashkenazim*] speak German, the inhabitants of Turkish lands speak Turkish, and so on. But the great wonder is what happens among the Jews in all Sicily, who not only speak the local language or Greek, as do those who dwell there with them, but have preserved the Arabic tongue which they had learned in former times, when the Ishmaelites were dwelling there.[48]

---

[47] Bresc, *Monde méditerranéen*, 2:628; H. Bresc and S. D. Goitein, "Un inventaire dotal de juifs siciliens (1479)," *Mélanges d'histoire et d'archéologie de l'École française de Rome* 82 (1970): 903–17.

[48] Abraham b. Samuel Abulafia, *Ozar 'Eden ganuz*, extract edited by A. Neubauer in *Revue des études juives* 9 (1884): 149, from a MS in Oxford; also cited in C. Roth, *The History of the Jews of Italy* (Philadelphia, 1946), p. 82, without further identification. For the extraordinary career of Abraham Abulafia of Saragossa, see in particular the four-volume set of studies by Moshe Idel, of which the first part is *The Mystical Experience in Abraham Abulafia* (Albany, 1988). Abulafia visited southern Italy and Sicily, after an attempt in 1280 to convince the pope of his undoubtedly remarkable abilities, and is last heard of in 1291 on the island of Comino, off Malta. He appears to have been influenced by the view (reported in Nahmanides' disputation before King James I of Aragon) that the true Messiah would go to Rome and show himself to the pope.

In Erice, in the extreme west of Sicily, the Jews lived mixed together with Christians around 1300; the Jewish quarter [*rabato*] of the town evolved later, perhaps under the influence of a new wave of ill-feeling (of Spanish importation) toward the Jews.[49] A similar picture originally obtained in Mdina-Notabile, capital of Malta, and in Rabat, capital of Gozo, though in the latter case the Jews lived below the citadel and in the former they had a synagogue at the highest point of the citadel. In time they found themselves concentrated in particular areas of the two towns.[50] As elsewhere in the medieval Jewish world, the Jews of Sicily harnessed a borrowed language for their own use; they judaized it, and this, no less than their adherence to the dietary laws of *kashrut* and other observances, helped them retain their cohesion. Yet the range of occupations among the Jews of Erice seems comparable to that found among Christians. There are, certainly, several Jewish physicians, as in other parts of Sicily; the gold and silversmith's art, too, may have been a special Jewish interest, though in Palermo the silver bells of the Torah scrolls were on occasion actually made for the Jews by Christians.[51] They functioned as carpenters; they owned vineyards; they made improvement loans—but in the same way as their Christian neighbors.

The Jews of Sicily formed part of North African Jewry; some were in fact thirteenth-century settlers from Tunisia or nearby, invited by Frederick II to reintroduce date and indigo cultiva-

---

[49] David Abulafia, "The Jews of Erice (Monte San Giuliano) in Sicily, 1297–1304," *Zion* 51 (1986): 295–317 [in Hebrew; summary in English] and in the *Archivio storico per la Sicilia orientale* 1986 [in Italian]. See also various articles by E. Ashtor on the Sicilian Jews in his *The Jews and the Mediterranean Economy, 10th to 15th Centuries* (London, 1983).

[50] Wettinger, *Jews of Malta*. There has been much speculation about the possible influence of late medieval hostility to the Jews in Malta on Christopher Marlowe's play *The Jew of Malta*, but to little effect.

[51] G. Bresc-Bautier, *Artistes, patriciens et confrères: production et consommation de l'oeuvre d'art à Palerme et en Sicile occidentale (1348–1460)* (Rome, 1979), pp. 115–16. The example of the *rimonim* (bells) is very late—the end of the fifteenth century. Interestingly, the *rimonim* now preserved in the Cathedral Treasury in Palma de Mallorca are probably of Sicilian origin, brought to Majorca after the expulsion and expropriation of the Sicilian Jews.

tion. His invitation to the Jews of "Garbum" is usually understood to signify the Jews of the fertile island of Jerba, but more probably it means the Jews of the Maghreb as a whole, for the term "Garbum" was often used to describe the entire area between the Algarve or Andalusia and Cyrenaica: "Debent in eis seminare alchanam et indicum et alia diversa semina que crescunt in Garbo nec sunt in partibus Sicilie adhuc visa crescere."[52]

The fact that Frederick was trying to restore the cultivation of crops once produced on the island is of some significance. The existence in late medieval Sicily of sugar plantations and of other "exotic" products does not prove that Islamic agricultural technology survived in Sicily, as it certainly did in Valencia; again and again it was necessary to restore what had been lost, in both know-how and labor reserves, after the destruction of Sicilian Islam.[53] Evidence from the Monreale estates suggests a sharp decline in the specialized agricultural skills practiced before 1200 by the Muslim peasantry of Sicily.[54] Frederick's recourse to North African Jews was a clever way to import Arab technology without reimporting Muslim personnel; it was not so much a policy favorable to the Jews as one unfavorable to the Arabs.[55] (Equally, Frederick's statement in the *Constitutions of Melfi* that the Jews and Saracens were "too greatly persecuted at present" does not mean he was opposed to all persecution; merely that, in accordance with the prescriptions of canon law,

---

[52] *Constitutiones regum utriusque Siciliæ mandante Friderico II Imperatore per Petrum de Vinea Capuanum Prætorio Præfectum et Cancellarium . . . et Fragmentum quod superest Regesti eiusdem Imperatoris Ann. 1239 & 1240*, ed. Cajetanus Carcani (Naples, 1786), pp. 290–91 [this is the only effective edition of the register]; cf. A. Watson, *Agricultural Innovation in the Early Islamic World* (Cambridge, 1983) for the transplantation of eastern crops to Sicily and Spain; and Bercher et al., "Une abbaye latine," for the break in continuity in western Sicily.

[53] See the studies of the production of sugar and other Levantine commodities in late medieval Sicily by C. Trasselli, such as his *Storia dello zucchero siciliano* (Caltanissetta, 1983), his *Siciliani fra quattrocento e cinquecento* (Messina, 1981), and more generally his *Mediterraneo e Sicilia all'inizio dell'epoca moderna (Ricerche quattrocentesche)* (Cosenza, 1977).

[54] Bercher et al., "Une abbaye latine," pp. 525–47.

[55] Abulafia, *Frederick II*, pp. 335–36.

Frederick wished to curtail unjust and violent persecution.[56]) In any case, the Maghribi Jews had difficulties with the native Jews of Palermo and had to be granted reserved use of a dilapidated synagogue.[57] Even so, all the Sicilian Jews looked to North Africa for religious leadership and for a model liturgy. Those few Jews who appeared at Frederick II's court were not in fact Sicilians: Moses ben Solomon of Salerno was at least a southern Italian, but the main figure, the translator Jacob Anatoli, had reached the royal court via Provence, while his relatives, the Ibn Tibbons, were Provençal Jews of Spanish descent.[58]

The same non-Sicilian origin had applied to a high proportion of the Greeks and Muslims at the court of Roger II a hundred years earlier. There were Calabrian Greeks such as the Maleinoi, and probably some Sicilian Muslims and Greeks too, but the non-Sicilian element carried the most weight, if not in numbers, at least in influence. The Norman and Hohenstaufen courts were accessible to talented administrators and men of learning (often these were the same) from around the known world, men in search of gold and honors. George of Antioch had been born in Syria but became minister to North African rulers before reaching the court of Roger II, and thus clearly spoke Arabic as well as Greek; Philip of Mahdia, born a Muslim in North Africa, had converted to Christianity in the hope of achieving high office under Roger, but (as has been seen) was executed by Roger in 1154 for backsliding. Countless Westerners were present too, of course, such as Thomas Brown who later served under Henry II of England, Peter of Blois, and Adelard of Bath. North African poets, disappointed at the response to their verses in Mahdia and Tunis, offered flattery in Arabic to Roger II in the hope of acquiring a wealthy and appreciative patron; it is unlikely that Roger understood anything

---

[56] *Liber Augustalis* [various eds., 1475, 1568, 1786, etc.], I, tit. 28 (32); Abulafia, *Frederick II*, p. 209.

[57] Carcani, *Registrum*, p. 290; Abulafia, *Frederick II*, p. 335.

[58] Ibid., pp. 255–57; C. Sırat, *A History of Jewish Philosophy in the Middle Ages* (Cambridge, 1985), pp. 212–32.

they were saying.⁵⁹ But the real stars seem in this period to be the Muslim Idrīsī and the Greek Doxapatrios—both arriving from outside the kingdom, but both patronized partly at least for political reasons.

Idrīsī, a refugee prince from Morocco, was given the task of describing the produce and natural resources of each region of the world, and of making a great silver map of the world. The map was destroyed during the sacking of the royal palace by rioters in 1161; but his *Book of King Roger* still survives, a mixture of travelers' tales, of Arabic geography books, and of personal observation.⁶⁰ Its wealth of detail and reliability decrease somewhat the further north the coverage extends. Idrīsī had some awareness of the physical geography of northern Europe, and no doubt he did consult Western Europeans based at or visiting the royal court. But he seems not to make use of Latin or Greek sources; he is certainly happier with antiquated Arabic accounts of Europe than with up-to-date eyewitness testimony. This was not unusual in any twelfth-century writer; but it hardly suggests the syncretism lyrically attributed to the Sicilian court—an ability to cross cultural boundaries, to create an eclectic mix of the best or boldest ideas to be found in Greek, Latin, Arabic, and Hebrew sources. Nor, for that matter, did Idrīsī's book have any known influence on later writers at this or other European courts. Its future readership lay solely in the Arab world. For Muslim and Christian to exist side by side at court was not to observe and instruct one another.⁶¹

---

⁵⁹ For their works, see Amari, *Biblioteca arabo-sicula*. Modern studies of cultural life among the Muslims of Sicily include U. Rizzitano, *Storia e cultura nella Sicilia saracena* (Palermo, 1975); and M. Amari, *Storia dei Musulmani di Sicilia*, 2d rev. ed., 3 vols. (Catania, 1930–1939).

⁶⁰ See *L'Italia descritta nel "Libro del Re Ruggero" compilato da Edrisi*, eds. and trans. M. Amari and C. Schiaparelli (Rome, 1883), for the sections dealing with Italy and Sicily. See also *India and the Neighbouring territories in the Kitab Nuzhat al-Mushtaq fi'khtiraq al-'afaq*, trans. S. Maqbul Ahmad (Leiden, 1960); *Description de l'Afrique et de l'Espagne*, eds. and trans. R. Dozy and M. J. de Goeje (Leiden, 1886); and other studies of Idrīsī's comments on regions as remote as Finland. A new edition is in progress: *Opus geographicum, sive Liber ad eorum delectationem qui terras peragrare studeant*, eds. E. Cerulli et al. (Naples–Rome, 1971–).

⁶¹ This agrees in some measure with N. Daniel, *The Arabs and Medieval Eu-*

So too among the Greeks: Neilos Doxapatrios's career had begun at the imperial court in Constantinople, though he may have been of Sicilian ancestry. His *History of the Five Patriarchates* laid heavy stress on the claims of jurisdiction of the patriarchs of Constantinople in Sicily and southern Italy. It was not, at first sight, the message Roger II might have expected, but in fact the work provided him with a useful stick with which to beat the pope.[62] In 1142/43 Roger was involved in one of the periodic rows with the papacy over his claim to exercise the legatine authority he had inherited from his father, and it is precisely at this time that we see the appearance of Doxapatrios's work, the renewal of diplomatic contact with Byzantium, and the portrayal of Roger II in the Martorana mosaic as a king crowned by Christ, receiving his power directly from heaven without papal mediation. Thus Doxapatrios's book has to be placed in the context of his uneasy relationship with a papacy insistent on its overlordship over the kingdom of Sicily; and of his occasional aspirations for a negotiated peace with Constantinople, in which even a renewed orthodox Sicilian church might be dangled as bait. Equally, the presence of distinguished Greek poets and rhetoricians, arriving at the Norman court from Constantinople or the Peloponnese, flattered Sicilian kings who wished to present their monarchy as comparable to that of Byzantium: indeed Roger was accused of wishing to secure from the one true Roman emperor recognition of the title of *basileus*, though more probably he was merely trying to secure acceptance of the plenitude of his authority as a territorial king.[63] But the real significance should

---

rope (London–Beirut, 1975), pp. 146–47, though he greatly overstates his case.

[62] The work on the five patriarchates appears in Migne, *Patrologia Græca*, 132: cols. 1083–1114. For Doxapatrios, see F. Giunta, *Bizantini e bizantinismo nella Sicilia normanna*, 2d ed. (Palermo, 1974), pp. 87–88.

[63] Joannes Cinnamus, *Epitome rerum ab Ioanne et Alexio Comnenis gestarum*, ed. A. Meinecke (Bonn, 1836); *The Deeds of John and Manuel Comnenus, by John Kinnamos*, trans. C. M. Brand (New York, 1976), p. 75, reports Roger's wish to gain recognition of his "equal plane of greatness" to the *basileus*, implying that Roger was placing impossible demands in the way of peace. But cf. the position implicit in W. Ullmann, "Rulership and the Law in the Middle Ages:

not be exaggerated; no firmly based local school of Greek literature was created. Just as again and again the mosaicists for the great churches had to be brought from Constantinople, so too the men of letters were lured thence by promises of pensions and patronage. It seems that even the great cycle at Monreale was the work of Byzantine mosaicists, and that the native Sicilian contribution consisted more of adaptation to Latin iconographical requirements than of real workmanship.

Finally, the much-acclaimed work of translation at the Sicilian court must be seen as a less glorious moment in Greco-Latin intellectual contact than is often supposed. Precisely because the court at Palermo was not a hive of Greek philosophers at home with Plato's texts and ideas, it proved necessary to render the Greek texts newly acquired from Constantinople into more familiar Latin. Plato's *Meno* and *Phaedo* and Ptolemy's *Almagest* were translated by or for William I's minister Henry Aristippus in the mid-twelfth century; the last of these was, in fact, to be retranslated under Frederick II. These works were being taken out of the Byzantine world into a cultural orbit in which classical Greek was not widely understood, despite the contemporary use of vernacular Greek in royal charters. Translation signifies, in this case, the removal of the text from its cultural context. The Sicilian court was not particularly interested in contemporary Byzantine scholarship; it wanted ancient texts for their philosophical content, not because they were important components in the syllabus of Constantinople.

In other words, the court as well as the country was being Latinized in the twelfth century. The eclecticism of Roger II's time—eclecticism in a slightly pejorative sense, given the lack of real contact between cultures—gave way to a heavy emphasis

---

The Case of Norman Sicily," *Acta Juridica* (1978), where Roger's place as practitioner of the theory of the king as "emperor in his own kingdom" is forcefully argued (a view explicitly propounded in the late thirteenth century commentaries on the laws of Roger II, William II and Frederick II). In other words, Roger aimed to secure recognition that neither the Greek ruler, nor the pope, nor the German king had any authority over one who was "*a Deo coronatus*"; and in that sense he would be the equal of the *basileus*, not in the whole world but within his kingdom.

on Latin culture, magnificently displayed in the rich neoclassical Latin of "Hugo Falcandus," the historian, at the end of the century.[64] There were, indeed, survivors of an earlier age. Admiral Eugenius, last of a family of Greek servants of state, continued to write elegant Greek poetry; but he too participated in the Latinization of court culture, by translating a Byzantine version of the Sibylline oracles into Latin.[65] The late twelfth century shows a significant expansion of Latin political influence at court: the Norman and southern Italian baronage gained a place in the government of the kingdom, placing further pressure on the Greek and Muslim remnants in the civil service. These Greeks and Muslims had been major patrons of Greek or Arabic culture, and as they disappeared the range of the court's cultural links contracted sharply. The same period sees the creation of close political and cultural bonds between the Sicilian and English courts, each harping on its Norman antecedents; this emphasis around 1180 was actually something new, and forms part of that process of Sicily's integration into the Latin world.[66]

This is not to deny the existence of a later revival in contact with the Muslim world under Frederick II; Frederick corresponded with leading Muslim scholars such as Ibn Sab'īn, and with Spanish Jewish philosophers as well. But he had no Muslim intellectuals permanently at court and few Greeks; the Saracens of Lucera were soldiers, not philosophers. Some of Frederick's closest advisers, such as the bureaucrat Uberto Fallamonaca, seem to have been of Muslim descent; but Frederick's main contact with Muslim culture was achieved either through correspondence, or through the mediation the Spanish-trained philosopher and astrologer Michael Scot, or

[64] *La Historia o Liber de Regno Sicilie e la Epistola ad Petrum Panormitane Ecclesie Thesaurarium*, ed. G. B. Siragusa (Rome, 1897).

[65] On Admiral Eugenius, see E. M. Jamison, *Admiral Eugenius of Sicily: His Life and Work* (London, 1957).

[66] E. M. Jamison, "The Sicilian-Norman Kingdom in the Mind of Anglo-Norman Contemporaries," *Proceedings of the British Academy*, 24 (1938); cf. R. H. C. Davis, *The Normans and Their Myth* (London, 1976).

through the translation work of Jews such as Jacob Anatoli.[67] Some of the cultural figures associated with him, such as the young prodigy Judah ha-Cohen and the mathematician Leonardo Fibonacci, met him only briefly and knew the emperor through correspondence rather than through close personal contact. Toledo was the great source of texts; and this side of the cultural life of Frederick's court was partly in a Spanish shadow.[68] It was their Spanish links and their understanding of Arabic as well as Western languages that brought the Ibn Tibbons and Judah ha-Cohen to Frederick's attention; but the Jews served increasingly as the channel of communication between the Sicilian court and the culture of Islam. No work symbolizes these links more than the Latin translation of Maimonides' *Guide for the Perplexed*, a great work of Jewish philosophy originally addressed (in Arabic) to philosophically minded Jews, but known too at Frederick's court through the efforts of Michael Scot and by the brilliant escapee from that court, Thomas Aquinas.[69] In any case the days of a Palermo-based court were long since over; Frederick's court was itinerant, and Naples rather than Palermo was the intellectual center of his Sicilian realm. Frederick's was really a hand-luggage court, whose main equipment consisted of manuscripts of works on zoology that the emperor carried on his Lombard campaigns, such as the Arabic treatise of the falconer Moamyn, which Frederick was studying during the siege of Faenza in 1240/41 and which Master Theodore of Antioch, Scot's successor, translated for him.[70]

---

[67] L. Thorndike, *Michael Scot* (London, 1965), pp. 32–39. Scot actually seems to have followed Frederick on his travels around Italy.

[68] For this view of Frederick's court, see Abulafia, *Frederick II*, esp. pp. 251–67. For the Greek men of letters, see M. B. Wellas, *Griechisches aus dem Umkreis Kaiser Friedrichs II* (Munich, 1983).

[69] Moses Maimonides, *The Guide for the Perplexed*, trans. M. Friedländer, 2d ed. (London, 1904).

[70] Abulafia, *Frederick II*, p. 268; C. H. Haskins, *Studies in the History of Mediaeval Science* (Cambridge, Mass., 1924), p. 318. An especially bleak view must be presented of Latin letters at Frederick's court. Haskins, *Studies in Mediaeval Culture* (Oxford, 1929), pp. 129–48, does not really prove that there was very much happening at any one time; many of his examples are from

Indeed, the cultural flavor of Frederick's court is in one very important way entirely Western: the appearance of a school of lyric poets writing imitations of the Provençal love-songs under the emperor's patronage in an Italian dialect signals an interesting shift. Not merely Provençal but German poetry may have inspired the *Scuola Siciliana*—Frederick's father is supposed to have been a *Minnesinger* as well as an emperor. Looking more closely at the authors of these poems, one sees striking similarities. Guido delle Colonne, Giacomo da Lentini, Rosso Rosso, Mazzeo di Ricco of Messina—again and again they are the ruler's intimates, judges, and notaries in the imperial civil service or prominent landlords, in all these cases inhabitants of eastern Sicily or the tip of Calabria. (Others, such as Rinaldo d'Aquino, are southern Italians.) They represent the new Latin (or Latinized) population of the area in the kingdom where Islam had always been weakest, and where Latin immigration had long been strongest.[71] Iacopo Mostacci is described both as a Messinese and as a Pisan, but this is no problem, since so many of Messina's inhabitants were of northern Italian origin by the early thirteenth century. Maybe the prominence of Messina in the *Scuola Siciliana* reflects accidents of manuscript survival, but in fact it seems that the bustling, prosperous port with its large settler population provided an ideal environment for the importation of European fashions—not merely fashions in textiles, but fashions in speech and literature. Just after 1200 the Provençal troubadour Peire Vidal certainly visited eastern Sicily, and composed poems in praise of the Genoese adventurers who had seized control of Malta and Syracuse.[72] But it was in

---

Frederick's youth or of cases where personal contact with the emperor was very limited. On this, see Abulafia, *Frederick II*, pp. 264–66.

[71] See B. Panvini, *La scuola poetica siciliana: le canzoni dei rimatori nativi di Sicilia* (Florence, 1955); and, for a valuable selection, F. Jensen, *The Poetry of the Sicilian School*, Garland Library of Medieval Literature, vol. A 22 (New York, 1986). For an overall interpretation, see Abulafia, *Frederick II*, pp. 270–79.

[72] Abulafia, "Henry, Count of Malta," pp. 113–14, repr. in David Abulafia, *Italy, Sicily and the Mediterranean, 1100–1400* (London, 1987), chap. 3, with additional nn. referring to later literature. See also J. Brincat, "Le poesie 'maltesi' di Peire Vidal." *Melita Historica* 7 (1976):65–89.

Italian that the Sicilian poets wrote, not in Provençal. They used an Italian that had been fused out of a mélange of southern Italian, Ligurian, and Tuscan dialects; and, though what survives is perhaps a literary rather than a spoken form of Italian, it still stands as testimony to the massive cultural and ethnic transformations that had taken place in Sicily between 1100 and 1250.

The repopulation of the cities by Italian immigrants, the settlement of eastern Sicily by Lombardi, and the expulsion or assimilation of the Muslims are one side to the Latinization of the island of Sicily. In lesser measure the same applies to parts of the southern Italian mainland; here it was the Greeks who were under immediate pressure, and there was also heavy immigration in the twelfth and thirteenth centuries, still revealed in the Franco-Provençal dialect of a tiny area of northern Apulia. In Calabria Greek gave way to Italian, and there were even some Provençal settlers there by the mid-fourteenth century. Arguably the survival of Greek Orthodoxy in southern Italy and Sicily was as much the work of the Albanian migrations of the fifteenth century as it was the result of tenacious traditionalism among the residue of Hellenophone Sicilians and Calabrians. The Muslim community of Lucera, founded by Frederick II, did not and was not intended to flourish as an outpost of Islamic culture in continental Europe. Frederick had transplanted about twenty thousand Muslims from Sicily to the northern parts of his kingdom in order to isolate them from the rest of the Muslim world, to ensure that the damaging links between the Saracen rebels in Sicily and their coreligionists in North Africa could not be duplicated. Lucera was too far away and its inhabitants were fully dependent on the favors of the emperor.[73] In fact Frederick declared that he was pleased that the Dominicans were prepared to work for the conversion of the Luceran Saracens, and (at least for a time) he may have expected the colony to become fully assimilated into the surrounding Christian society.[74] By 1233 some Luceran Muslims

[73] Abulafia, *Frederick II*, pp. 146–48, 252.
[74] See the discussion by James M. Powell in chap. 5. But for much of his

were familiar with Italian; in fact it is quite possible that Italian had been gaining ground among them even before they left Sicily.⁷⁵

Although Frederick made extensive use of the royal castle at Lucera, he never made it into one of the cultural centers of his kingdom; perhaps he did live there surrounded by oriental ceramics, trumpeters, and dancing-girls (who doubled as concubines), but the men of Lucera were encouraged either to serve in the imperial bodyguard or to sow the fields around the town, for which purpose Frederick supplied plough-teams in 1239/40.⁷⁶ The emperor's idea was to bind the Saracen colony to the soil, "as was the case in the time of King William [II]"—to transform a settlement of restive, transplanted rebels into industrious peasants who could perform the same agricultural tasks as they had done when resident in Sicily, and who could help repopulate an area that, like other parts of the *Regno*, was lightly settled and therefore unable to realize its potential as a source of saleable foodstuffs. The Luceran Saracens became a *casus belli* when the popes began to declare the war against the Hohenstaufen a crusade: Innocent IV cited the Luceran Sara-

---

reign Frederick appears to have tolerated Islam at Lucera, as did his successors. He probably knew canon law well enough to resist the temptation to convert by force. He possibly assumed that the problem would take care of itself and that Islam in Lucera would be even less resilient than that close to Africa in Sicily. But embattled minorities can resist assimilation very fiercely. J. M. Martin's "La colonie sarrasine de Lucera et son environment: quelques réflexions," *Mediterraneo medievale; scritti in onore di Francesco Giunta*, 3 vols. (Soveria Mannelli, 1989), 2:795–811, appeared too recently to be discussed in the text, but deserves mention because of its extensive coverage of the literature.

⁷⁵ See J. L. A. Huillard-Bréholles, *Historia diplomatica Friderici secundi*, 12 vols. (Paris, 1852–1861), 4:452, for Italian speakers at Lucera. Powell suggests that the Luceran Saracens may have started to contaminate the local Christians with their beliefs.

⁷⁶ See David Whitehouse, "Ceramici e vetri medioevali provenienti dal Castello di Lucera," *Bollettino d'Arte* (1966): 171–78, for finds of Chinese celadon ware of the eleventh to thirteenth centuries. Clearly their main value was as curios and they could have arrived long after their manufacture—most probably via Egypt, where a delayed reaction to Chinese models led to the extensive imitation of Far Eastern pottery styles. For the Saracen farmers, see Carcani, *Registrum*, p. 307; Abulafia, *Frederick II*, pp. 334–35.

cens as proof that the hated Manfred was an ally of Islam.⁷⁷ But even Charles I of Anjou never fulfilled his promise to uproot the Luceran Saracens; it was left to his son Charles II to close down the Muslim colony in 1300, at a time when not merely the Muslims but the Jews of southern Italy were being subjected to calls for their conversion or expulsion. By the end of the thirteenth century the Muslim colony at Lucera had become an utter anomaly—a community that had lost touch with the Islamic world but had continued to resist attempts to integrate it into the Latin world, rebuffing visiting preachers and maintaining itself as an exclusively Islamic entity. Yet even after the re-Christianization of Lucera, there were still Muslim inhabitants scattered around Apulia, who complained to the royal court about their persecution and lack of protection, and were evidently caught in the theological and canon law vice that explicitly guaranteed the right of the Infidel to live unconverted under Christian rule, but used every method short of forced conversion to draw him into the Christian faith.⁷⁸

After 1300 Islam had still not entirely vanished from Sicily and the south, for the expansion of the slave trade, in which the rising merchants of Catalonia and Majorca had a large stake, brought unknown numbers of unfree Muslims to Palermo,

⁷⁷ N. Housley, *The Italian Crusades: The Papal-Angevin Alliance and the Crusades against Christian Lay Powers* (Oxford, 1982), pp. 40, 62, 65, 243; and yet there were also Saracens of Lucera in the Angevin armies resisting Peter of Aragon after the Sicilian Vespers! See p. 158.

⁷⁸ J. Muldoon, *Popes, Lawyers and Infidels: the Church and the non-Christian World, 1250–1550* (Liverpool, 1979), pp. 1–28. For the fate of the expelled Saracens, see P. Egidi, *Codice diplomatico dei Saraceni di Lucera* (Naples, 1917), §166, 168, 241, 349, 350, 390, 450, where it is stated that the Christians of Apulia "multos graviter atque letaliter percusserunt et aliquos inhumane ac impie occiderunt." But the dominating flavor was one of relentless persecution of the Saracens, stopping just short of extermination. See P. Egidi, "La colonia saracena di Lucera e la sua distruzione." *Archivio storico per le province napoletane*, 36 (1911): 597–694; 37 (1912): 71–89, 664–96; 38 (1913): 115–44, 681–707; 39 (1914): 132–71, 697–766. Similar measures were also being adopted in the kingdom of Naples against the Jews. Financial considerations at a time of rising war costs may be one insalubrious motive; peace with the Aragonese was still a couple of years away. Cf. Housley, *Italian Crusades*, p. 243.

Trapani, and other centers.[79] In the period 1280 to 1310 there was an emphasis on the handling of Saracen slaves, but the slave markets were packed with Greek slaves over the next half-century, and by Tatar slaves between about 1360 and 1400. As in other areas of the western Mediterranean, the years after 1440 saw a return to African sources, by now primarily black African. Bresc warns against exaggerating the importance of the slave trade of late medieval Sicily, both in relation to the island's overall trade and as far as their numbers and functions are concerned.[80] It is probable that slaves never played the same part in the agricultural economy of Sicily that they played in contemporary Valencia, where slave gangs were set to work on the soil. They were either domestic slaves (including concubines) or they arrived in transit, awaiting sale in the slave markets of Palermo and elsewhere, before reexport, possibly back into the Muslim world. The Catalan slave handlers were middlemen who exploited the position of Sicily close to the slave sources in Cyrenaica, but who appear to have thought little about the religious affiliation of the purchaser. As for those slaves who remained in Sicily, it is unlikely that the unfree Muslims created their own religious communities, as the Christian unfree in North Africa had perhaps managed to do until the twelfth century;[81] many certainly converted to Christianity, and in the process could expect to gain their freedom, or at least gain the right to buy it. Among those who did not convert were Saracens of Lucera, sold as slaves in Sicily after the colony was disbanded by Charles II of Anjou.[82]

In Jewish households there was a special interest in Muslim slaves. The fourteenth-century kings of Sicily insisted that Jews

[79] C. Verlinden, *L'esclavage dans l'Europe médiévale*, vol. 2, *Italie, Colonies italiennes du Levant, Levant latin, Empire byzantin* (Ghent, 1977); C. Verlinden, "L'esclavage en Sicile au bas moyen âge," *Bulletin de l'Institut historique belge de Rome* 35 (1963).

[80] Bresc, *Monde méditerranéen*, 1:439–75.

[81] Ibid., 2:583, argues that "il n'y a pas de communauté, pas de lieu de culte: c'est un monde en survie précaire."

[82] Ibid., 2:582. It would be interesting to know how such Saracens reached Sicily, since the colony was dispersed during the War of the Vespers when southern Italy and Sicily had few trading links.

should not exercise power over Christians, but it remained permissible to own Muslim slaves. In addition, the use of circumcised Muslims may have made it possible for Jews to circumvent the complex religious laws concerning the handling of wine by non-Jews, since some rabbinic authorities allowed *kosher* wine to be poured by any circumcised person, not merely by a male Jew.[83] Thus as late as the fifteenth century there were some Muslims in Sicily, but virtually all were unfree and of non-Sicilian origin. Rare instances of Muslim merchants resident in Sicily come as little surprise: Asmectus (Aḥmad) Bursarius, a maker of bags and pouches, lived in Palermo with his wife Fatima from 1307 to 1309, and Saracens appear in the notarial acts of these years and as late as 1329 making oaths "tacto pane ad legem Muhamet" (swearing oaths in the Muslim fashion while holding bread). Salem de Messana, resident at Palermo, appears to have been the last prominent Muslim merchant; he died in 1345. After that, references to Muslims are very scarce; in 1402 a Muslim was functioning as headman (*raysi*—itself an Arabic word still in use in Sicily) in tunny-fisheries in western Sicily, but when the government of Sicily needed translators for Arab documents or embassies it had to turn to Jews, Muslim slaves, and Christians of Pantelleria.[84] It is striking, too, that Arabic left few marks on the Italian spoken in Sicily to compare with its impact on Castilian; about two hundred words of Arabic origin survive in Sicilian Italian, providing testimony to the reality of the cultural break between Islamic and Christian Sicily. There was thus no return of the Muslims to Sicily, such as occurred in late medieval Andalusia or indeed Castile proper, where the Muslim settlements in the major towns often contained new immigrants unconnected, it appears, with the original, expelled Moorish population.

Several dimensions to the Latinization of the Sicilian kingdom have been identified in this study. It has been seen that the cultural complexion of the court underwent significant changes between 1100 and 1250. The relative openness of Roger II had

[83] Abulafia, "Jews of Erice," p. 312. However, there was and is no consensus on this.

[84] Bresc, *Monde méditerranéen*, 2:582–84.

not resulted in the removal of existing cultural barriers; after him, interest in Greek and Arabic culture became more and more selective, with an emphasis on the acquisition of ancient texts preserved by Byzantines or Muslims rather than on the achievements of contemporary scholars outside the Latin orbit. Under Frederick II contact was restored, mainly by post, but the Sicilian court itself was heavily Latinized. These were developments in which the inhabitants of Sicily played little part. Their own cultural preferences can perhaps be gauged by the continuing interest in Byzantine-type icons even among the Latin citizens of Palermo as late as 1400; these icons were still being made, and demand for them was strong.[85] And in Messina and eastern Sicily the Greek language and liturgy survived beyond 1500, even if the number of Greek speakers continued to shrink rapidly. Thus on an island where the Greeks had—even under Norman rule—still constituted the vast majority of all Christians, they were now a minority, overtaken by the Latin settlers from further north. Italian became the *koiné* of nearly all the Sicilians.

In a famous passage in his book *The Leopard*, Giovanni di Lampedusa makes one of his characters remark that the Sicilians are "old, very old."[86] Some striking continuities are visible: the grain traffic of the Greco-Roman world, active again in the Middle Ages and the sixteenth century; the long sequence of foreign rulers, bewailed in the same passage by Lampedusa. But between 1100 and 1300 Sicily did change; it was renewed—in population, language, culture, and religion—in massive degree. When in 1282 the king of Aragon conquered the island he gained command, if not over a new country, at least over a new people.[87]

---

[85] Bresc-Bautier, *Artistes, patriciens et confrères*, p. 72.

[86] Giuseppe di Lampedusa, *The Leopard*, trans. A. Colquhoun (London, 1963), p. 145; D. Mack Smith, *Medieval Sicily, 800–1713* (London, 1969), p. xiii, uses this quotation as a starting-point for his analysis of Sicilian society.

[87] And indeed Bresc ("Formazione"; *Monde méditerranéen*, 2:*passim*) argues that by 1282 there had developed a consciousness of a Sicilian *populus*, revealed, for instance, in the attempt that year to replace King Charles of Anjou with a confederation of Sicilian communes.

4

THE SUBJECTED MUSLIMS
OF THE FRANKISH LEVANT

Benjamin Z. Kedar

THE PHASE OF LATIN RULE over subjected Muslims had a different long-term significance in the western and central Mediterranean on the one hand and in the Levant on the other. In the Iberian peninsula and Sicily, the Latin conquest ushered in the crucial stage in the history of the local Muslims at the end of which they were to disappear completely. By comparison, Frankish rule over Levantine Muslims constituted a relatively brief episode, which ended in Muslim triumph and the total eradication of the Frankish population. At most this episode may be considered to have lasted from the conquest of Antioch in 1098 to the fall of Acre in 1291, but when specific localities are considered, its duration was shorter still: for instance, Antioch was Frankish from 1098 to 1268, Tyre from 1124 to 1291, Caesarea from 1101 to 1187 and from 1191 to 1265, Jerusalem from 1099 to 1187 and from 1229 to 1244, and Nablus from 1099 to only 1187. Moreover, the Franks came repeatedly under attack by outside Muslim powers and suffered several setbacks at their hands, and therefore their rule was much more precarious than that of the Latin conquerors of Spain and Sicily. This precariousness resulted primarily from the adverse geopolitical situation of the Frankish states in the Levant, established as they were in the midst of

---

I would like to thank the Alexander von Humboldt-Stiftung for a grant which enabled me to write this chapter in the summer of 1987 at the Monumenta Germaniae Historica, Munich.

Oriental Islam, but also from the limited influx of Catholic Europeans which markedly differed from the considerable immigration to the closer and safer regions wrested from the Muslims in the western and central Mediterranean. A further characteristic of the Frankish Levant was its origin in, and permanently close linkage with, Christian holy warfare. The religious factor was, of course, also present in Sicily and Spain—Pope Gregory VII exhorted Count Roger of Sicily to extend "the worship of the Christian name" among the pagans (the Muslims), and Pope Urban II urged the first Latin archbishop of Toledo, Bernard of Sédirac, "to endeavor by word and example to convert, with God's grace, the infidels to the faith"[1]—but it was only in the Levant that Latin states came into being as a result of a papally conceived and initiated military expedition whose declared aims were religious, namely, to put an end to Infidel defilement of the Holy Places and to liberate Oriental Christians from the Infidel yoke.

Short and precarious duration, limited European immigration, and linkage to holy warfare are some of the major peculiarities of the Frankish Levant. An examination of the subjected Levantine Muslims in the framework of a comparative perspective calls, therefore, for an assessment of the extent to which these and other peculiarities shaped the fate of these Muslims differently from that of subjected Muslims elsewhere in the Mediterranean. But since the evidence on these Levantine Muslims, some of which has come to light rather recently, is less well known than that on their Sicilian or Spanish coreligionists, a somewhat extensive presentation of the documentation must come first.[2]

---

[1] *Das Register Gregors VII*, ed. E. Caspar (1920), in *MGH Epp.* 2, 1:272; D. Mansilla, ed., *La documentación pontificia hasta Inocencio III (965–1216)*, Monumenta Hispaniae Vaticana, Registros 1 (Rome, 1955), doc. 27, p. 44, and docs. 45, 101, pp. 65, 121. For the context, see my *Crusade and Mission: European Approaches toward The Muslims* (Princeton, 1984), pp. 42–57.

[2] There is no monograph on the Levantine Muslims subjected to Latin rule. The most recent discussions are Joshua Prawer, *The Latin Kingdom of Jerusalem: European Colonialism in the Middle Ages* (London, 1972), pp. 47–52; idem, "Serfs, Slaves and Bedouin," in *Crusader Institutions* (Oxford, 1980), pp. 201–14; idem, "Social Classes in the Latin Kingdom: The 'Minorities,' " in *A*

Documentation and Reality

The collapse of the Frankish states of the Levant entailed the destruction of most archives. The narrative sources also yield little information. The Frankish chroniclers, focusing on political developments, refer to the fate of the Muslims at the time of the crusader conquest, but have very little to say about them thereafter. All but one of the Muslim chroniclers lived beyond the boundaries of the Frankish states. To be sure, Ḥamdān b. ʿAbd al-Raḥīm al-Athāribī (ca. 1071–1147/48), the one Muslim chronicler who did live within these boundaries, was eminently qualified to write on Muslims under Frankish rule, as he himself made a remarkable career both under Frankish and Muslim rulers. It is symptomatic, however, that Ḥamdān's *History of the Franks who came forth to the Land of Islam*, like the one Frankish attempt to write a history of the Muslim East—William of Tyre's *Historia orientalium principum*—has not survived, and only quotations from it appear in some later works.[3] Other Muslim chroniclers bring somewhat more details than their Frankish counterparts on the fate of their coreligionists during the crusader conquest; interestingly enough, their accounts are occasionally less gruesome than those of the Franks.[4] The

---

History of the Crusades, ed. Kenneth M. Setton, 6 vols. (Madison, 1989), 5:61–65, 101–15; H. E. Mayer, "Latins, Muslims and Greeks in the Latin Kingdom of Jerusalem," *History* 63 (1978): 175–92; J. Richard, *The Latin Kingdom of Jerusalem*, trans. J. Shirley (Amsterdam, 1979), pp. 130–36 (this is an updated version of the French original); Claude Cahen, *Orient et Occident au temps des croisades* (Paris, 1983), chap. 13, pp. 167–70.

[3] On Ḥamdān b. ʿAbd al-Raḥīm, see Claude Cahen, *La Syrie du Nord à l'époque des croisades et la principauté franque d'Antioche* (Paris, 1940), pp. 41–42, 343–44, 405, n. 2, 540, n. 45; F. Rosenthal, *History of Muslim Historiography*, 2d ed. (Leiden, 1968), pp. 62, 466. The publication of the fragments of Ḥamdān's chronicle remains a desideratum. On William of Tyre's lost work, see H. Möhring, "Zu der Geschichte der orientalischen Herrscher des Wilhelm von Tyrus," *Mittellateinisches Jahrbuch* 19 (1984): 170–83.

[4] Cf., e.g., the accounts of the Frankish conquest of Tripoli in 1109: Roger Le Tourneau, *Damas de 1075 à 1154, Traduction annotée d'un fragment de l'Histoire d'Ibn al-Qalānisī* (Damascus, 1952), p. 86; Ibn al-Athīr, *RHC. Or.*, 1:274; *Fulcheri Carnotensis Historia Hierosolymitana (1095–1127)*, ed. H. Hage-

Muslim chroniclers also refer far more often to the activities of the subjected Muslims during Saladin's reconquest campaign. But they, too, concentrate on political developments and therefore shed little light on the internal affairs of the Muslims who lived under Frankish rule. Only one Arabic narrative deals exclusively with subjected Muslims. This is the short account by Ḍiyāʾ al-Dīn Muḥammad b. ʿAbd al-Wāḥid al-Muqaddasī (1173–1245) of the flight of Ḥanbalī peasants from the Nablus area to Damascus from the 1150s on; however, it reflects the attitudes of a tiny, radical minority. In addition, there were a few Muslim visitors to the Frankish states who wrote down their impressions and, like other travelers of that age, tended to report in considerable detail on the kinsmen they encountered. Consequently, a substantial part of our knowledge about the subjected Muslims of the Frankish states derives from the account of a single Muslim traveler, Ibn Jubayr of Granada, who was in the kingdom of Jerusalem for just thirty-two days, thirteen of which he spent on a ship in Acre harbor, waiting for a favorable wind.

On the whole, then, the evidence is sketchy; the secondary literature is, perhaps, even more meagre than the sources warrant. Because of the haphazard nature of the documentation, modern historians often find themselves constrained to generalize from a single testimony. For instance, mosques in full Muslim possession are attested for just one town of the kingdom of Jerusalem, namely Tyre. Does it follow, therefore, that elsewhere in the kingdom mosques and public Muslim worship were not permitted? Some historians have been inclined to think so.[5] But we should recall that the Muslim-owned mosques of Tyre are mentioned only in the account of Ibn Jubayr, who visited just two towns, Tyre and Acre. In Tyre he rested in a mosque that remained in Muslim hands and learned about others which were in their possession; in Acre he saw a small oratory in the erstwhile main mosque where Muslims

---

meyer (Heidelberg, 1913), p. 533; Albert of Aachen, in *RHC. OCC.*, 4:668–69.

[5] See Mayer, "Muslims," pp. 185–86; and, less definitely, Cahen, *Orient*, p. 167.

MUSLIMS OF THE FRANKISH LEVANT 139

from outside the town could "congregate to perform the obligatory prayers," as well as the mosque at ʿAyn al-Baqar, in Frankish possession and with a Frankish-built eastern apse, where Muslims and Christians assembled to pray, each in the customary direction.[6] Had Ibn Jubayr not visited them, we should not have known of the existence of the Tyre mosques as well as of the oratory in Acre's former main mosque.[7] Had he visited even one other town, the information at our disposal might have been quite different. By the same token, if Ibn Jubayr had been our only source on Frankish hospitals, the only ones known would have been those he mentions having seen in Acre and Tyre. In these circumstances, then, it is rather risky to generalize from the data available.

One could approach the problem from a different angle, by examining the statement on the restoration of the Islamic cult after Saladin's reconquest in 1187. The most detailed information is to be found in the florid account of Saladin's secretary, ʿImād al-Dīn. In Acre, he says, prayer took place on the first Friday after the battle of Ḥaṭṭīn and the "interrupted custom" was reestablished; at Nablus the call to prayer was restored; in Sidon the Friday public prayer was reestablished; and so forth.[8] But what are the facts behind these statements? Are we to conclude that, under the Franks, there were no mosques in any of these places and the Muslims were not able to worship publicly? Possibly, but not necessarily, for Muslim worship under Christian rule could assume various forms. Let us turn to Ibn Jubayr's account about the Muslims of Sicily. Ibn Jubayr stayed in Sicily from December 9, 1184, to March 25, 1185, about four times longer than he did in the kingdom of Jerusalem, and

[6] Tyre: *The Travels of Ibn Jubayr*, trans. R. J. C. Broadhurst (London, 1952), p. 321; Acre: ibid., p. 318. (The Arabic original states explicitly that the Muslims of Tyre owned several mosques in addition to the one in which Ibn Jubayr took his rest.)

[7] The mosque at ʿAyn al-Baqar outside of Acre is also mentioned by ʿAlī al-Harawī, *Guide des lieux de pèlerinage*, trans. Janine Sourdel-Thomine (Damascus, 1957), p. 57.

[8] ʿImād al-Dīn al-Iṣfahānī, *Conquête de la Syrie et de la Palestine par Saladin*, trans. Henri Massé (Paris, 1972), pp. 33, 36, 40; see also ʿImād al-Dīn, in Abū Shāma, *RHC. Or.* (Paris, 1895), 4:309.

during this time he gathered detailed information and changed his initially favorable opinion on the situation of the local Muslims. In Palermo, he says, there was a *qāḍī* to judge the Muslims, teachers of Koran, countless mosques, and the call to prayer was distinctly heard, but the Muslims were unable to hold public prayer on Fridays, as they were not allowed the *khuṭba* (the address which includes a prayer for the well-being of the Muslim sovereign and all the faithful, and constitutes a condition for the validity of the Friday prayer). Only on the days of festival could Muslims perform the public prayer with a *khuṭba* in which the name of the 'Abbāsid caliph was invoked.[9] Consequently, distinctions must be made between the continued existence of a mosque, the public call to prayer (which was formally forbidden throughout Latin Christendom in 1311), the gathering in a mosque, and the Friday prayer with the *khuṭba*. 'Imād al-Dīn's statements could therefore have referred to anything from the reintroduction of Muslim worship as such to the performance of the Friday prayer with all its politico-religious dimensions. In fact, while 'Imād al-Dīn exulted at the restoration of the call to prayer at Nablus, another Muslim author, Ḍiyā' al-Dīn, related that under Frankish rule Ḥanbalī Muslim peasants of the Nablus region used to gather in the village of Jammā'īl for Friday prayers at which the *khuṭba* was delivered.[10]

[9] *Travels of Ibn Jubayr*, pp. 340, 348–49. On his change of opinion, see Michele Amari, *Storia dei Musulmani di Sicilia*, ed. C. A. Nallino (Catania, 1937), 3, 1:54–42, who, however, somewhat misunderstood the limitations on the *khuṭba* (p. 543); for a correct appraisal, see Dietlind Schack, *Die Araber im Reich Rogers II* (Berlin, 1969), pp. 42–43.

[10] Ḍiyā' al-Dīn, Sabab hijrat al-Maqādisa ilā Dimashq, in Ibn Ṭūlūn, Shams al-Dīn Muḥammad ibn 'Ali, *al-Qalā'id al-jawharyya fī ta'rīkh al-Ṣāliḥiyya*, ed. M. A. Duhmān, 2 vols. (Damascus, 1980), 1:68; partial English translation in Joseph Drory, "Ḥanbalīs of the Nablus Region in the Eleventh and Twelfth Centuries," in *The Medieval Levant: Studies in Memory of Eliyahu Ashtor (1914–1984)*, eds. B. Z. Kedar and A. L. Udovitch, (Haifa, 1988), pp. 95–112. As Ḍiyā' al-Dīn (in Ibn Ṭūlūn, 1:69) mentions land which belonged to the mosque of Jammā'īl, one may assume that the mosque remained intact and that the Friday prayers took place in it. (I am indebted to my student Muḥammad al-Ḥajjūj for having drawn my attention to this passage.) For a similar conjecture on the fate of mosques in the Frankish Levant, see Joshua Prawer,

Only one *qāḍī* is mentioned in the documentation. This has been taken as proof that, as a rule, the subjected Muslims had no *qāḍīs*, just as they had no mosques. But let us examine more closely the circumstances under which this single *qāḍī* makes his appearance. Muslim chroniclers of Saladin's 1188 campaign in northern Syria report that Manṣūr b. Nabīl, the *qāḍī* of the harbor town of Jabala, appeared in the sultan's camp and urged him to advance on his hometown. Ibn al-Athīr reports that the *qāḍī* had been a confidant of Bohemond III of Antioch and exercised authority over all the Muslims of Jabala and its surroundings, indeed of the entire Principality of Antioch, but religious zeal moved him to offer Saladin help in the reconquest of Jabala, Laodicea, and other northern towns. When Saladin appeared under the walls of Jabala the *qāḍī* handed over the town to him and then negotiated the surrender of the Franks who had taken refuge in the citadel. He took Frankish hostages who were to remain in his hands until Bohemond released the Muslim hostages he had taken from him earlier—a procedure which suggests, incidentally, that the relationship between the two was less straightforward than initially stated. Later, the *qāḍī* was instrumental in bringing about the capitulation of Laodicea. Saladin, reports ʿImād al-Dīn, heaped eulogies and honors on the *qāḍī*, instituted a pious foundation in his name, guaranteed the possessions of his family, and appointed him to fulfill administrative and judicial functions.[11]

The name of Manṣūr b. Nabīl, *qāḍī* of Jabala, has evidently been preserved only because of his significant role in Saladin's

---

The History of the Jews in the Latin Kingdom of Jerusalem (Oxford, 1988), p. 106, n. 43.

[11] Ibn al-Athīr, in *RHC. Or.*, 1:717–19; ʿImād al-Dīn, in Abū Shāma, *RHC. Or.*, 4:352–53, 357–58. Bahā al-Dīn ascribes to the *qāḍī* a less prominent role (*RHO. Or.* [Paris, 1894], 3:110–11; 4:355–56. I would like to thank Etan Kohlberg of the Hebrew University of Jerusalem for having checked the translation of these and other passages. For discussion, see René Grousset, *Histoire des croisades et du royaume franc de Jérusalem* (Paris, 1935), 2:825–26; Cahen, *Syrie du Nord*, pp. 428, 462; idem, "La féodalité et les institutions politiques de l'Orient latin," *Accademia Nazionale dei Lincei. Atti del XII Convegno "Volta"* (Rome 1957), p. 186, repr. in idem, *Turcobyzantina et Oriens christianus* (London, 1974), chap. G, p. 186.

reconquest of Jabala and Laodicea, a role unparalleled throughout the Latin states. The mere fact that he was a *qāḍī* would hardly have warranted mention, as neither Muslim nor Frankish chroniclers (or jurisprudents) exhibited an interest in the judicial or, for that matter, any other internal arrangements of the subjected Muslim population. (Nor do they mention the judicial arrangements of the subjected Jews; were it not for the Jewish responsa literature, the existence of rabbinical courts in the Frankish kingdom of Jerusalem would have remained unknown.) Moreover, Manṣūr's sudden emergence in the documentation must not be taken to indicate that his unique status in the Principality of Antioch was a recent innovation, or an outgrowth of Bohemond III's imprudent Muslim policy, "by which the elite of the Frankish society uncontrollably abandoned itself to its sympathies toward the indigenous."[12] Rather, Manṣūr's status may have been at least partially traditional. In the latter part of the eleventh century, when Jabala was under Byzantine rule, another man named Manṣūr served as headman of the local Muslims and judged cases which came up among them. Manṣūr's son, the *qāḍī* Abū Muḥammad 'Ubayd Allāh, ruled the town at the turn of the twelfth century. He exhibited a distinct taste for martial activities, repulsing several Frankish attacks, but in 1101 he felt constrained to call upon the Damascenes for help and then left the town. A few years later, the *qāḍī* Ibn 'Ammar of Tripoli seized Jabala and ruled it until Tancred's conquest in 1110, a conquest which appears to have been mild.[13] It is symptomatic for the history of the Muslims subjected to Frankish rule that nothing is known of the Muslims of Jabala in the period between the departure of the *qāḍī* Ibn 'Ammar after his surrender in 1110 and the activities of the *qāḍī* Manṣūr b. Nabīl in 1188. Possibly, then, there were *qāḍī*s in the intervening period, too.

These two examples should suffice to illustrate how risky it can be to equate a single mention in the documentation on the

[12] Grousset, *Histoire*, 2: 826.

[13] Ibn al-Athīr, in *RHC. Or.*, 1: 204–6, 256, 274; see also Ibn al-Qalānisī, p. 87.

subjected Muslims with a single occurrence in reality. It is preferable to concede that the history of these Muslims, of so little interest to their contemporaries, remains in many important respects unknown, and to present as fully as possible the meagre data on which tentative approximations of their history may be founded. On the positive side, one may note that the documentation, especially that written in Arabic, is not necessarily finite. Less than fifty years ago Claude Cahen brought Ḥamdān b. ʿAbd al-Raḥīm to the attention of historians of the Crusades, and only about two decades ago Emanuel Sivan first utilized the account about the exodus of Ḥanbalī villagers from the Nablus area.[14]

The Frankish Conquest and the Modes of Muslim Exitence

For reasons spelled out above, one of the relatively well-documented facets of the history of the subjected Levantine Muslims is their fate during the Frankish conquest. The sources warrant the generalization that the mode of Frankish takeover largely determined their fate in each case. When a town was taken by assault, Muslim and Jewish inhabitants were usually massacred or enslaved. The best-known example is Jerusalem, stormed on July 15, 1099, where, as a Frankish eyewitness puts it, "some of the pagans were mercifully beheaded, others pierced by arrows plunged from towers, and yet others, tortured for a long time, were burned to death in searing flames. Piles of heads, hands, and feet lay in the houses and streets, and indeed there was a running to and fro of men and knights over the corpses."[15] Similar scenes occurred in other towns stormed by the Crusaders, such as Maʿarrat al-Nuʿmān in 1098, Haifa in 1100, Caesarea in 1101, Beirut in 1110, and Bilbays in 1168.

---

[14] For Ḥamdān b. ʿAbd al-Raḥīm, see n. 3 above; on the Ḥanbalīs, see E. Sivan, "Réfugiés syro-palestiniens au temps des croisades," *Revue des études islamiques* 35 (1967): 138–39; and Drory, "Ḥanbalīs," pp. 35–112.

[15] Raymond d'Aguilers, *Historia Francorum qui ceperunt Iherusalem*, trans. John Hugh Hill and Laurita L. Hill (Philadelphia, 1968), p. 127.

The massacres were hardly ever total, however. In Jerusalem, for example, the Fāṭimid commander was allowed to depart with his garrison swelled by civilians, while other Jerusalemites were left alive and forced to dump the corpses of their fellow citizens beyond the city walls. The Cairo Geniza reveals that some Qaraite Jews were ransomed by their coreligionists. Muslim sources relate that the Franks took captive Abu 'l-Qāsim al-Rumaylī, the most celebrated Palestinian ḥadīth expert of his age and author of tracts on the merits of Jerusalem and Hebron, and offered to set him free for a ransom of one thousand dinars. When the money was not forthcoming, they stoned him to death.[16] Elsewhere, too, some survivors of crusader massacres succeeded in reaching Muslim territory, while others were taken captive.[17]

Fear of massacre led some Muslims to flee for safety even before the advent of the Crusaders. The two regional capitals of Ramla and Tiberias were deserted when the Franks entered them in 1099, and the same was true of Jaffa, the region at the southern edge of the Dead Sea, and some Syrian localities. Probably some of the refugees returned to their hometowns with the consolidation of Frankish rule.

The third mode of takeover, following a formal act of surrender, was equally bloodless and did not entail Muslim dislocation. Nablus was the earliest instance. A few days before the fall of Jerusalem, the crusader leaders Tancred and Eustache of Boulogne went on a foraging expedition during the course of which they reached Nablus. The Muslim inhabitants fled to the

---

[16] On the dumping of corpses, see e.g., *Gesta Francorum et aliorum Hierosolimitanorum*, ed. K. Mynors, trans. Rosalind Hill (London, 1962), p. 92. The Geniza evidence has been summarized, for the English-reading public, by S. D. Goitein, "Geniza Sources for the Crusader Period: A Survey," in *Outremer. Studies in the History of the Crusading Kingdom of Jerusalem Presented to Joshua Prawer*, eds. B. Z. Kedar, H. E. Mayer, and R. C. Smail (Jerusalem, 1982), pp. 308–12. On Abu 'l-Qāsim al-Rumaylī, see Rosenthal, *History*, pp. 464, 468; E. Sivan, "The Beginnings of the Faḍā'il al-Quds Literature," *Israel Oriental Studies* 1 (1971): 264. The primary sources, all in Arabic, are listed by Moshe Gil, *Palestine during the First Muslim Period (634–1099)*, 3 vols. (Tel Aviv, 1983), 1: 350, n. 630 (in Hebrew).

[17] Evidence summarized by Sivan, "Réfugiés," p. 136.

Turkish-garrisoned castle leaving the Franks free to pillage the town, though native Oriental Christians dissuaded them from setting it on fire. Thereupon the inhabitants who had taken refuge in the castle promised Tancred and Eustache that they would hand Nablus over to them should the Crusaders conquer Jerusalem. True to their word, after the fall of Jerusalem they sent messengers to announce that the Turks had left Nablus and that Tancred and Eustache were welcome to take possession of it.[18] It is probable that Tancred, a Norman from southern Italy, played the leading role. After the conquest of Jerusalem, Tancred attempted to take Muslim prisoners, but could not prevail against the objections of the other crusader chieftains.[19] A few days after this setback, Tancred was instrumental in setting the precedent for Frankish rule over an indigenous, largely Muslim population. His awareness of Norman rule over Sicilian Muslims presumably affected his attitude.

Siege culminating in negotiated surrender was another mode of Frankish takeover. The terms of surrender varied. At Arsuf in 1101, Acre in 1104, Tripoli in 1109, and Ascalon in 1153, the Muslims were permitted to leave for Muslim territory, but

---

[18] This reconstruction of events is based on the detailed account by an anonymous adapter of the chronicle of Baudri of Dol: Baldricus ep. Dolensis, *Historia Jerosolimitana*, MS G, in *RHC. Occ.*, 4:100, n. 13; 105, nn. 15, 16, 19. (The adapter's version, pieced together from the main text and the variants, appears in Benjamin Z. Kedar, "The Frankish Period," in *The Samaritans*, ed. Alan D. Crown [Tübingen, 1989], p. 82, n. 1.) See also William of Tyre, *Chronique*, 9, 11, ed. R. B. C. Huygens, Corpus Christianorum. Continuatio Mediaevalis 63 (Turnhout, 1986), p. 434. On *reguli* (headmen) *de montibus Samarie in quibus urbs Neapolitana sita est*, who came to Godfrey of Bouillon in 1100 to submit their villages but were suspected of spying, see William of Tyre, 9, 20, p. 446.

[19] See Albert of Aachen, 6, 28–30, in *RHC Occ.*, 4:482–84. William of Tyre writes that, in his own days (ca. 1180), Tancred was still remembered with gratitude in Galilee (William of Tyre, 9, 13, p. 438). But it appears from the context that the gratitude referred to Tancred's generous donations to churches rather than to his lenient treatment of the indigenous population. Tancred's biographer, Raoul of Caen, describes his hero's conquest of the vicinity of Bethsan in harsh terms: "cetera per circuitum municipia spoliat, aratra disjungit, jugum a bove ad rusticum transfert, claudit mercibus vias, urbibus portas" (*Gesta Tancredi*, c. 139 in *RHC. Occ.*, 3:704).

at Acre and Tripoli the Franks' Genoese allies turned the Muslim exodus into a massacre. At Sidon in 1110 and Tyre in 1124, the Muslims were given the choice of either going into exile or remaining under Frankish rule. In the towns which surrendered to Tancred in the region of Antioch, most inhabitants apparently chose to stay.

The linkage between assault and massacre suggests that the crusader leaders followed, or were largely bound by, prevailing customs of warfare. Their intentions at the stage of conquest can therefore be perceived through the terms of surrender which they proposed. Hence the significance of the offers purportedly made in 1100 to the Muslim and Jewish defenders of Haifa either to convert to Christianity and retain all rights and possessions, or retain their religion, lose their possessions, and choose between subjection to Frankish rule or exile.[20] Haifa was besieged by the Franks and their Venetian allies, but Tancred, one of the leaders who hoped to obtain possession of the town upon its conquest, probably had a say in the formulation of these terms. Yet the defenders rejected capitulation, the siege went on, and Haifa was eventually stormed and the population massacred. It was only in 1110, in the kingdom of Jerusalem, that the Muslim inhabitants of a besieged town were actually given the opportunity to choose between exile or life without conversion under Frankish rule. This happened at Sidon where, as Fulcher of Chartres relates, the Muslim defenders suggested that the local peasants be allowed to stay so that they might cultivate the land to King Baldwin I's advantage.[21] Perhaps the offer originated with the king, but Fulcher considered it too controversial to ascribe to him. Indeed, in the first re-

---

[20] *Monachi Littorensis Historia de Translatione S. Nicolai*, in *RHC. Occ.*, 5: 276; Albert of Aachen, 7, 22–25, in *RHC. Occ.*, 4:521–23. It should be noted that according to William of Tyre the Saracens of Acre capitulated in 1104 on the terms that they might choose between exile and life under Frankish rule (William of Tyre, 10, 27, p. 487). But the contemporary chroniclers Fulcher of Chartres, Albert of Aachen, and Ibn al-Qalānisī, who do not mention such choice, should be preferred.

[21] Fulcher of Chartres, 2, 44, 6–7, p. 548: the besieged asked the king for safe conduct ("et si ei [= regi] placeret, agricolas ad excolendum terras causa utilitatis suae in urbe retineret").

daction of the chronicle, probably written in Baldwin's lifetime, the advantage to accrue from the peasants' work is not yet ascribed to the king.[22] In any case, the offer was accepted and a considerable number of the Muslims chose to stay; somewhat later, Baldwin extracted a large sum of money from them.[23] By contrast, Tancred, then ruler of Antioch, exhibited a marked, unequivocal interest in enlarging the Muslim manpower at his disposal. Kamāl al-Dīn, describing events which took place at Athārib in northern Syria within months of the surrender of Sidon, explicitly states that Tancred made efforts to persuade Muslim workers to stay, and even negotiated the repatriation of their wives who had fled to Aleppo.[24]

The treatment meted out to the Levantine Muslims at the time of the Frankish conquest resembled, in general terms, that of the Moors in Spain. There, too, the mode of takeover was decisive, with conquest by assault leading to slaughter and enslavement, and siege terminating in surrender leading to exile or subjection.[25] But the massacres in the Levant were often more ferocious, probably because most Crusaders—unlike many Spaniards—had never before encountered Muslims, or because of the frenzy inherent in holy warfare. The one unique measure was the decision taken after the conquest of Jerusalem to forbid Infidels—Muslims and Jews—to reside in the Holy City.[26] This was an obvious outgrowth of the desire to put an

[22] "Ac si placeret, agricolas ad excolendum terras causa utilitatis in urbe retineret." See Hagenmeyer's apparatus to the passage quoted in the preceding n.

[23] Ibn al-Qalānisī, pp. 100–101; Ibn al-Athīr, in *RHC. Or.*, 1:276.

[24] Kamāl al-Dīn, in *RHC. Or.*, 3:597–98, utilized by Cahen, *Syrie du Nord*, p. 343.

[25] See O'Callaghan in the present volume, Chap. 1. For the similarity of Christian reconquest argumentation vis-à-vis the Muslim population, see the purported retort by the patriarch of Jerusalem at the siege of Caesarea in 1101 and the appeal of the archbishop of Braga during the siege of Lisbon in 1147 (Caffarus, *Annali Genovesi di Caffaro e de'suoi continuatori*, ed. L. T. Belgrano 5 vols. [Genoa, 1890–1929], 1:9–10; and *De expugnatione Lyxbonensi*, ed. and trans. C. W. David [New York, 1936], pp. 114–18).

[26] On this decision, see Joshua Prawer, "The Latin Settlement of Jerusalem," in his *Crusader Institutions*, p. 90, n. 21. (The original version of this article appeared in 1952.)

end to Infidel desecration of the Holy Places, a core component of the idea of the crusade.

At the present stage of research it is not possible to assess the number of Muslims who remained under Frankish rule after the initial massacres and emigrations. However, the order of magnitude, for the kingdom of Jerusalem only, may be roughly estimated. Ernoul, a Frankish chronicler well-versed in Palestinian affairs, relates that in the mid-1160s King Thoros of Armenia proposed that King Amalric of Jerusalem evict the Saracen peasants of his realm and replace them with 30,000 trustworthy Armenian warriors, who would come with their families to populate and defend the country.[27] If Thoros (or Ernoul) had in mind a replacement on a one-to-one basis, it would follow that the contemporary estimate of the number of subjected Muslim households in the countryside amounted to about 30,000. It should be noted that a present-day independent estimate based on a multiplier of 5 posits, for the kingdom of Jerusalem at its demographic zenith in the 1180s, a Frankish, mostly urban population of 100,000 to 120,000 and a subjected, Muslim and Oriental Christian population of 300,000 to 360,000, and 250,000 of whom lived in the countryside.[28] In the kingdom of Acre, which came into being as a result of the Third Crusade and lasted from 1191 to 1291, the number of subjected Muslims must have been considerably smaller than in the twelfth-century kingdom of Jerusalem, since Frankish rule had been restricted during most of this period to the coastal plain. The Frankish/indigenous ratio and the Frankish/Muslim ratio must therefore have become more favorable to the Franks.[29]

Whether Muslims constituted the majority of the subjected, indigenous population of the crusading kingdom of Jerusalem is a moot point, since the few explicit references in the narrative sources are at odds with each other. The Andalusian writer Ibn

---

[27] *Chronique d'Ernoul et de Bernard le Trésorier*, ed. M. L. de Mas Latrie (Paris, 1871), pp. 28–29.

[28] Joshua Prawer, *Histoire du royaume latin de Jérusalem*, trans. G. Nahon, 2 vols. (Paris, 1969), 1:498, 568–72.

[29] Cf. Cahen, "La féodalité," pp. 189–90.

al-ʿArabī, who stayed in Jerusalem between 1093 and 1095—a few years before the advent of the First Crusade—remarked that "the country is theirs [the Oriental Christians']; they till its estates, attend to its monasteries and maintain its churches."[30] On the other hand, the Frankish chronicler Ernoul relates that King Thoros of Armenia stated, during his visit to Jerusalem in the mid-1160s, that Saracens inhabited all villages of the Frankish kingdom, and the Granadan pilgrim Ibn Jubayr, who passed through Galilee in 1184, made a similar observation.[31] It is not easy to reconcile these statements even when some exaggeration is allowed for on both sides. The notion of an Oriental Christian majority in the Palestinian countryside giving way, under Frankish rule, to a Muslim one, is patently untenable. Perhaps the statements should be taken to apply to different regions. Ibn al-ʿArabī may have been referring to the surroundings of Jerusalem, and Iby Jubayr's statement evidently reflects the observations he made on his trip from Tibnīn to Acre. Consequently, one may assume that Muslims were in the majority in some, possibly most parts of the kingdom of Jerusalem, and Oriental Christians in others.[32] The fact that Saladin's secretary ʿImād al-Dīn, in his account of the Muslim reconquest of 1187, sees fit to point out that all the villagers in the surroundings of Nablus and the majority of the inhabitants of Sidon, Beirut, and Jubayl were Muslims,[33] appears to support this assumption. The situation was different in the northern Frankish states, where the indigenous population was preponderantly Oriental Christians—Jacobite and Greek Orthodox in the Principality of Antioch, Armenian in the County of Edessa—and Muslims apparently constituted the majority only in some enclaves.[34]

[30] Ibn al-ʿArabī, *al-Riḥla*, ed. I. ʿAbbās, p. 81, quoted and discussed by Gil, *Palestine*, 1:142.

[31] Ernoul, *Chronique*, p. 28; *Travels of Ibn Jubayr*, p. 316.

[32] For the assessment that the indigenous population was mainly Muslim with several Oriental Christian enclaves, see Prawer, *Histoire*, 1:570.

[33] ʿImād al-Dīn, *Conquête*, p. 36; ʿImād al-Dīn, in Abū Shāma, *RHC. Or.*, 4:309. See also n. 67 below.

[34] Cahen, *Syrie du Nord*, pp. 343, 514. On the importance of the Maronites

Beyond determining the immediate fate of the Muslims, the mode of Frankish takeover also largely shaped the future structure of their communities. When the terms of surrender allowed for a choice between staying or going into exile, members of the leading strata chose to leave. Ibn al-Athīr writes that "a large group of the important people" of Sidon left in 1110, and Fulcher of Chartres refers to the Muslims who remained there as peasants. Ibn al-Qalānisī writes that in Tyre, in 1124, the only Muslims who stayed were those too weak to embark upon a journey, and that at the surrender of Ascalon in 1153 all Muslims who were able to depart did so.[35] To some extent these statements may be exaggerations motivated by the desire to minimize the size and importance of the Muslim population that chose to remain under Frankish rule. Independent evidence contained in the guide to pilgrimage sites by ʿAlī al-Harawī, who visited the Frankish kingdom in the early 1180s, and in the history of Jerusalem and Hebron by Mujīr al-Dīn, a fifteenth-century Jerusalemite author, indicates, in any case, that the remaining Muslims were too weak to preserve the tombs of famous local personages, or too uninformed to uphold the traditions about their exact location. ʿAlī al-Harawī provides many details about pilgrimage sites throughout the mountainous region of the country as well as in the Jordan Valley east of it, but has very little to say about the towns of the coastal plain. He is aware of the difference between the two regions, remarking at one point that "in the cemetery at Ascalon, there are many saints and followers whose tombs cannot be recognized, and the same is true of Gaza, Acre, Tyre, Sidon and the entire coastal region."[36] Mujīr al-Dīn makes similar remarks with re-

---

in the County of Tripoli, see the diverging views of J. Richard, *Le comté de Tripoli sous la dynastie toulousaine (1102–1187)* (Paris, 1945), p. 86, and Prawer, "Social Classes," p. 92.

[35] Sidon: Ibn al-Athīr, p. 276; Fulcher of Chartres, 2, 44, 6–7, p. 548. Tyre: Ibn al-Qalānisī, p. 162; Ibn al-Athīr, p. 359. Ascalon: Ibn al-Qalānisī, p. 333 (William of Tyre [17, 29–30, pp. 802–3] speaks of a total evacuation, but at the time of the conquest of Ascalon he was still in Europe). ʿImād al-Dīn, in Abū Shāma, *RHC. Or.*, 4:409, refers to the subjected Muslims of Sidon, Beirut, and Jubayl as poor people.

[36] ʿAlī al-Harawī, *Guide*, p. 76. Followers (*tābiʿūn*) are those who did not know the Prophet personally but only as one of his Companions (*aṣḥāb*).

gard to Muslim tombs at Ramla (the capital of southern Palestine deserted by its Muslim inhabitants upon the advent of the Crusaders in 1099), stating that the tombs were no longer extant, or known, as a result of the Frankish occupation.[37] Both writers also make similar comments regarding tombs near the walls of Jerusalem.[38]

On the other hand, where the Frankish takeover was relatively peaceful, as in the Nablus region or in parts of northern Syria conquered by Tancred, Muslim society remained largely intact. (The same was probably true of the Bedouin tribes who came under Frankish rule.) In fact, none of the subjected Muslims appear as frequently in the documentation as those of the Nablus area. The account of the Ḥanbalī exodus throws light on religious life in some villages southwest of Nablus in the early 1150s. Aḥmad b. Muḥammad b. Qudāma, a Ḥanbalī jurisconsult from the village of Jammāʿīl, would undertake voyages to study ḥadīth, and then return home and recite Koran and ḥadīth to his followers. One of these was a *faqīh* (jurist) who went to Damascus on several occasions, while another was a *ḥājj*, a man who had performed the pilgrimage to Mecca. A third, Yaḥyā b. ʿUthmān from Yāsūf, the only Ḥanbalī in his village, would come on Fridays to Jammāʿīl for prayer; in 1156 he went to Damascus, possibly to study there. All this suggests an intact rural Muslim society.[39] Things came to a head only when the local Frankish seigneur—probably Baldwin of Ibelin, lord of Mirabel—learned that Aḥmad b. Qudāma's Friday sermons drew peasants from several villages and diverted them from work. He may also have objected to the sermons' contents, although Ḍiyāʾ al-Dīn, the author of the account and Aḥmad's grandson, does not say so. The lord decided to have Aḥmad killed, but one of his subordinates who, as Ḍiyāʾ al-Dīn puts it, "believed in Muslim holy men and was benevolent toward them," alerted Aḥmad. (The name of the subordinate has

---

[37] *Histoire de Jérusalem et d'Hébron. Fragments de la Chronique de Moudjir-ed-dyn*, trans. Henry Sauvaire (Paris, 1876), pp. 45–46, 63.

[38] ʿAlī al-Harawī, *Guide*, p. 68; Mujīr al-Dīn, *Histoire*, p. 63.

[39] For similar conditions in Muslim villages of contemporary Norman Sicily, see H. Bercher, Annie Courteaux, and J. Mouton, "Une abbaye latine dans la société musulmane: Monreale au XIIᵉ siècle," *Annales E.S.C.* 34 (1979): 533.

been tentatively read as Ibn Tasīr, which does not sound Semitic; perhaps he was a Frank.) Aḥmad promptly fled to Damascus—the year was 1156—and soon after ordered his relatives and disciples to follow him there, intimating that emigration from Infidel territory was their religious duty. Some 140 men, women and children came to Damascus between 1156 and 1173.[40] Fortunately, Ḍiyā' al-Dīn wrote down their names and interrelations, thereby affording a unique glimpse of Muslim rural family life and patterns of name-giving under Frankish rule.[41] For instance, Aḥmad himself had at least four sons and five daughters from two wives, each of whom had come to Jammā'īl from a different village; both wives had the same name, Sa'īda, which was also the name of one of Aḥmad's sisters. At the time of Aḥmad's flight, one of his sons was already the father of three, while two of his brothers-in-law had at least seven children each. His followers appear to have had smaller families; perhaps they were younger people.

Slavery

Other forms of Muslim existence under Frankish rule were captivity and slavery, with the dividing line between the two being rather blurred. Many Muslims were reduced to slavery during the crusader conquest and many others were captured and enslaved during subsequent rounds of Frankish-Muslim warfare. Again, the Frankish sources, with the exception of the legal ones, seldom refer to these Muslims, But Ibn Jubayr devotes some of his most emotional lines to a description of the captive Muslim men stumbling in shackles and doing hard labor like slaves, and the captive Muslim women plodding along with iron rings on their legs.[42] He also describes at some length the efforts at ransoming Muslim prisoners from the far-away Maghreb.

[40] Ḍiyā' al-Dīn, pp. 67–77, partially translated in Drory, "Ḥanbalīs," pp. 95–96.
[41] The names are listed in Drory, "Ḥanbalīs," app. 2, pp. 108–12.
[42] *Travels of Ibn Jubayr*, p. 322.

MUSLIMS OF THE FRANKISH LEVANT 153

The number of slaves was substantial. When Saladin appeared in 1184 at Sebaste during his raid of central Palestine, the local bishop saved his town by handing over eighty Muslim captives. Three years later, four thousand Muslim prisoners were said to have been set free in Acre, and some five thousand in Jerusalem. And 'Imād al-Dīn boasts that Saladin liberated twenty thousand captive Muslims during his reconquest campaign.[43] The first figure sounds realistic, the three others rather less so, but whatever the exact figures, enslaved Muslim manpower must have played a distinct role in the Frankish economy. In 1263, relates the anonymous Templar of Tyre, the Mamlūk sultan Baybars offered the Franks of Acre an exchange of Christian and Saracen slaves, but the military orders of the temple and the hospital rejected the proposal, arguing that "their [Saracen] slaves (*esclas*) were of great profit to them, for they were all craftsmen and it would have cost them dearly to hire other craftsmen" [if the slaves were exchanged]. Baybars, by the way, was perfectly aware of the Franks' motives, and rebuked them—so relates Al-Maqrīzī—for retaining the Muslim prisoners in order to exact labor from them rather than showing pity for the Frankish prisoners held by the Mamlūks.[44]

The customary law of the Frankish kingdom bestowed free status on a slave who decided to convert to Christianity. The origins of this law—which had a parallel in Catalonia and Valencia, though apparently not in Castile—are not known. Perhaps it stemmed from a missionary impulse, or a desire to enlarge the initially minuscule Frankish element with captured Turkish warriors whose martial valor was highly respected, or from the inability to conceive of Catholic slaves in a society

---

[43] Sebaste: Baldwin IV's letter to Patriarch Eraclius in Ralph of Diceto, *Ymagines Historiarum*, Rolls Series 68, 2, ed. W. Stubbs (London, 1876), 68, 2:28. Acre: Bahā al-Dīn, in *RHC. Or.*, 3:98. Jerusalem: 'Imād al-Dīn, in Abū Shāma, *RHC. Or.*, 4: 328–29. Twenty thousand captives: 'Imād al-Dīn, *Conquête*, p. 38.

[44] *Chronique du Templier de Tyr*, § 318, in *Les Gestes des Chiprois*, ed. Gaston Raynaud (Geneva, 1887), p. 167; Al-Maqrīzī, *Histoire des sultans mamlouks de l'Egypte*, trans. M. E. Quatremère (Paris, 1837), 1, 1:195. Cf. Maurice H. Chéhab, *Tyr à l'époque des croisades*, vol. 2, *Histoire sociale, économique et religieuse, Bulletin du Musée de Beyrouth* (Paris, 1979), p. 117.

bifurcated into Catholic masters and non-Catholic subjects. Though the origins of this law are obscure, there is ample evidence of efforts to limit its applicability or disregard it altogether. The *assises* of Jerusalem endeavored to restrict the law to bona-fide converts, and masters are known to have refused their Saracen slaves baptism, as they were not willing to lose their authority over them. Some even prohibited their slaves from attending Christian sermons. In 1237 Pope Gregory IX attempted to solve the problem by ruling that slaves wishing to convert ought to be allowed to do so, but that their servile status must not be altered thereby. This compromise between missionary impulse and slaveholder interest, which abrogated the customary law of the kingdom, appears to have been welcomed by Catalan masters who faced a similar custom; in any case, the same solution was adopted there, too. In the Frankish Levant, opposition to slave conversion continued despite the papal ruling, and therefore in 1253 a papal legate had to threaten noncomplying masters with excommunication. The legate Eudes of Châteauroux ordered that henceforth his statute be proclaimed twice a year in all the churches of the Frankish Levant and Cyprus, a further indication of the vigor of the masters' opposition. Indeed, the threat had to be repeated at the Synod of Nicosia in 1298.[45]

Rare Resistance, Limited Collaboration

Once it became evident that Frankish rule was there to stay, the subjected Muslims ceased their initial attempts at agricultural

---

[45] For a more detailed discussion, see my *Crusade and Mission*, pp. 76–78, 146–51, 212–15; also idem, "Ecclesiastical Legislation in the Kingdom of Jerusalem: The Statutes of Jaffa (1253) and Acre (1254)," in *Crusade and Settlement. Papers Read at the First Conference of the Society for the Study of the Crusades and the Latin East and Presented to R C. Smail*, ed. P. W. Edbury (Cardiff, 1985), pp. 225–26. For the Catalan *consuetudo bona*, see Raymond de Penyafort, *Summa de paenitentia*, I, 4, 7, eds. Xavier Ochoa and Aloysius Diez, Universa Bibliotheca Iuris 1/B (Rome, 1976), col. 316.

MUSLIMS OF THE FRANKISH LEVANT 155

boycott and occasional ambush,[46] and became largely docile. Of course, there was hatred. Ibn Jubayr refers to King Baldwin IV as *al-khinzīr* ("the pig") and to Baldwin's mother as *al-khinzīra* ("the sow"), and the context leaves little doubt that he picked up these telling epithets from the Muslims he encountered in Frankish Galilee. (Nothing of this kind in his report on Sicily!) There were some individual acts of violence. Usāma b. Munqidh relates that the Muslim mother of a young man of Nablus killed her Frankish husband and that the son, together with his mother, assassinated a number of Frankish pilgrims. There were also cases of flight to Muslim countries or, as Frankish law puts it, to *Païenime*. But open rebellion is attested for only one area, Jabal Bahrā east of Jabala in the Principality of Antioch, where the Nuṣayrī montagnards spontaneously revolted in the 1130s and again in the early 1180s.[47] Elsewhere the subjected Muslims were quiescent, daring to rise only when a Muslim army was invading the country. In 1113, when the men of Mawdūd of Mosul were roaming through northern and central Palestine, the subjected Muslims helped them harass the Franks, conveyed booty and supplies to their camp, and let Mawdūd know that they considered him their new overlord. The villagers of the Nablus area appear to have been especially active, for Fulcher of Chartres relates that the subjected Saracens who lived in the mountains helped the invaders sack Nablus. Similar scenes occurred during Saladin's reconquest three generations later. The doings of the *qāḍī* of Jabala have already been mentioned. In Galilee, local Jews and Muslims harassed the remaining Franks, as Roger of Howden reports. 'Imād al-Dīn relates that the Muslim peasants of the Nablus region fell upon the local Franks, looted their possessions, and forced them to take refuge in their fortresses even before the arrival of Saladin's men. And when, upon the advent of the Khwarezmi-

---

[46] On such attempts, see William of Tyre, 9, 19, p. 445, utilized by Prawer, "Social Classes," p. 62.

[47] *Travels of Ibn Jubayr*, p. 316; *An Arab-Syrian Gentleman and Warrior in the Period of the Crusades. Memoirs of Usāmah ibn Munqidh*, trans. Philip K. Hitti (New York, 1929), p. 168; *Livre des Assises de la Cour des Bourgeois*, c. 255, in *RHC. Lois* (Paris, 1843), 2:191; Cahen, *Syrie du Nord*, pp. 353, 428.

ans in 1244, the Franks left Jerusalem, "Saracen rustics of the mountain area" fell upon them, killing many and capturing others.[48] Evidently the subjected Muslims were willing to rise when the risks were, or seemed to be, extremely low.

Spontaneous uprisings against the Franks were rare; active collaboration with them was limited. As in other areas of Catholic reconquest, some Muslims entered into the service of their conquerors and assumed their religion. In August 1099, a former Saracen ruler of Ramla accompanied his crusader allies to the battle of Ascalon and was persuaded by Godfrey of Bouillon to become a Christian. In November 1100, Saracen converts to Christianity advised Baldwin I on the feasibility of an expedition to the Dead Sea. Baldwin also raised a Saracen from the font, gave him his name, and took him into his intimate service until he became "almost a chamberlain." But in 1110 this ex-Muslim was caught conspiring with the besieged Muslims of Sidon, and was promptly executed. A somewhat legendary account has it that in about 1112 Baldwin left another baptized Muslim in temporary charge of Jerusalem. As none of these former Saracens is mentioned for his own sake but only because of his role in royal affairs, there might have been even more converts in the king's service.[49] The phenomenon appears, however, to have been limited to the early years of the kingdom, for no such cases are mentioned later on.

One Muslim is known to have risen to some prominence in Frankish service. This was the aforementioned chronicler Ḥamdān b. ʿAbdval-Raḥīm, who, having succeeded in healing Alan, the first Frankish lord of Atḥārib in the Principality of Antioch, received from him the village of Mār Būniya as a pres-

---

[48] 1113: Fulcher of Chartres, 2, 49, 11, p. 572; Ibn al-Qalānisī, p. 125. Galilee, 1187: Benedict of Peterborough (= Roger of Howden, first redaction), *Gesta regis Henrici secundi*, Rolls Series 49, 2, ed. W. Stubbs (London, 1867), p. 93. Nablus, 1187: ʿImād al-Dīn, in Abū Shāma, *RHC. Or.*, 4:301–2; ʿImād al-Dīn, *Conquête*, pp. 35–36. 1244: Letter of the patriarch of Jerusalem, in Matthew Paris, *Chronica Majora*, Rolls Series 57, 4, ed. H. R. Luard (London, 1877), p. 339.

[49] Albert of Aachen, 6, 42–44, pp. 491–93; Fulcher of Chartres, 2, 4, 4, pp. 374–75; William of Tyre, 11, 14, p. 518; Guibert de Nogent, in *RHC. Occ.*, 4:262.

ent, and thereby became one of the very few Muslim landlords of the Frankish Levant. (Other known cases are those of the Shaykh of Banū Sulayḥa in the Principality of Antioch, and the emirs of the Gharb region south of Beirut.) Ḥamdān fulfilled for the Franks administrative tasks in the Jazr region, and later directed for them the *diwān* at Ma'arrat al-Nu'mān. But his loyalty to his Frankish masters was hardly greater than that of King Baldwin's ex-Muslim intimate. After Zengi's entry into Aleppo in 1128, Ḥamdān went there, later to become governor of the reconquered Jazr.[50]

Some Muslim scribes were employed by the Franks, since the Arabic language was used for several purposes and as some elements of the previous Muslim administration survived into Frankish times.[51] Most Arabic-writing clerks, though, appear to have been Oriental Christians. Ibn Jubayr reports that the clerks of the Acre customs house who wrote and spoke Arabic were Christians.[52] Of seventeen indigenous scribes mentioned in Frankish charters, nine bear unequivocally Christian names like Jurj b. Ya'qūb (George, son of Jacob), Boteros (Peter), or are otherwise known to have been Christians. Six bear names like Brahim (Ibrāhīm) or Seit (Sa'īd) which could equally well

[50] On Ḥamdān b. 'Abd al-Raḥīm's career, see Cahen, *Syrie du Nord*, pp. 41–42, 343–44; his standing with the Franks may be compared with that of the *scribani* discussed by Jonathan Riley-Smith, "Some Lesser Officials in Latin Syria," *English Historical Review* 87 (1972): 23–26. On Roger of Antioch's grant of three villages to the Banū Ṣulayḥa in 1118, see Cahen, *Syrie du Nord*, p. 278; the 1180 grant of Bohemond III of Antioch to the military order of Santiago excepts the villages "quos concessimus habendo vetulo Assidaeorum" (*Bullarium equestris ordinis S. Iacobi de Spatha*, ed. J. López Agurleta [Madrid, 1719], p. 22, noted by Cahen, *Syrie du Nord*, pp. 5, 462). On the grants of 1255 and 1280 to the emirs of the Gharb, whose allegiance vacillated between Franks and Muslims according to the shifts in the balance of power, see Ch. Clermont-Ganneau, "Deux chartes des Croisés dans les archives arabes," *Recueil d'archéologie orientale* 6 (1905): 1–30. On the rather slight possibility that Muisse Arrabit (or Arrabi), a vassal of Hugh of Ibelin, may have been of Muslim origin, see my *Crusade and Mission*, pp. 75–76, n. 95.

[51] See Jonathan Riley-Smith, "The Survival in Latin Palestine of Muslim Administration," in *The Eastern Mediterranean Lands in the Period of the Crusades*, ed. P. M. Holt (Warminster, 1977), pp. 9–22.

[52] *Travels of Ibn Jubayr*, p. 317.

have been Oriental Christian or Muslim, and only one, Nasser, bears a typically Muslim name.[53] The presumed predominance of Oriental Christians may have been an inheritance from the pre-Frankish period, for Al-Muqaddasī, writing in the late tenth century, observed that in Syria all the scribes were Christians.[54] Although in 1012 the caliph Al-Ḥākim ordered the Christian scribes to be replaced by Muslims, it is possible that at the turn of the twelfth century most were still Christian.

Unlike in Norman Sicily, Hungary, or Valencia, there were no Muslim troops in Frankish service, unless one counts the Saracen archers whom Adelaide of Sicily brought in 1113 as a marriage gift to her future husband, Baldwin I of Jerusalem.[55] Some converted Muslims served the Franks as mounted archers or turcopoles.[56] Only once, and as late as 1264, are subjected Muslims mentioned as participating in a power struggle on behalf of their masters. The Templar of Tyre relates that during a Venetian attack on Tyre the local lord, Philip of Montfort, ordered "the sergeants, archers, Saracens, villeins of his lands" to come to Tyre.[57] Significantly, Philip attempted to use his Saracens in a struggle with Christians, not Muslims. Evidently, the subjected Muslims could not have been relied upon to fight their coreligionists. Both sides suspected them of spying, probably with good reason.[58] For instance, in 1263 the sultan Baybars imposed a large fine on the Muslims of the partly recon-

---

[53] Charters mentioning names of indigenous scribes are listed by Clermont-Ganneau, "Deux chartes," pp. 15–16; Riley-Smith, "Lesser Officials," p. 23, n. 2; idem, *The Feudal Nobility and the Kingdom of Jerusalem, 1174–1277* (London, 1973), p. 256, n. 145. The Oriental names, in addition to those quoted in the text, are Sororius Syrus, Youseph, Huissetus, Ferry, Geiggus or Georgius, Petros, Georgius Surianus, Soquerius (with relatives called Johannes and Georgius), Johannes Bogalet, and Belhes (or Belheis).

[54] Al-Muqaddasī, *Description of Syria Including Palestine*, trans. Guy Le Strange, in *Palestine Pilgrims' Text Society* (London, 1896), 3, 3:77.

[55] Albert of Aachen, 12, 13, in *RHC. Occ.*, 4:697.

[56] For details, see *Crusade and Mission*, p. 76.

[57] Templier de Tyr § 322, p. 170; see also § 283, p. 154, where the lord of Tyre used "ccc. archers vilains de sa terre," also in an internal struggle. Both passages noted by Chéhab, *Tyr*, 2:115.

[58] See Cahen, *Syrie du Nord*, p. 714.

quered coastal plain of Palestine as well as of the region of Nablus, because of the information they had allegedly supplied to the Franks.[59] In Sicily, suspicion of collusion with outside Muslims was also present and occasionally justified. ʿAlī al-Harawī relates that when he was in Sicily, Abu 'l-Qāsim b. Ḥammd—the leader of the local Muslims whom Ibn Jubayr also met—gave him letters for the sultan (presumably Saladin), intending to incite him to conquer the island.[60] Nevertheless, the Normans had no substantial reason to fear any outside Muslim power, while, on the other hand, the scope for their use of the subjected Muslims in inter-Christian warfare was considerable.[61]

In all, the Muslim role in the Frankish body politic was negligible, and Hans Eberhard Mayer did not exaggerate much when he quipped that "the only occasions when the Muslims were allowed to participate in public life were when they mourned a dead king."[62] The reverse side was that, with no Muslim officials or courtiers, there was no anti-Muslim resentment as in Sicily, no auto-da-fé like that of the ex-Muslim (or crypto-Muslim) Philip of Mahdiyya toward the end of Roger II's reign, no outbreaks of anti-Muslim violence as in Palermo in 1160/61. But in the Frankish Levant, too, preference shown to Muslims over Franks, no matter of how restricted a nature, would trigger an angry response. Perhaps the only instance was Frankish recourse to Muslim and other Oriental physicians, which aroused stark resentment. William of Tyre complained that the Frankish nobles, influenced by their wives, despised Latin medicine and trusted only the utterly ignorant Jews, Samaritans, Syrians, and Saracens, and the author of the Old French version of William's chronicle knowingly added that these Orientals gave poison to all the great men of the realm.

---

[59] Maqrīzī, *Histoire*, 1, 1:199. Maqrīzī adds that Baybars decided to impose the fine rather than execute them, seeing that they were peasants and shepherds.

[60] ʿAlī al-Harawī, *Guide*, p. 126. On Saladin as the sultan in question, see the translator's introduction, pp. xv, xvii.

[61] For a divergent comparison of the Levant and Sicily in this respect, see Cahen, "Féodalité," p. 190.

[62] Mayer, "Muslims," p. 180.

The resentment did not remain verbal only. One of the constitutions of the Latin church of Nicosia, Cyprus, probably dating from the early 1250s and possibly depending on some earlier enactment in the kingdom of Jerusalem, formally prohibited having recourse to a Jewish or Saracen physician or taking medicine on his advice.[63] It should be noted, however, that Latin and Muslim physicians sometimes acknowledged each other's achievements. The enigmatic Benvenutus of Jerusalem writes that a Saracen physician succeeded in curing a bishop's brother whom neither he nor any other physicians could help, while Gilbertus Anglicus proudly relates that he cured Bertranninus, the son of Hugh of *Jubiletum* (Gibelet, Jubayl), who almost lost his sight and of whom "both illustrious Saracens as well as Syrian Christians had despaired."[64] Occasionally, at least, professionalism proved stronger than prejudice.

The Causes of Docility

The Muslims' docility and divorce from the body politic were, to a very large extent, of the Franks' making. The initial massacres certainly taught the surviving Muslims to hold their new masters in awe. These masters also erected numerous castles throughout the country, which served as efficacious bases for the demonstration and exercise of power and the routine control of the adjacent population.[65] The Franks allowed the Mus-

---

[63] William of Tyre, 18, 34, p. 859; Eracles in *RHC. Occ* , 1:879: "qui riens ne savoient de fisique, et si donnoient poisons a touz les hauz homes de la contrée"; *Constitutiones Nicosienses*, c. 14 in Mansi, *Concilia*, 26:314.

[64] Benvenutus, *Practica oculorum*, Vat. Lat. 5373 (s. XV), in Giuseppe Albertotti, ed., "Cenni intorno ad altri codici dell'opera di Benvenuto," *Memorie della R. Accademia di scienze, lettere ed arti in Modena, Memorie della sezione di lettere*, 3d ser. 4 (1902): 128; Gilbertus Anglicus, *Compendium medicine*, Clm 28187 (s. XIV), fol. 76va; ed. Lyon, 1510, p. 137a. See also Usāma b, Munqidh, p. 162. These texts will be discussed in detail in the study mentioned in n. 103 below.

[65] See R. C. Smail, "Crusaders' Castles of the Twelfth Century," *Cambridge Historical Journal* 10 (1950–1952): 133–49; idem, *Crusading Warfare (1097–1193)* (Cambridge, Eng., 1956), pp. 60–62, 204–15; Cahen, *Orient*, p. 169.

lims to adhere to their religion and administered justice fairly. In addition, there were relatively few Frankish rural foundations,[66] and therefore, unlike in Catalonia or Sicily, the Muslim peasants had no reason to fear large-scale eviction by Frankish settlers. Moreover, the Frankish variant of feudal economy did not know much demesne land and therefore the amount of *corvées* or labor services imposed on the Muslim serfs—or *villeins*, as they were called in the Frankish Levant—was limited. Taxation was onerous but not altogether intolerable, and apparently some Muslim *villeins* under Frankish rule were better off than their coreligionists in neighboring Muslim countries. It is worthwhile taking up these points in some detail.

Even as bitter a foe of the Franks as 'Imād al-Dīn concedes that they let the subjected Muslims practice their religion. Writing of the Muslims in the Nablus area, he remarks that the Franks "did not change a single law or cult practice,"[67] a statement vividly substantiated by the account of Ḥanbalī religious life in that same region. The crusaders, initially bewildered at the array of non-Catholic beliefs they encountered in the Levant, soon evolved the realistic policy of letting each group observe its "law,"[68] which, as far as the Saracens were concerned, was the law of detested Muḥammad. Thus the laws of the kingdom of Jerusalem take it for granted that in Frankish-administered courts a Saracen would give his oath "sur le Coran de sa lei."[69]

As in Spain and Sicily, the Latin conquerors used to convert mosques into churches. In Jerusalem the Dome of the Rock became the *Templum Domini*, while the Al-Aqṣa mosque became first the royal residence and then the headquarters of the Knights Templar. In Caesarea the main mosque became St. Pe-

[66] See Joshua Prawer, "Colonization Activities in the Latin Kingdom," in his *Crusader Institutions*, pp. 103–42. (The article originally appeared in 1951.)

[67] D. S. Richards, "A Text of 'Imād al-Dīn on 12th-Century Frankish-Muslim Relations," *Arabica* 25 (1978): 203.

[68] See, e.g., the statement of the pilgrim Wilbrand of Oldenburg: "Quilibet eorum suas leges observant" (J. C. M. Laurent, ed., *Peregrinatores medii aevi quatuor* [Leipzig, 1873], p. 172).

[69] *Assises des Bourgeois*, c. 241, p. 172.

ter's Cathedral; in Ascalon, the Green Mosque—which, before 937, had been the Church of Mary the Green—became the church of *Sancta Maria Viridis*.[70] As for the prayer places left to the subjected Muslims, the evidence of Ibn Jubayr with regard to Tyre and Acre has already been reviewed. Beyond the boundaries of the kingdom of Jerusalem there is mention, as early as 1108/9, of the restoration of the mosques of Sarūj, the second largest town of the County of Edessa, by powerful Muslim allies of Count Baldwin, the future King Baldwin II of Jerusalem.[71]

Muslims were also allowed to pray at shrines which formed part of Christian sanctuaries. Usāma b. Munqidh, the Syrian emir who left behind a vivid description of his encounters with the Franks, both friendly and otherwise, relates that in about 1140 he visited the crypt of John the Baptist at Sebaste. At that time the crypt was still outside the church, but even when it was incorporated into the new cathedral, Muslims were allowed to pray at it, and the clerics—it is 'Imād al-Dīn who supplies this detail—grew rich from the sumptuous gifts they extracted from the Muslims for permission to do so. Usāma was even allowed to pray in the small church the Templars had attached to the Al-Aqsa mosque, but this was an exceptional arrangement.[72]

The fifteenth-century Egyptian chronicler Al-Maqrīzī remarks that the Franks used to coerce Muslims into converting to Christianity,[73] but this appears to be a gross exaggeration, as

---

[70] On the vicissitudes of the Ascalon sanctuary, see *Histoire de Yaḥyā ibn Sa'īd d'Antioche*, in *Patrologia Orientalis*, eds. and trans. I. Kratchkovsky and A. Vasiliev (Paris, 1924), 18, 5:719; Joshua Prawer, "The Town and County of Ascalon during the Crusades," *Eretz-Israel* 5 (1958): 229 (in Hebrew).

[71] Ibn al-Athīr, in *RHC. Or.*, 1:263.

[72] Sebaste: The relevant passage from Usāma's *Kitāb al-'Asā* is edited and translated in Hartwig Derenbourg, *Ousâmah ibn Mounkidh*, un émir syrien au premier siècle des croisades (1095–1188), première partie: *Vie* (Paris, 1889), pp. 189, 528–29; 'Imād al-Dīn, in Abū Shāma, *RHC. Or.*, 4:302. Al-Aqsa: Usāma b. Munqidh, pp. 163–64. In Frankish Ascalon, 'Alī al-Harawī was able to sleep in the mashhad of Ibrāhīm and leave an inscription on its wall ('Alī al-Harawī, p. 76).

[73] See Chéhab, *Tyr*, 1:536.

documented cases of enforced baptism are extremely rare.[74] Even Ibn Jubayr, who is peculiarly attentive to this issue as far as Sicily is concerned, reports nothing of the sort with regard to the Frankish Galilee which he traversed. True, there were some efforts at persuading Muslims to convert. The first recorded case occurred during the siege of Jerusalem in 1099, when Baldwin of Bourg (the later King Baldwin II) and other crusading leaders tried to convince a captive Saracen warrior to accept Christianity and, when he failed to comply, had him decapitated in front of the Muslim-held Tower of David. The customary law which called for the manumission of a slave who consented to convert is further evidence of some missionary tendency. From the very beginning there were Muslims who accepted Christianity, like the above-mentioned converts in the entourage of the first two rulers of Jerusalem. In later years, cases of voluntary conversion from Islam are described or referred to by men as different as Fulcher of Chartres and Usāma b. Munqidh, Pope Innocent III and 'Imād al-Dīn, and sources as diverse as the Frankish *assises*, a rare testament drawn up at Acre, Mamlūk-Frankish treaties, and an Arabic-French glossary. (Since several sources report also on Frankish conversion to Islam, it is evident that the dividing line between the religions was crossed on numerous occasions.)[75] It would appear that Muslim conversion to Christianity, especially on the lower rungs of Muslim society, gained momentum in the last fifty years or so of the Frankish presence in the Levant. At that time, mendicants were engaged in missionary activity (they appear to have been behind Gregory IX's decision on slave conversion) and Frankish rule was limited to an ever-shorter strip in which the Latin element was proportionately larger than ever before, and faced a relatively small number of Muslims who had lived under Frankish rule for several generations.

But for the *qāḍī* of Jabala, there is no documentary evidence for internal Muslim jurisdiction, but it is plausible to assume

[74] See *Crusade and Mission*, pp. 62, 153.
[75] For details on conversion in both directions, see ibid., pp. 74–83, 145–54.

that the Muslims, like other subjected communities, had institutionalized ways of settling their own affairs, whether by *qāḍīs* or not. For instance, a headman (*rays*, *raycius* or *regulus* of the Frankish charters, the Arabic *ra'īs*), of a Muslim community might well have exercised jurisdiction over his coreligionists as Manṣūr, headman of the Muslims in late eleventh-century Jabala, is explicitly said to have done during the Byzantine rule over his town. The same was probably true of the village headmen and Bedouin chieftains who represented their villages and tribes vis-à-vis the Franks and presumably continued to exercise their traditional authority.[76] In the towns, cases concerning life and limb would come before the Frankish Court of Burgesses, while other cases involving members of different communities would come before the Cour de la Fonde, or Market Court, which had competence over all the subjected, non-Frankish population, whether Christian or not.[77] The *assises* reminded the four Syrian and two Frankish jurors who, together with the presiding Frankish *bailli* composed that court, that Syrians, Greeks, Jews, Samaritans, Nestorians, and Saracens "are also

[76] On Manṣūr of Byzantine Jabala, see Ibn al-Athīr, in *RHC. Or.*, 1:204. On the *rayses*, see the detailed discussion of Riley-Smith, "Lesser Officials," pp. 1–15; idem, *Feudal Nobility*, pp. 47–49, 90–91; Prawer, "Social Classes," pp. 103–4. It is an open question to what extent a *rays* of urban Muslims must have been a Muslim himself. Sadé, *rays* of the Saracens of Tyre in 1181, had a brother bearing the Romance name "Guillaume" (J. Delaville Le Roulx, "Inventaire de pièces de Terre-Sainte de l'Ordre de l'Hôpital," *Revue de l'Orient latin* 3 [1895]: 66; cf. Riley-Smith, "Lesser Officials," p. 5, n. 3 and p. 6, n. 7). The *ra'īs* of the largely Muslim town of Sarūj in the County of Edessa was an apostate from Islam, whom County Baldwin of Bourg put to death after he had insulted Islam in front of his Muslim allies (Ibn al-Athīr, in *RHC. Or.*, 1: 263). On the possibility that some form of internal Muslim jurisdiction did exist, see also Riley-Smith, "Survival," p. 10; Prawer, "Social Classes," pp. 104–5. It should be noted that while Fulcher of Chartres (2, 9, 7, p. 403) speaks of the *qāḍī* of Caesarea, captured in 1101, as the city's *episcopus*, known in the Saracen language as *archadius*, William of Tyre (10, 15, p. 472) describes him as "iuridicus, qui iuri dicendo preerat, qui etiam lingua eorum Cadius appellatur."

[77] On the relationship of the Cour de la Fonde to the Cour des Syriens, see the diverging views of Riley-Smith, "Lesser Officials," pp. 1–9; idem, *Feudal Nobility*, pp. 89–91; and Prawer, "Social Classes," pp. 102–6.

men like the Franks" ("si sont il auci homes come les Frans") and therefore equally liable to heed the verdicts meted out to them.[78] Ibn Jubayr, too, notes the equitable justice of the Franks—but he does so with apprehension lest the subjected Muslims thereby be led astray from their faith.

Nevertheless, it appears that the Muslims were treated not only as inferior to the Franks (as were all the indigenous), but also as inferior to the Oriental Christians. The very composition of the Cour de la Fonde—four Syrians, three Franks, no Muslims—is a case in point. And the *assise* which deals with this court and starts by enumerating the various Christian and non-Christian groups for which it is competent, later lumps all Christians together as against the Saracens, stipulates stiff penalties for a Saracen who beat up a Christian man or woman (presumably in court), and prescribes death by hanging in case of repeated offense.[79] Nothing is said about the reverse case of Christian aggression, and this omission must be significant, as elsewhere the *assises* neatly balance each case with its reverse to the point of repetition.[80] Inequality between Muslim and Oriental Christian was not restricted to the Cour de la Fonde. This is attested by the charter by which Bohemond III of Antioch (whom Grousset rebuked for his soft "politique musulmane"), granted several possessions to the Order of the Hospital in 1186. Bohemond deals there also with the issue of fugitive serfs, and sets down that any Saracen serfs fleeing from his possessions to those of the hospital must be returned, whereas the Oriental Christian fugitives may stay there if compensation is agreed upon within fifteen days.[81]

The only Frankish legislation dealing specifically with the subjected Muslim population appears in the decisions of the Council of Nablus which convened in 1120 at a calamitous

---

[78] *Assises des Bourgeois*, c. 241, p. 172.

[79] *Travels of Ibn Jubayr*, pp. 316–17; Assises des Bourgeois, c. 241, p. 173.

[80] E.g., ibid., cc. 59–65, pp. 53–56.

[81] *Cartulaire général de l'Ordre des Hospitaliers de Saint-Jean de Jérusalem*, ed. J. Delaville Le Roulx, 4 vols. (Paris, 1894), 1: no. 783, 495, utilized by Cahen, *Syrie du Nord*, p. 343, n. 51 (but the charter refers to the hospital, not to churches in general); and Prawer, "Social Classes," p. 109.

juncture and attempted to forestall further disasters by curbing vices such as adultery, sodomy, and larceny among the Franks. Four canons forbid sexual intercourse between Christians and Muslims. Male transgressors, whether Christian or Saracen, were threatened with castration, while female transgressors, if they consented to the act, were to suffer nasoctomy. Rape of one's own female Saracen was to entail castration; rape of a Saracen belonging to another man was to be punished by castration and exile.[82] This is the earliest legislation of its kind in the Latin world, and, compared with later legislation in the West, is striking for the equal punishment meted out to Christian and Muslim transgressors.[83] The subsequent canon forbids the wearing of Frankish dress by Saracen men and women.[84] It is noteworthy that this first dress regulation for Infidels in the Latin world differs from later legislation, in that it does not forbid specific items of clothing or prescribe a certain type of haircut, as did the mid-thirteenth-century Castilian legislation, for example. By 1120, Frankish and Muslim dress in the Holy Land were so different that the mere prohibition of dressing "according to Frankish custom" ("Francigeno more") was deemed sufficient. No reason is given for this dress regulation, but as it follows immediately upon the legislation against sexual intercourse with Muslims it is reasonable to assume that it aimed primarily to ensure immediate recognition and avoidance of intimacy. If implemented, this legislation might have accorded some protection to Muslim women vis-à-vis Frankish men, their Frankish lords included, and, more generally, might have hampered contacts between Franks and Muslims. Yet it is not certain that any of the canons pertaining to Muslims was carried out. As Charles Verlinden has observed, they were not incorporated into the *assises* of the kingdom of Jerusalem.[85]

The oppressive Frankish rule over the Muslim serfs is per-

---

[82] *Concilium Neapolitanum*, cc. 12–15, in Mansi, 21:264. A critical edition will appear in my "William of Tyre and the Council of Nablus, 1120," *Annuarium historiae conciliorum* (forthcoming).

[83] See, e.g., the laws discussed by O'Callaghan, chap. 1 above.

[84] *Concilium Neapolitanum*, c. 16, in Mansi, 21:264.

[85] Verlinden, *L'esclavage dans l'Europe médiévale*, 2 vols. (Gent, 1977), 2:968.

MUSLIMS OF THE FRANKISH LEVANT 167

haps the most widely discussed aspect of the history of the subjected Levantine Muslims. Like so much else, the discussion hinges largely on a remark by Ibn Jubayr. Speaking of the Muslim peasants he encountered on his way from Tibnīn to Acre, Ibn Jubayr remarks that they lived prosperously with the Franks and owned their houses and other possessions. Then he goes on to say:

> But their hearts have been seduced, for they observe how unlike them in ease and comfort are their brethren in the Muslim regions under their (Muslim) governors. This is one of the misfortunes afflicting the Muslims. The Muslim community bewails the injustice of a landlord of its own faith, and applauds the conduct of its opponent and enemy, the Frankish landlord, and is accustomed to justice from him.[86]

Modern historians have ascribed diverging measures of importance to these sentences. Two examples will suffice. In 1935 René Grousset regarded them as statements of fact, especially impressive as they came from the pen of an enemy of the Franks, and proposed to consider them "le plus bel éloge de la colonisation francaise."[87] Claude Cahen, who wrestled with this passage in publications which span half a century and include even an encyclopedia entry, warns against accepting it at face value or as applicable to Muslims everywhere under Frankish rule, depending as it does on conversations with a few people in a given place and time. Ibn Jubayr, he argues, traversed one of the richest parts of the Frankish Levant, the region of Tyre where Muslims might have fared better than elsewhere owing to the favorable terms on which Tyre had capitulated in 1124. Cahen also points to contrary evidence such as the Muslim legal status, their emigrations and uprisings, and finally suggests that Ibn Jubayr, who as a proponent of jihād would have preferred a Muslim exodus or uprising, here puts his subjected coreligionists to shame on account of their faintheartedness. But Cahen, too, concedes that Ibn Jubayr could not have

---

[86] *Travels of Ibn Jubayr*, p. 317.
[87] Grousset, *Histoire*, 2:754.

written his *fameuse page* if the Frankish regime were unmistakably harsher than that in the adjacent Muslim countries, and that he attests that Muslim peasants did not have a systematically unfavorable opinion of this regime.[88]

The preoccupation with Ibn Jubayr's statement has eclipsed the contrary if somewhat enigmatic remark made by Gautier, chancellor of Antioch in the second decade of the twelfth century. In one of the prologues to his *Bella Antiochena*, Gautier observes that the sinful ways of the inhabitants of Syria had not been corrected by the oppression at the hands of the Byzantines, the Turks, or the "more intolerable" (*intolerabilior*) rule of the Franks.[89] Gautier speaks of the subjugated population in general, not of the subjected Muslim peasantry; yet his remark ought to be read alongside Ibn Jubayr's *fameuse page*.

How, then, did the Frankish rule appear from the angle of the subjected Muslim peasant? A major change which the Franks introduced was the extension of the poll tax to the Muslims. For Oriental Christians and Jews this tax was no different from the one they had had to pay as *dhimmīs* to their Muslim rulers. For the Muslims, though, it was a form of degradation, a symbol of the demotion of the religious group to which they belonged from dominant to subjected status. But it was more than a symbol. The poll tax amounted to one dinar according

---

[88] Claude Cahen, "Indigènes et croisés. Quelques mots à propos d'un médecin d'Amaury et de Saladin," *Syria* 15 (1934): 356–58, repr. in idem, *turcobyzantina*, chap. F; idem "Le régime rural syrien au temps de la domination franque," *Bulletin de la Faculté des Lettres de Strasbourg* 29 (1951): 308–9, repr. in *turcobyzantina*, chap. H; idem, "Crusades," in *Encyclopaedia of Islam*, 2d ed. (Leiden, 1963); idem, *Orient et Occident*, pp. 168–69.

[89] "Graecis namque regnantibus ipsorum imperio seruisse conuincuntur eisdem ex Asia propulsis Parthorum regnantium cessere dominio; tandem, Deo uolente, intolerabiliori succubuere Gallorum potestati" (Galterius Cancellarius, *Bella Antiochena*, 1, Pr. 6, ed. Heinrich Hagenmeyer [Innsbruck, 1896], pp. 62–63). For *Praefati Syri*, refer back to *accolarum Syriae*, 1, Pr. 2, p. 61. For the identity of the nations mentioned, see Hagenmeyer's commentary, pp. 124–26, who believes that Frankish rule was more intolerable on account of widespread warfare and the earthquake of 1114. *Intolerabilior* may also mean "more irresistible," but the other instances in which Gautier uses this term tend to vindicate Hagenmeyer's assumption that he means here "more intolerable."

to Ḍiyā' al-Dīn and to 1 5/24 dinar according to Ibn Jubayr.[90] Contrary to previous assumptions, S. D. Goitein and Hans Eberhard Mayer have convincingly shown that, far from being a trifle, this tax constituted a heavy burden for the poorer parts of the subjected population.[91] Moreover, a harsh Frankish lord (or a Frankish lord in urgent need of money, say for the ransom of a captive relative), could exact much higher sums. Ḍiyā' al-Dīn reports that the Frankish lord of Jammā'īl and adjacent villages levied four dinars from everyone.[92] In addition to the poll tax paid by all Muslims, Muslim peasants paid up to one-half of their crops, as well as other customary fees.[93] The significant fact, however, is that taxation in Muslim-ruled Syria appears to have been still more onerous. There the peasant had to pay a

---

[90] Ḍiyā' al-Dīn, p. 67, English trans. in Drory, "Ḥanbalīs," p. 95; *Travels of Ibn Jubayr*, p. 316. Like in other Christianized areas of the Mediterranean, the Muslim peasants of the Frankish Levant did not pay tithes (Ernoul, *Chronique*, p. 30).

[91] S. D. Goitein, *A Mediterranean Society: The Jewish Communities of the Arab World as Portrayed in the Documents of the Cairo Geniza*, 5 vols. (Berkeley, 167–88), 2: 380–93; Mayer, "Muslims," pp. 181–82.

[92] An eighteenth-century Damascene author familiar with Ḍiyā' al-Dīn's work asserts that while a Frank paid one dinar, a Muslim had to pay four times as much (Muḥammad b. 'Īsā b. Maḥmūd b. Kannān, *al-Murūj al-sundusiyya al-fasīḥā fī talkhīṣ ta'rīkh al-Ṣāliḥiyya*, ed. Muḥammad Aḥmad Duhmān [Damascus, 1947], p. 2).

[93] See the discussion by Mayer, "Muslims," p. 183. Mayer also believes that the main burden of the emergency tax of 1183 fell largely on the (Muslim) peasants, who had to pay both an income tax and a property tax (ibid., pp. 177–80). The argument hinges largely on the equation of *loca* in William of Tyre's text of the tax decree (*Chronique*, 22, 24, p. 1044) with *casiaus* in the Old French version printed in *RHC. Occ.*, 1:1111. But another version of the Old French text, which is superior on several counts, translates *loca* with *leus entor* (*Guillaume de Tyr et ses continuateurs*, ed. Paulin Paris, 2 vols. [Paris, 1879–80], 2:450). Besides, if *villeins* were really expected to pay the property tax, the four ad hoc assessors would have had to enter the villages belonging to the various lords and assess the worth of every single peasant hearth in the kingdom—a cumbersome procedure for an emergency measure. That speed was essential can be deduced from the method of collecting the income tax: the lords, who must have known the wealth of their *villeins* much better than an outside assessor, were instructed first to pay the state one bezant for each peasant hearth, and only later, to reimburse themselves by distributing the payment among the peasants as equitably as feasible.

land tax which could amount up to three-fifths, or even two-thirds, of the crops, and in addition he had to hand over up to one-tenth of the crops as obligatory alms.[94] Thus, Ibn Jubayr was quite right in considering the taxes which the Franks imposed on their Muslim peasants as relatively light.

Except for the introduction of the poll tax, the Franks did not significantly change the economic and social routine of the Muslim (and other indigenous) peasantry. They systematized the existing links of servitude, and since they largely dispensed with demesne exploitation and the concomitant *corvées*, the modes of cultivation, internal land distribution, village organization, and obligations of the peasants remained basically unaltered. The Frankish lord lived mostly in the town, and the peasants did not face him daily. Rather, they had to deal with the village *ra'īs*, who apparently acted both as the lord's representative and as head of the village community.[95] Still, the lord's intimidating presence was never far away. As Ḍiyā' al-Dīn saw it, the Franks used to punish and jail the Muslims who worked the lands for them; the harshest of them, the lord of Jammā'īl, would also mutilate their legs. Nevertheless, the overwhelming majority of Muslim peasants remained. At Jammā'īl, despite the quadruple poll tax and corporeal punishments, none of the peasants left before Aḥmad b. Qudāma fled to Damascus to save his life, and Aḥmad's call to follow him was heeded by only a small group whose members had to keep their intentions secret. When these became known, the other villagers tried to dissuade Aḥmad's followers and finally alerted the Franks, who attempted unsuccessfully to stop the fugitives near the Jordan.[96]

The fact that only a few Muslim peasants fled to neighboring Muslim countries does not necessarily reflect contentment with Frankish rule. The average Muslim peasant clung to his land as long as he could, and was willing to suffer indignation rather

---

[94] For details, see Nikita Elisséeff, *Nûr ad-Dîn. Un grand prince musulman de Syrie au temps des croisades*, 3 vols. (Damascus, 1967), 3:796–801.

[95] Cahen, "Régime rural syrien," esp. p. 309; Riley-Smith, *Feudal Nobility*, pp. 45–46; Prawer, "Social Classes," pp. 103–10.

[96] Ḍiyā' al-Dīn, pp. 67–69, English trans. in Drory, "Ḥanbalīs," pp. 95–96.

than go into exile as a landless refugee. He paid his taxes because—and only when—Frankish coercion was effective. Fulcher of Chartres relates that Saracen peasants near Beirut refused to pay their dues until 1125 when King Baldwin II erected a castle in the neighborhood; thereafter they were constrained to yield the revenue.[97] But as soon as the peasant had grounds to believe that the Franks were loosening their grip, he would try to dodge his obligations. In 1263, when the Mamlūks were threatening Lower Galilee, a Frankish charter took into account the possibility that the village of Kafr Kāna—the Cana of the biblical wedding—might be occupied by the enemy, or its *villeins* might become disobedient to their masters, the Knights Hospitaller.[98] It is not known which eventuality materialized first, but Frankish rule over the region collapsed soon after.

Ruthless Frankish control of the countryside coupled with the realization that, with no massive colonization by European peasants in sight, the least frictional way of obtaining the all-important produce was to let the indigenous peasants maintain their routines; Muslim resignation to the fact that the price for staying put was to hand over a sizeable part of the harvest—these appear to have been the basic elements of the typical lord-peasant relationship, a relationship beset with suspicion and hostility exacerbated by the fact that the lord was also an Infidel. Thus the absence of large-scale Frankish rural colonization, besides minimizing friction between settlers and indigenes, set the stage for relatively stable though definitely coercive Frankish-Muslim coexistence in the countryside. In the coastal towns, the Frankish-Muslim relationship was also stable, but for different reasons. With the Muslim population killed or driven into exile, Frankish immigrants settled in the towns and obtained burgess status there, and members of Italian com-

[97] Fulcher of Chartres, 3, 45, pp. 771–72, utilized by Smail, "Crusaders' Castles," p. 143.
[98] *Cartulaire*, ed. Delaville Le Roulx, 3 vols. (Paris, 1899), 3:64, No. 3051. Cahen noted this charter ("Régime rural syrien," p. 308, n. 3) but did not dwell on its context.

munes established their quarters in the main commercial centers. The Frankish nobility, too, was largely city-dwelling. Under these circumstances, the Muslims who returned to these towns some time after the conquest or who were allowed to stay in some of them played only a modest role in the urban economies dominated by Franks and Italians, and there is nothing to indicate that this role changed perceptibly during the duration of Frankish rule.[99]

The low proportion of Franks in the general population of the Latin states and the precarious political situation of these states evidently interacted.[100] The precariousness also hampered the mobilization of Muslim manpower and expertise; since war with the outside Muslim powers was always imminent, the subjected Muslims could not be entrusted, as they were in Sicily or Hungary, with military or administrative functions. Only some of the Normans in the Principality of Antioch, who not only had been acquainted with Muslims before their move to the Levant but also faced a smaller subjected Muslim population, appear to have acted differently. The precariousness and the low proportion of the Western element also worked against total Muslim resignation to life under the Franks and against assimilatory tendencies.

The impact of the idea of the crusade on the relationship between the Franks and the Muslims subjected to them was most

[99] For interesting details on Muslim merchants in Frankish Acre in about 1184, apparently overlooked by economic historians, see *The Book of the One-Thousand-Nights-and-One-Night*, 4 vols. (London, 1972) nights 894–904, 4: 230–59; also as an independent text, edited by Varsy, "Anecdote des croisades," *Journal asiatique* 4, 16 (1850): 75–92. For a letter of protection which King Baldwin III issued to "Bohali f. Ebinesten," a merchant from Tyre setting out by ship to Egypt, see Hans Frh, von Soden, "Bericht über die in der Kubbet [sic] in Damaskus gefundenen Handschriftenfragmente," *Sitzungsberichte der Königlich Preussischen Akademie der Wissenschaften zu Berlin* (1903), p. 827. (Von Soden erroneously ascribed the letter to Baldwin IV, and was followed by R. Röhricht, *Regesta regni hierosolymitani* [Innsbruck, 1893–1904], No. 598a.) Some of the Oriental merchants of Acre and Tyre mentioned in Genoese acts of 1268 and 1271 may have been Muslims; three of them are said to have originated in Damascus (L. de Mas Latrie, *Histoire de l'île de Chypre*, 3 vols. [Paris, 1852–62], 2:74–79).

[100] See the remark by William of Tyre, 10, 20, p. 479.

pervasive. It was the idea of the holy war which led to the initial frenzied massacres. These left a legacy of revulsion and hatred, and directly or indirectly vacated the conquered areas of their indigenous Muslim elites. No Muslims of intellectual stature are known to have stayed permanently under Frankish rule, whereas Muslim refugees and fugitives from the conquered regions—among them a son and a nephew of Aḥmad b. Qudāma, both born in Jammā'īl—played a considerable role in the dissemination of the idea of anti-Frankish jihād.[101] Again, it was the crusading idea of liberating the Holy Places from their Infidel desecrators which led to the prohibition of Muslim settlement in the new kingdom's capital, a prohibition which rendered Muslim employment at the royal court even more unlikely. The continued appeal of the idea of the crusade in Western Europe ensured a continuous if numerically limited influx of newcomers from the West who felt that all Saracens were detested enemies and who significantly slowed down the incipient "orientalizing" tendencies on the part of the old-timers.[102]

The centrality of the Holy Places in the genesis of the kingdom of Jerusalem as well as in its subsequent history also affected the intellectual temper of the Frankish Levant. The clerics who went on the First Crusade or who went East in the following decades, were by no means a representative sample of the European clergy of their time. Many of them came from regions with major schools, but none is known to have been a prominent man of learning. Those who joined the crusade or later emigrated to the Frankish Levant were chaplains attached to the leaders of the expedition, men driven by the wish to live in the country sanctified by the ministry and passion of Christ, men attracted to, and preoccupied by, holy places, holy relics, and the traditions pertaining to them. On the other hand, cler-

[101] See Sivan, "Réfugiés," pp. 140–44. Al-Qāḍī al-Fāḍil, secretary and counselor to Saladin, was born in Ascalon eighteen years before the Frankish conquest of 1153; his father was a native of Baysān (Bethsan), which the Franks conquered in 1099; see A. Helbig, *al-Qāḍī al-Fāḍil* (Heidelberg, 1908).

[102] For a cognate argument on the "occidental" character of the kingdom, see Cahen, "Féodalité," pp. 188–89.

ics interested in theological and philosophical speculation, the application of dialectic to Roman and canon law, the study of scientific tracts translated from the Arabic or the Greek—in short, clerics attracted by the new intellectual trends of the age, stayed behind in Europe. (Stephen of Pisa, later of Antioch, is a lone exception.) In other words, the clerics who settled in the Frankish Levant established there only one part of the ecclesiastical world from which they had come: they constituted a fragment of the European clergy of the age, a fragment characterized by lowbrow religiosity. These men were not interested in, or capable of, intellectual give-and-take with Oriental Christian or Muslim scholars. Many or perhaps most of the latter were massacred during the crusader conquest or left later for the lands of Islam. It should also be noted that the Crusaders never conquered a major Islamic cultural center and that of the numerous native communities they subjugated, none spoke both Arabic and a Romance language. For all these reasons, the contribution of the Frankish Levant to the transfer of Arabic learning to the West was considerably more limited than that of Spain or southern Italy, though somewhat less negligible than usually assumed.[103]

[103] The issues touched upon in this paragraph will be dealt with in detail in my forthcoming study of intellectual activities in the Frankish Levant.

5

THE PAPACY AND THE MUSLIM

FRONTIER

James M. Powell

IN THE DEBATE over the medieval frontier, the role of the papacy has been peripheral to broader questions regarding the impact of the frontier on expanding Western societies. Even in the discussions of those churches that were at the borders of Western Christendom, there is often little recognition that the popes faced distinctive problems. Works such as Peter Linehan's *Spanish Church and the Papacy*, Josef Déer's *Papsttum und Normannen*, Jean Decarreaux's *Normands, papes et moines*, and Kenneth Setton's massive *Papacy and the Levant* devote little space to these issues.[1] James Muldoon has explored

[1] For the debate over the frontier thesis, see Peter Linehan, "Segovia: A 'Frontier' Diocese in the Thirteenth Century," *English Historical Review* 96 (1981): 481–508, esp. pp. 481–82 and nn. Linehan's *Spanish Church and the Papacy in the Thirteenth Century* (Cambridge, 1971) seems overly critical of papal efforts to support the Spanish churches without providing a sufficient analysis of the reasons for that failure. Josef Déer, *Papsttum und Normannen: Untersuchungen zu ihren lehnsrechtlichen und kirchenpolitischen Beziehungen* (Cologne, 1972) places the relationship between the papacy and the Normans in the framework of western feudalism and imperial/papal rivalries in Italy, but does not discuss the Muslim frontier in any detail. Jean Decarreaux, *Normands, papes, et moines: Cinquante ans de conquêtes et de politique religieuse en Italie méridionale et en Sicile* (Paris, 1974) focuses on monastic chronicles. G. A. Loud, "Royal Control of the Church in the Twelfth Century Kingdom of Sicily," *Studies in Church History* 18 (1982): 147–59, argues that the papacy and the Normans enjoyed a good relationship, largely due to the moderate policies of such kings as William I and William II. The Muslim frontier plays no part in his analysis of this relationship. Loud also discusses the relationship between the papacy and the Norman princes in his *Church and Society in the Norman*

the development of canon law regarding the sovereign rights of Muslim rulers in their own lands, but touches on Muslim communities under Christian rule only in passing. In *Crusade and Mission*, Benjamin Kedar wonders at the slowness of progress in the work of leading Muslims to Christianity.[2] Robert I. Burns alludes to the attitudes and the efforts of the popes in his numerous studies of the Muslim frontier in the kingdoms of Valencia and Aragon, as does Joshua Prawer in his work on the Latin kingdom of Jerusalem.[3] While a number of these studies are suggestive, none confronts the role of the papacy directly. The purpose of this essay is to define more precisely the impact of the interaction between the popes and the Muslim frontier. The guiding concerns in this relationship were papal rights of jurisdiction over local churches and the defense of orthodox belief among neighboring Christian populations. The limited nature of these aims helps to explain the significant role accorded to secular rulers in ecclesiastical affairs on this frontier and the emphasis on separation of Christians from Muslim and Jewish communities in the Middle Ages.

During the ninth and tenth centuries, the papacy, along with almost every other power in the West, was on the defensive against the Muslims. Its attitude may well be summed up by

---

Principality of Capua, 1058–1197 (Oxford, 1985), esp. pp. 55–65. While critical of Josef Déer, he argues (p. 58) that "feudal links provided an effective imagery for a political relationship in a way that claims of papal *potestas* in a general sense did not." Lynn White's *Latin Monasticism in Norman Sicily* (Cambridge, Mass., 1936), pp. 58–59, has some interesting remarks regarding the role of the monasteries in the conversion of the Muslims. Kenneth Setton, *The Papacy and the Levant*, 4 vols. (Philadelphia, 1976–1984), despite its title, deals only with the Byzantine Empire. See also Allan and Helen Cutler, *The Jews as Allies of the Muslims* (Notre Dame, Ind., 1986).

[2] James Muldoon, *Popes, Lawyers, and Infidels* (Philadelphia, 1979); Benjamin Z. Kedar, *Crusade and Mission: European Approaches toward the Muslims* (Princeton, 1984), pp. 45–57.

[3] See, e.g., Robert I. Burns, *The Crusader Kingdom of Valencia*, 2 vols. (Princeton, 1967), and idem, *Islam under the Crusaders: Colonial Survival in the Thirteenth Century Kingdom of Valencia* (Princeton, 1973), which examine the church on the frontier and relations between Muslims and Christians, respectively. For the Latin kingdom of Jerusalem, see Joshua Prawer, *Crusader Institutions* (Oxford, 1980).

the building of the Leonine Wall in Rome to protect the Church of St. Peter from the fate recently suffered by St. Paul outside the Walls. In 971, John XIII raised the church of Vich to metropolitan status on the grounds that the archepiscopal see of Tarragona was under Muslim rule "et pastore destituta, nullum recuperandi locum, aut inhabitandi usque hactenus reperire valeat."[4] Yet, within another fifty years, the tide had begun to turn against the Muslims in the western Mediterranean. Along a broad front, from Spain through Sardinia and southern Italy, the followers of Muḥammad began to lose the European footholds they had gained during previous centuries and the long process of reconquest got underway. By the mid-eleventh century, Leo IX, the guiding spirit of the papal reform movement, in anticipation of the reconquest of Sicily, commissioned Humbert of Moyenmoutier to preach the Word of God to the Sicilians as their archbishop. In the same letter, he granted the Normans of southern Italy all the lands they could conquer in Calabria and Sicily to be held from St. Peter "hereditali feudo."[5]

Leo IX's claim to feudal overlordship signaled the direction in which the papacy would move to advance its claims to ecclesiastical jurisdiction in the lands reconquered from the Muslims. Leo obviously had little direct knowledge of conditions in Sicily. He acted in anticipation of Norman military action. His assertion that these lands should be held as a hereditary fief of St. Peter was a recognition that the papacy was dependent on the success of a secular power. The claim of papal overlordship was in fact an effort to safeguard papal ecclesiastical jurisdiction. Obviously, this claim had considerable political ramifications. Historians have often emphasized the threat it posed to secular authority, but have tended to overlook the fact that it conferred legitimacy on the project to conquer Calabria and Sicily.[6] It established a contractual basis of reciprocal rights and obligations in the relationship between the papacy and the

[4] Demetrio Mansilla, ed., *La Documentación pontificia hasta Innocencio III (965–1216)* (Rome, 1955), pp. 1–2.

[5] *IP*, 10:186.

[6] But see Déer, *Papsttum und Normannen*, pp. 107–27.

Normans. In the past, the stress on the political nature of this relationship has not sufficiently recognized the difficulties that confronted the eleventh-century papacy in establishing its hegemony over the churches in these lands. Assertion of the right of feudal overlordship provided a mechanism whereby the theoretical superiority of the spiritual power, embodied in such texts as that of Pope Gelasius I (492–496) on the accountability of the clergy for the souls of kings, obtained a concrete form in law. Clumsy and unsuitable as the claim to feudal overlordship was for this purpose, it was virtually the only means in feudal custom that offered protection for ecclesiastical liberty and it was, therefore, to become quite important in those regions where political instability and unsettled ecclesiastical arrangements threatened the future of papal jurisdiction. Despite its shortcomings, some of which were evident to contemporaries, the papacy found in the claim to feudal overlordship a valuable means of asserting and protecting its jurisdiction during the twelfth and early thirteenth centuries.

The claim to feudal overlordship by Leo IX was premature, but set an important precedent for his successors in their dealings with the Normans of southern Italy and with various Spanish rulers. It was, however, only one of the means adopted by the eleventh-century papacy in its effort to establish its rights. For example, Gregory VII worked assiduously for the establishment of the liturgy of the Roman rite in Spain. In a letter to Alfonso VI of Castile and Sancho IV of Navarre, Gregory summarized the papal view of the historical ties between Spain and Rome: "Your diligence should not be ignorant of the deep agreement that Spain has had with Rome in religion and in the ordering of the divine office."[7] While stressing religious ties between Spain and Rome, Gregory also based his demand for conformity to the Roman rite on the Donation of Constantine, arguing that Spain was the "jus et proprietatem" of the Roman Church.[8] He did not refer to an earlier papal claim of overlordship in the kingdom of Aragon, which dated

[7] Mansilla, *Documentación*, p. 15.
[8] Ibid., pp. 12, 24.

from the reign of Sancho Ramirez (1068).⁹ Nor did he advance a claim to feudal overlordship over Castile and Navarre. His appeal to the Donation may, however, have been meant to serve as a basis for such claims. The Donation, founded on the supposed transfer of temporal power in the West to Pope Sylvester and his successors by the emperor Constantine, provided a juridical basis for Gregory's assertion that the victories of the Spanish rulers over the Muslims reestablished the ancient position of the Roman Church.[10] His aims were the same as those which had led Leo IX to advance the claim to feudal overlordship in southern Italy and Sicily. Behind the facade of the Donation of Constantine and feudal overlordship lay the ideology of the reform papacy summed up by Gerhart Ladner in the concept "reformatio in pristinum."[11] It was this vision of a restored church that informed Gregory's policy.

The meaning of the papal use of the Donation and of feudal overlordship is illustrated in the feudal oath in Sicily. The oaths of vassalage taken by the Norman princes from the time of Leo IX seem always to have contained a clause surrendering jurisdiction over the church of their dominions to the pope. The form of these oaths suggests that they were actually treaties, the terms of which were spelled out in the language of the oath.[12] These terms demonstrate that the form utilized, namely, the oath of vassalage, had been adapted to ecclesiastical needs. There is no indication that it was intended to limit the political jurisdiction of the Norman princes. It would be wrong, however, to ignore the risks inherent in the use of this form by the

---

[9] Ibid., p. 54, n. 32, and pp. 58–59.

[10] Ibid., p. 24.

[11] Gerhart B. Ladner, "Terms and Ideas of Renewal," in *Renaissance and Renewal in the Twelfth Century*, eds. Robert L. Benson and Giles Constable (Cambridge, Mass., 1982), pp. 1–33; see esp. p. 18.

[12] Jesef Déer, ed., *Das Papsttum und die süditalienische Normannenstaaten, 1053–1212* (Göttingen, 1969), pp. 17–18, 21–22, 23, 31–32. "Omnes quoque ecclesias que in mea consistunt dominatione cum earum possessionibus dimittam in tuam potestatem et defensor ero illarum ad fidelitatem sancte Romane ecclesie, et nulli iurabo fidelitatem nisi salva fidelitate sancte Romane ecclesie" (from the oath of Robert Guiscard to Nicholas II, August 1059; Déer, *Papsttum*, pp. 17–18).

papacy; certainly, the princes were aware of this meaning of the oath. Robert Guiscard used it to his advantage in his negotiations with the representatives of Henry IV. He expressed his willingness to become Henry's vassal, "sempre salvant la fidelite de l'Eglize." He thereby used his oath to the papacy to escape the dominance of a great temporal lord. Moreover, the proimperial pamphleteer, Peter Crassus, accused Gregory VII of seeking temporal benefits by promising a kingdom to Robert Guiscard.[13] The same kinds of risks were attendant on the use of the Donation as a basis for papal claims in Spain.

In Sardinia and Corsica, Gregory asserted the rights of the Roman Church along the same lines as in Spain, taking into account the local political situation.[14] His appointment of Landulf, bishop-elect of Pisa, as papal vicar in Corsica asserted the Donation of Constantine as the basis for papal jurisdiction.[15] Throughout the western Mediterranean lands liberated from Muslims, the papacy had, by the end of Gregory's pontificate, put in place mechanisms aimed at strengthening papal ties to local churches. In each case, the goal was to limit the ability of local secular powers to dominate the churches in their lands.

Gregory's pontificate witnessed increased papal involvement in the reconstitution of churches freed from Muslim rule. Following the death of Nicodemus, the last Greek archbishop of Palermo, who had received a papal privilege from Alexander II, Gregory confirmed the ancient privileges of the church of Palermo, "quicquid dignitatis antiquitus tenuisse probatur," for the new Latin archbishop, Alcerius. He made special provision for the reestablishment of suffragan sees, including those which had been destroyed during the Muslim occupation. The tenor of this letter leaves the details in local hands, as when Gregory

---

[13] Ibid., p. 24.

[14] *IP*, 10:380, 469. On Gregory's effort to reconstitute the church in North Africa, see C. Courtois, "Gregoire VII et l'Afrique du Nord," *Revue Historique* 195 (1945): 97–122, 193–226; and R. S. Lopez, "A propos d'une virgule: Le facteur économique dans la politique Africaine des papes," *Revue Historique* 198 (1947): 178–88.

[15] *IP*, 10:469.

concedes the pallium "according to the ancient usage of his church."[16]

Claims to overlordship asserted by the papacy seem to have had little impact on day-to-day relations between the popes and secular rulers. Nor were they uniquely aimed at the problems of the Christian-Muslim frontier. They were advanced elsewhere on the frontiers of Latin Christendom, where papal ecclesiastical jurisdiction might be imperiled by the changing policies of secular rulers. Such claims did not alter the dependence of the papacy on secular rulers. For example, Gregory VII's chief concern in Spain was the acceptance of the Roman rite in place of the local Spanish liturgy. He pressed for its acceptance by the Spanish bishops attending the Roman synod of 1074. Opposition to the Roman rite seems to have been strongest among the Spanish aristocracy. Gregory enlisted royal support, which proved critical to his limited success. When, as in the case of his support for the expedition of Ebles de Roucy against the Muslims in Spain, Gregory called upon French knights to join in the war without linking his efforts to those of the Spanish rulers, his attempt failed. Spanish monarchs saw papal overlordship as a means of gaining papal favor and promoting their influence over the church in their realms.[17] While the claim to overlordship was a cornerstone of the ecclesiastical policy of the reform papacy, its value lay more in securing cooperation from secular rulers in return for papal support of their policies than in its juridical effect.

The eleventh-century papacy's claims to universal jurisdiction over the church applied as much on the Rhine as in Sicily, Sardinia, or Spain. But it became clear that the unique conditions found along the Muslim-Christian frontier had a limiting effect on direct papal intervention in the affairs of churches in

[16] Ibid., 10:229.

[17] Joseph O'Callaghan, *A History of Medieval Spain* (Ithaca, 1975), pp. 201–2; Mansilla, *Documentación*, pp. 58–59. See also the discussion by Peter Linehan, "Religion, Nationalism and National Identity in Medieval Spain," *Studies in Church History* 18 (1982): 161–99, esp. pp. 186–87, on Portugal, where he states: "The king of Portugal controlled the Portuguese church under papal license, because of not in spite of Portugal's feudal subjection to Rome."

newly conquered lands. The reestablishment of bishoprics in these lands was, in any case, very gradual and depended not only on the pace of the reconquest but on other factors as well. It was not always possible to restore suffragan sees to each metropolitan. Changes during the period of Muslim occupation sometimes meant that former episcopal cities had declined or even been destroyed. Papal letters reestablishing bishoprics often give only the slightest hint of the negotiations that preceded papal action. When the city of Toledo was captured from the Muslims in 1085, Alfonso VI of Castile delayed the appointment of its archbishop until 1088. Pope Urban II's letter of October 10, 1088, confirming the appointment of Bernard as archbishop and primate of all Spain, opened with the famous quotation from Pope Gelasius I concerning the superiority of spiritual to temporal power.[18] But this statement did nothing to conceal the reality that Urban accepted the candidate proposed by Alfonso.[19] Moreover, Urban's recognition of the primacy of Toledo raised an immediate controversy because of the threat it posed to the claims of other Spanish prelates, especially the Aragonese archbishopric of Tarragona.[20]

Urban II's relations with the Normans in southern Italy and Sicily furnish the classic example of the limitation of papal jurisdiction by the secular power. Examination of this case illustrates the concern of Roger I, count of Sicily, to prevent direct papal intervention in the ecclesiastical affairs of the island in the years after the final conquest of Sicily in 1091 because of the complex religious issues confronted by the comital government. During the previous fifty years, the papacy had grown increasingly dependent on the military strength of the Normans to maintain its position in Rome. The election of Urban, a Frenchman, injected a new factor into that relationship. Urban recognized his need for Norman support, but wanted to distance himself somewhat by creating an independent base of power within the city.[21] At the same time, he cooperated with

---

[18] Mansilla, *Documentación*, p. 39.
[19] Ibid., p. 40.
[20] Ibid., pp. 48–52.
[21] Alfons Becker, *Papst Urban II (1088–1099)* (Stuttart, 1964), pp. 114–15.

Roger I in the restoration of Sicilian dioceses. In his letter of March 9, 1092, confirming the election of the bishop of Catania, Urban stated that Count Roger had offered the "city with the whole diocese" to Peter.[22] But, in his letter to Roger, bishop of Syracuse, Urban states that Roger, who had been dean of the cathedral, had been chosen "consilio episcoporum illius provinciae," making no mention of any role of Count Roger. On the other hand, Count Roger is shown acting with the counsel of Urban in the building of the Church of St. Nicholas in Messina, which he handed over to Bishop Robert.[23] All of this suggests that relations with Roger were generally good. Certainly, Urban had been able to hold synods in southern Italy in relative freedom. Nevertheless, his decision to appoint Robert, bishop of Troina and Messina and a close adviser of Count Roger, as papal legate in Sicily suggests that he was not entirely satisfied with Count Roger's ecclesiastical policy.[24] Roger reacted quickly by arresting the bishop, thus precipitating a crisis in his relations with the papacy.[25]

The account of subsequent events by Geoffrey Malaterra throws a cloud over the issues discussed by the pope and the count in their meeting at Salerno (1098) and stresses the resolution of the dispute rather than its causes. The most that can be said is that Urban was more concerned with ecclesiastical matters than with his political relations with the Normans.[26] The terms of Urban's letter, confirming the settlement of the dispute, conferred on Roger and his son Simon, or another heir, a special privilege, that no papal legate would be appointed without his approval and that he could determine which bishops and how many should be sent in response to a

[22] *IP*, 10:290.
[23] Ibid., 10:337.
[24] Salvatore Fodale, *Comes et legatus Siciliae* (Palermo, 1970), pp. 137–38.
[25] Hans-Walter Klewitz, "Studien über der Wiederherrstellung der römischen Kirche in Süditalien durch das Reformpapsttum," *Quellen und Forschungen aus italienischen Archiven und Bibliotheken* 25 (1933–1934): 105–57; esp. pp. 137–39.
[26] Déer, *Papsttum*, pp. 47–48.

papal summons to a council.[27] This was the famed "apostolic legation" of the Sicilian monarchy that would become a major bone of contention between the kings and the papacy from the fifteenth to the nineteenth centuries. But, as Fodale has shown, that later debate has little relevance for the actual grant made by Urban and, therefore, need not concern us here. On the other hand, it served ultimately as a precedent for the grant of the *patronato real* over the still to be conquered kingdom of Granada to Ferdinand and Isabella in 1486. Urban justified his privilege on the grounds that Roger had extended the church at the frontier with the Saracens. Fodale has shown that the English monarchy enjoyed a similar privilege at this time. This suggests that the grant was perceived in Rome as justified by particular and special circumstances such as might be found in postconquest England or in Sicily. In both cases, the motivation lay in the need to support the reconstruction of the church during a critical period.[28] In Sicily, Urban limited the privilege to the life-time of Roger and his immediate heir. So much of the discussion of this issue has centered on papal-Norman relations and the further development of the apostolic legation of the Sicilian kings that its special significance to the Muslim frontier has been neglected. When Pope Paschal II discussed this privilege in his letter to Roger II in 1117, he not only emphasized, as had Urban, that it arose from the problems created by the Muslim invasion and stressed the need for efficiency in meeting the needs of the church (per tuam industriam) but set out to describe Roger II's role in detail. Paschal provided as a model for Roger II the "good emperors" and his own father, protectors of the church and venerators of the bishops as "vicars of God."[29] This imagery eschews the symbols of feudalism to stress that of the church of the Constantinian and post-Constantinian age. It was much more fitting as a basis for the description of Roger's relation with the church than that of feudal investiture. Paschal's letter preserves the Gelasian character of

[27] Ibid., pp. 48–49.
[28] Fodale, *Comes et legatus*, pp. 134–139.
[29] Déer, *Papsttum*, p. 51.

this relationship, but in so doing makes clear that Roger, as "protector," acted as an executor of ecclesiastical authority for the papacy.

What emerges from the evidence presented thus far is the consistency of a papal policy in which papal claims of overlordship were balanced by the realities of papal dependence on secular support. Rome strove for recognition of its jurisdiction, but it also worked to ensure that the reconstruction of local churches would be carried out as effectively as possible. Realistically, this meant a considerable degree of cooperation with secular powers, which in turn, meant that local initiative was of greater importance than centralized administration.[30] The policies of Urban II and Paschal II recognized the *de facto* situation that obtained during the first phase of the reconquest of Muslim territories in the western Mediterranean as well as in the Holy Land after the First Crusade from the mid-eleventh to the mid-twelfth centuries.[31]

The presence of large Muslim populations along with native Christians and Jews in these lands created a new problem for their Latin rulers and the papacy. As previous chapters in this volume have shown, it became necessary to regulate relations between the dominant Latin Christians and these minority groups. Treaties, terms of surrender, existing laws regarding Jews, and the state of relations between the Latin Church and the Byzantines played significant roles in establishing the status of these groups. Certain features, however, were common to all. The most basic was the status of each minority as a separate

---

[30] The flexibility of papal policy regarding the reconstitution of churches in newly conquered lands as well as the deference shown to the interests of temporal powers is also illustrated in the establishment of the Latin hierarchy in the Holy Land. See J. G. Rowe, "Paschal II and the Relation between the Spiritual and Temporal Powers in the Kingdom of Jerusalem," *Speculum* 32 (1957): 470–501; and idem, "The Papacy and the Ecclesiastical Province of Tyre, 1110–1187," *Bulletin of the John Rylands Library* 43 (1962): 160–89. Yael Katzir ("The Patriarch of Jerusalem, Primate of the Latin Kingdom," in *Crusade and Settlement*, ed. Peter Edbury [Cardiff, 1985], pp. 169–74) illustrates the pressures that prevented the papacy from consistently applying various earlier models to the establishment of a Latin hierarchy in the East.

[31] Fodale, *Comes et legatus*, pp. 83–109.

community under its own laws and religious practices. Individuals within these groups obtained their status as members of these communities. To move from one community to another, even through religious conversion, raised complex issues that affected not only the subordinated communities but the ruling group as well. Moreover, the resolution of such difficulties remained almost exclusively a local affair. Benjamin Z. Kedar has asked why the Latin Church abstained from efforts to convert Muslims to Christianity for so long a period.[32] If this question poses a problem with respect to areas under direct Muslim rule, it raises even more perplexing issues when applied to those areas in which Christians ruled over Muslims. Certainly, the advantages realized by Christian rulers from their Muslim subjects did create an impediment to conversion, but another reason must be sought in barriers erected by the separate communities.[33] In a society which placed such stress on religious orthodoxy, preservation of believers from possible contamination was of prime importance. The precedent for such separatism lay in the relations of Christians and Jews. In the course of the twelfth century, subjugated Muslims and Jews came to be viewed as coordinate communities. Very aptly, Kedar has cited the view of Bernard of Clairvaux: "If the Saracens were subjugated to Christian rule as the Jews are, the Christians would await their conversion as they await that of the Jews."[34] This position is only understandable if the two communities are seen in essentially the same terms. Something of this attitude may be seen in Peter the Venerable, whose emphasis was on the conversion of both groups.[35]

---

[32] Kedar, *Crusade and Mission*, p. x.

[33] Ibid., pp. 145–54. Burns places great stress on the role of community in the preservation of Muslim religious practices (*Islam under the Crusaders*, pp. 184–219).

[34] Kedar, *Crusade and Mission*, p. 60.

[35] James Kritzeck, *Peter the Venerable and Islam* (Princeton, 1964), pp. 21–22. The views expressed in this essay differ substantially from those presented recently by R. I. Moore in *The Formation of a Persecuting Society* (Oxford, 1986). Moore argues that persecution grew because clerical intellectuals desired to increase their control over society. This essay stresses the breakdown of community boundaries, in part a product of the incorporation of minorities

While popes did call for the conversion of Muslims in Spain, they undertook no major initiatives. Their words of encouragement were directed chiefly at the efforts of others. Moreover, this continued to be the case even when the mendicant missions began in the early thirteenth century. Conversion was, as Kedar shows, subordinated to the needs of the local situation. The needs of local landholders and their rulers were an important impediment to conversions in Valencia. But, as we shall see in the case of Lucera discussed below, conversion was also a means of protecting local Christians from the contamination of error.

By the mid-twelfth century, we can discern several different patterns in the relationship between Christian rulers and their Muslim subjects. Previous essays in this volume have shown that the situation of Muslims in the kingdom of Aragon, in Castile, in Sicily, and in the eastern lands conquered by the Crusaders depended chiefly on local economic conditions. In some areas, the Christian landholding class was more dependent on Muslim labor, both free and slave. Immigration of

along the frontiers of Christendom and in part characteristic of the social mobility that characterized this period, as the source of those concerns and fears that created the climate for persecution. Clerical intellectuals were not unanimous or alone in feeling these concerns. Interestingly, Moore does not deal with Muslim minorities. My colleague, Kenneth Pennington, has called my attention to the *consilia* of Oldradus da Ponte, written in the early fourteenth century. His discussion of the status of the Jews in *consilium* 36, Oldradus, *Consilia* (Rome, 1472), no. 36 (unfoliated); Munich, Staatsbibl., Lat. (Clm) 3638, fol. 23v (no. 35); Clm 5463, 40v–41r (no. 72, olim 79) centers on the relapse of a Jewish convert. He asks the question: "Sed numquid excusabitur quia Iudaeus?" In his response, he cites 1 Cor. 5:12—"Nichil ad nos de hiis qui foris sunt"—as the classicus locus for the argument that the Jews do not fall under the jurisdiction of the church's courts. But he goes on to argue that this does not apply in the case of a relapsed Jew. In *consilium* 51, ibid., Rome, 1472; Clm 3638, 29r–29v; Clm 5463, 105r (167), dealing with the conversion of a Jew to Islam, he cites the same verse, arguing that "Judaei et Saraceni constitutionibus non ligantur." He further states: "etiam ad fidem Catholicam que veritatem colit et in qua perfecte salus invenitur nemo compellitur." These *consilia* provide a valuable summary of the communitarian basis for toleration of Jews and Muslims. At the same time, they reveal the practical pressures against the maintenance of this position.

Christian peasants into newly conquered areas was often encouraged, but seems to have been more successful in some parts of the kingdoms of Aragon and Sicily than elsewhere. Such immigration not only filled areas vacated by fleeing Muslims, but also created pressures against Muslims who remained. Very naturally, Christian rulers tailored their relations with their Muslim subjects to fit the needs of their Christian subjects. Given the fluidity of the situation on the frontier, as well as an emphasis on local solutions to local problems, the role of the papacy was limited to settling appeals of issues that eluded local solution and ratifying policies that found their expression in the constitutions of general councils of the church. The main thrust of legislation in this period was the maintenance of the separate identity of the subject communities in order to protect Christians from contamination by error or to prevent them from being subjected to Muslims or Jews. It is important to emphasize this frame of reference, since there has been a strong tendency to judge this legislation by its impact on the subject communities, rather than from the viewpoint of the legislators, who focused on the Christian community virtually to the exclusion of any other.

The period before the Third Lateran Council in 1179 provides evidence of problems arising from the intermingling of Muslim and Christian populations. For example, in the kingdom of Sicily the archbishop of Palermo sought the advice of Pope Alexander III in 1167 because King William I had handed over to the bishops jurisdiction over Muslims accused of the rape or murder of Christian women and children. Alexander responded that the bishops could levy a money fine in such cases but that they should refer serious crimes to the king. Alexander also decided that a Muslim man and a Christian woman, from whom he had children, should receive serious punishment.[36] In another letter he established that money resulting from usury could not be used to ransom poor captives from the Muslims.[37]

[36] *IP*, 10:232.
[37] Ibid., 10:234.

The Third Lateran Council (1179) dealt with two issues that arose directly from Christian penetration into the Muslim world. The first concerned trade in war materials by Christians. Promotion of the crusade emerged during the twelfth century as a major concern, but there was still no coherent body of law dealing with it. The enactment of canon 22 by Lateran III was not aimed at the crusade alone, but regulated trade between Christians and Muslims all along the frontier. The depth of interpenetration of the two societies is suggested by the prohibition against Christians captaining Muslim ships.[38] Another decree (canon 26) dealt, inter alia, with Jewish and Muslim ownership of Christian slaves. Linkage of Jews and Muslims became a common feature in the ecclesiastical legislation of this period. But this approach posed a difficult problem for the church. It is easy enough to trace the roots of this view in early Christian theology, but impossible to do more than suggest how it corresponded to the realities of the Muslim-Christian frontier. Most probably, the views of secular rulers regarding the usefulness (*utilitas*) of Muslim subject populations carried some weight in the formulation of the linkage between the Muslim and Jewish communities. Further, efforts to restrict Muslim/Jewish and Christian relations, which got underway during the late twelfth century, reflect the uneasiness of the ecclesiastical leadership about the dangers inherent in the presence of such communities. Canon 26 also contains regulations concerning the testimony of Jews before ecclesiastical courts. In this instance, the law seems to pertain only to Jews. The final section of this canon deals with the right of converts to keep their property following conversion. Again, the law itself does not make clear whether it applies to Muslims as well as Jews, though this was an important issue in both Muslim and Jewish conversions. The joining of these regulations in a single title without resolution of the question of their applicability to both communities suggests that this decree may have been drawn from sources in which Jews alone were the subject of concern.[39]

[38] *Conciliorum Oecumenicorum Decreta* (Bologna, 1973), pp. 223–32.
[39] Ibid., pp. 233–34. For a discussion of the problems in interpreting

The existence of these minorities on the Mediterranean frontier marked a new stage in the involvement of the papacy with the Muslims and their Latin rulers. This does not mean that the problems of institution building and the restoration of ecclesiastical order ceased to be important. They continued to be a priority for the papacy in the late twelfth and early thirteenth centuries, but the presence of Muslim communities under Christian rule raised issues which were both new and dangerous to the Christian community. It was against these dangers that the church and the papacy began more and more to react in the early thirteenth century.

Decisive measures to regulate the relationship between Muslims and the dominant Christian community were taken during the pontificate of Innocent III (1198–1216). The most important of these is found in the decree of the Fourth Lateran Council regulating dress of Jews and Muslims. The aim of this legislation is the separation of the communities with a view to preventing mixed marriages.[40] This decree refers to the existence of a requirement that Jews (and Muslims?) should wear a distinctive garb in "some provinces." It also refers to an injunction found in the biblical books of Leviticus and Deuteronomy. Most previous discussion has centered on its implications for relations between Christians and Jews in the thirteenth and fourteenth centuries. The badge became a symbol of opprobrium to Jews and, already in the early thirteenth century, some Jews tried to gain exemption from the requirement to wear it.[41] It is not surprising, therefore, that scholarly interest has chiefly centered on this development and its linkage with the increasing persecution of Jews from the inception of the Crusades. Many scholars have associated canon 68, which contains this provision, directly to the attitude of Innocent III toward the Jews.

There is no clear precedent for canon 68 in the literature. The

---

changes in Christian attitudes toward the Jews, see Jeremy Cohen, *The Friars and the Jews: The Evolution of Medieval Anti-Judaism* (Ithaca, 1982), pp. 19–32.

[40] *COD*, p. 266.

[41] Salo W. Baron, *A Social and Religious History of the Jews*, 2d ed., 18 vols. (New York, 1957–83), 11:96–106.

synodal legislation of Eudes de Sully, bishop of Paris, shows that in 1208 there was a requirement that Jews should wear a distinguishing badge in the shape of a wheel, but this legislation makes no mention of Muslims.[42] Others have pointed to a Muslim source requiring Jews to wear a distinctive sign on their garb. Although precedents of this kind cannot be ruled out, neither are they conclusive. What is more indicative of the manner in which this canon was formulated is the linking of Jews and Muslims which had become quite common in the conciliar legislation and the decretals of the late twelfth century. Lateran IV follows these precedents. Moreover, its opposition to the mixing of Christians and non-Christians was already reflected in previous legislation. What was new was the requirement of an identifying badge. Here, it seems reasonable to suggest that the canon of the Paris Synod of 1208 points to the influence of the French bishops as a source for such a decree at the Fourth Lateran Council.[43]

The inclusion of a prohibition against Jews and Muslims appearing in public during Holy Week was adapted from an earlier law that referred only to the Jews. Lateran IV was the culmination of a process in which the treatment of Muslims and Jews was linked. This development makes it difficult to understand this legislation since it is often impossible to distinguish an element that arose out of the Muslim-Christian experience from one that resulted from the Jewish-Christian relationship. It does seem, however, that the latter influence played a more direct role in the shaping of these laws.

What is more understandable, if still not entirely susceptible of proof, are the reasons why this kind of legislation increased in the late twelfth and early thirteenth centuries. During a pe-

---

[42] Mansi, 22:685. See also Baron, *Social and Religious History of the Jews* 11: 97–98; Ulysse Robert, *Les signes d'infamie au moyen âge* (Paris, 1891), pp. 10–11. The Council (*Parlement*) of Nablus (1120) forbade the wearing of clothing, *Francigeno more* (in Frankish style), by Muslims (Mansi, 21:264, esp. xvi).

[43] Both Baron and Robert point to France. My research on the Fifth Crusade indicates that the role of the French bishops at the Fourth Lateran Council was even more influential than has previously been suggested (*Anatomy of a Crusade, 1213–1221* [Philadelphia, 1986], pp. 46–47; 49, n. 31).

riod of substantial economic and demographic expansion, with an influx of population into towns and cities, the church found itself confronted by numerous pressures. The rise of heresy in this same period intensified concerns about the defense of true belief. The rights of believers appeared to be in conflict with the rights of minority communities. The problem lay in the breakdown of traditional communities, particularly in the intermixing of Christians with Jews and Muslims in Spain, Sicily, and the Latin East. Just as heretics threatened the church from within, the breakdown of the barriers between minority groups and the dominant Latins raised in some minds the specter of the decline of Christianity. The resultant fear drew strength from contemporary concerns about the Last Days and the approach of the end of the world. Against the background of this eschatological climate, pressures to protect the faithful from peril increased. The new period narrowed the rights of minority communities without denying them the right to exist. The restrictions that were the hallmark of this effort were designed to enforce the separation of minority communities from Latin Christians. Muslims and Jews were perceived as a more serious threat to Christianity in the early thirteenth century than they had been a mere fifty years earlier. Robert Grosseteste, at the first Council of Lyons in 1245, reflected how the church had emerged from obscurity to triumph during her first centuries, now to find herself surrounded by enemies and attacked from within.[44] The Fourth Lateran Council signals the emergence of a growing awareness of the problems confronting the church not merely within Europe but also along the Muslim-Christian frontier.

There is no evidence that the papacy was an innovator of new policy for Muslim-Christian relations. The increased emphasis on separation between Christians and Muslims and Jews, evident in the decrees of Lateran IV, signaled the emergence of a

[44] Richard W. Southern, *Robert Grosseteste: The Growth of an English Mind in Medieval Europe* (Oxford, 1986), p. 278. Peter Linehan ("Religion, Nationalism and National Identity in Medieval Spain," pp. 192–93) cites Diego Garcia's *De Planeta*, dedicated to Archbishop Rodrigo of Toledo, as arguing that proximity to the Muslims had a corrupting influence on the clergy.

response that would link the futures of Muslims and Jews in Europe from the thirteenth to the sixteenth centuries. To study the development of this response in the thirteenth century, the remainder of this essay will focus not only on papal and conciliar legislation but also on papal reaction to a specific Muslim community, that of Lucera, founded by Frederick II in 1223 or 1224 on the frontier of the papal state near Foggia. It is particularly valuable to compare changes in the papal attitude toward Lucera with the evolution of regulations in successive collections of canon law from the promulgation of the *Decretales* of Gregory IX in 1234 to promulgation of the *Extravagantes Communes* of Pope John XXII in the early fourteenth century. The foundation of Lucera has long been regarded as a direct provocation of the papacy by Emperor Frederick II, king of Sicily. Canonistic sources, which loomed so significantly in the public life of the church in the thirteenth century, offer a way of tracing the official status of Jews and Muslims in the eyes of the papacy. The study of Lucera throws light on the development of canon law, while the study of canon law enables us better to understand the papal attitude toward a Muslim colony on its doorstep.

The foundation of Lucera was a royal solution to a political and military problem that had long festered in the kingdom of Sicily. In 1223, Frederick was in the midst of preparations to fulfill his long-delayed vow to go on crusade.[45] His projected marriage to Yolande, the heiress of the kingdom of Jerusalem, was a culmination of an effort to bring the crusade more directly under his control. But he was also confronted by rebellion among the Muslims of western Sicily and by some of his barons on the mainland. Frederick secured the surrender of a part of the Muslims who had taken up arms in the mountains of Sicily, and ordered them to be transported to Lucera.[46] In early March 1224, he wrote to Pope Honorius III, seeking a further postponement of his crusade vow on the grounds that

[45] Powell, *Anatomy of a Crusade*, pp. 196–97.
[46] Ryccardus de Sancto Germano, *RISS*, 7:2, 110–12, 120; H.-B., 2:392–94.

the Muslim rebellion still did not permit his departure from the kingdom.[47] There is no evidence at this time that the establishment of the colony at Lucera evoked any opposition from the pope.

In fact, Frederick's relocation of Muslims in Lucera was based entirely on economic and military considerations and was certainly not directed against the papacy. Despite his postponement of his crusade vow, Frederick enjoyed a positive relationship with the pope and the curia. Even granted that patience in Rome was wearing thin after the disastrous defeat of the crusade army at Damietta in 1221, he had no reason to threaten the pope or the cardinals at this time. In fact, such a move would have seriously compromised his own plan for the crusade.[48] The transfer of Muslims from Sicily to Lucera was in support of this plan. It removed a large body of Muslims from a mountainous and remote area where they were able to find support from their fellow religionists and placed them in an area where their presence threatened the unruly northern barons, who had often proved difficult for Frederick and his Norman predecessors. Moreover, they were an agrarian colony in a region where their labor would bring a good income to the Crown; they were a military colony, whose strong fortifications served royal interests in a politically unstable area.[49] Rebellion no longer offered a realistic alternative to faithful service of the Crown for this group of Muslims. While they enjoyed royal protection under their own $qā'id$, there is no reason to accept the rapturous paeans to Frederick's tolerance found in some historians.[50] Long ago, Amari wrote of the mistreatment of Sicilian Muslims under Frederick.[51] There is little reason for re-

[47] Ibid., 2:409–13.

[48] Cf. my views in *Anatomy of a Crusade*, pp. 197–200, with those of Thomas van Cleve, *The Emperor Frederick II of Hohenstaufen* (Oxford, 1972), pp. 153–54.

[49] Ruggiero Romano and Corrado Vivanti, eds., *Storia d'Italia*, 6 vols. (Turin, 1972–1976), 3:664.

[50] Van Cleve, *Frederick II*, pp. 154–55. See also Francesco Gabrieli, "La colonia saracena di Lucera e la sua fine," *Archivio storico pugliese* 30 (1977): 169–75.

[51] Michele Amari, *Storia dei Musulmani di Sicilia*, 2d ed., 5 vols. (Catania, n.d.), 3:615, 630–31.

garding the position of the Muslim serfs at Lucera in a light more favorable than their fellows in Sicily. Very likely, by 1224, Honorius knew Frederick's reasons for moving them to Lucera. If so, he did not raise any objections. Nor did his successor.

In a famous and much discussed incident, Pope Gregory IX wrote to Frederick in August 1233 to seek his cooperation in securing a peaceful reception for Dominican missionaries to convert the Muslims of Lucera. Gregory asked Frederick's support to convert the Muslims "who inhabit Noceria di Capitanata (Lucera) and who speak Italian fairly well."[52] The latter phrase is important because it shows why the Dominicans were called on. The fact that the Muslims could speak Italian suggests that they were a danger to the faith of the peasantry in the region. Their religious views might easily spread through the countryside. The Dominicans aimed at countering this problem by promoting the conversion and assimilation of the Muslim population. Frederick's reply supports this view, indicating that some Muslims had already been converted and expressing a desire for the conversion of the rest. He even suggested that he planned to be in that area in the near future, indicating a personal interest in the matter. Although the tone of Frederick's letter is high-blown, the facts suggest that he was quite willing to support the work of the Dominicans. From Gregory's side there was concern but no direct objection to the existence of the colony.

When Frederick returned to the kingdom of Sicily from Germany in 1236 following the abortive rebellion of his son Henry, he faced numerous complaints from the pope regarding the administration of the church in the *Regno*. He was also accused of laxness in his concern for the conversion of the Muslims of Lucera. In his reply, Frederick argued that he was the victim of gossip. He recounted how he had brought the Muslims to the mainland from the mountains of Sicily and replaced them there with Christian colonists. His report was perhaps

[52] H.-B., 4:452: "rogandam duximus et hortandam quatenus Sarracenis qui Capitanate Nocerium incolunt et italicum idioma non mediocriter ut fertur intelligunt."

overly optimistic in maintaining that one-third had already been baptized and more would soon follow. But his reference to the pressure he had applied to the *qā'ids* of the Luceran Muslims to encourage conversion rings true. He was here following precedents already set by his Norman predecessors in dealing with their Muslim subjects. This letter, which has been cited to show that Frederick had little interest in the conversion of the Luceran Muslims, actually demonstrates the opposite.[53]

The Muslim colony of Lucera also emerged as a subsidiary issue at the Council of Lyons in 1245, but in a context that suggests that the complaint was a repetition of the "gossip" referred to in Frederick's letter of 1236 to Gregory IX. Thaddeus de Suesa's refutation of charges against Frederick at Lyons followed the same line as Frederick's letter of 1236. At any rate, these charges were made chiefly to reenforce the accusation of heresy against Frederick and had no direct reference to the historical reasons for the establishment of the colony. They were part of the polemic that dominated these years. Nevertheless, the failure of efforts to convert the Muslims of Lucera seemed to justify these papal charges and to lend support to the view of some modern historians that the colony was aimed against the Papal States. The second half of the thirteenth century witnessed a hardening of the attitude toward the colony on the part of the popes. The loyalty of the Muslims to the Hohenstaufen during the reign of King Manfred, entirely understandable given their circumstances, was a principal cause of suspicion. Failure of the effort to convert them, even under the Angevins, and the willingness of Charles I to make use of their arms (as the papacy itself had earlier tried to do) contributed to an increased concern in Rome. This attitude had already manifested itself in the treaty between Urban IV and Charles, prior to his invasion of the kingdom, which commanded the preaching of the crusade against Manfred and the Saracens of Lucera.[54] On the very eve of the destruction of Lucera in 1300,

[53] Ibid., 4:831.

[54] Edouard Jordan, *Les origines de la domination angevine en Italie*, 2 vols. (Paris, 1909), 2:426.

Charles II had returned from Rome, where Pope Boniface VIII had reproached him for allowing this colony of pagans to exist for so long within his kingdom so near the Papal States.[55] In this connection, it is significant that Pope Clement IV wrote to James of Aragon, calling upon that ruler to expel the Muslims from his kingdom.[56] Charles, unlike James, felt compelled to take swift and decisive action. But it soon became obvious that he was not really committed to the program of destruction advocated by the pope. As Bevere has shown, within two years, Charles permitted the reconstruction of small communities of Muslims in the same region to his own economic benefit and that of his nobles, though he was careful to restrict the public observance of Islam by forbidding the muezzin's call to prayer.[57]

The case of Lucera is instructive because it provides insight into the grounds for papal concern about Muslim communities living in the midst of Christian populations and, at the same time, shows how, even under extreme conditions, the papacy was slow to involve itself in a matter that fell chiefly under the jurisdiction of a secular ruler. Concern for the faith of the nearby Christian population provided the chief impetus for efforts to promote the conversion of the Muslims. It was the slowness of progress in their conversion that aroused strong papal opposition to the continued existence of Lucera.

During this period, there was an increasing effort to isolate the Christian community from Muslims and Jews. Paradoxically, isolation and conversion, though based on essentially diverse premises, represented means toward the same goal. Emphasis on conversion denied the rights of subordinate communities, as it exalted the rights of the individual over those of the community. Sustained efforts at conversion, as at Lucera, placed these communities under considerable stress. The logical result of this pressure was the destruction of the

[55] R. Bevere, "Ancora sulla causa della distruzione della colonia saracena di Lucera," *Archivio storico per le province napolitane* 21 (1935): 222–28; see esp. p. 224, n. 2.

[56] Linehan, *Spanish Church and the Papacy*, pp. 178–79.

[57] Bevere, "Ancora," pp. 225–27.

community as a separate entity and its absorption into the larger society. Conversion was a solvent of the minority community. Failing conversion, isolation of subordinated communities from the dominant Christian community was the ultimate religious defense for both the dominant and the subordinated communities. But the existence of the Muslim frontier made possible a safety valve of another type for Muslims and, to some extent, also for Jews: a crossing of the frontier by flight or by expulsion.

The development of canon law in the thirteenth and early fourteenth centuries demonstrates, as did the experience of Lucera, the way in which papal concern for the protection of orthodoxy led to increasing efforts to restrict the public religious activities and personal lives of Muslims and Jews. The *Decretales* of Gregory IX, compiled by the Dominican Raymond of Penyafort and promulgated in 1234, was the first canonical collection to focus significant attention on Christian relations with subject Jewish and Muslim communities. Although much of this material was scattered through various books of the collection, book 5, title 6 was entirely devoted to matters, "De Iudaeis, Sarracenis, et eorum servis."[58] These materials, drawn mostly from the decretals and conciliar legislation of the late twelfth and early thirteenth centuries do not constitute a coherent body of regulation for Christians and Muslims. Nor, even if we include other materials scattered through the various books of the *Decretales*, does such a corpus of law emerge. Only those questions serious enough or sufficiently difficult to come to the attention of popes or councils found their way into these collections. Only those judged to have some lasting applicability passed muster with Raymond. Nevertheless, the *Decretales* does enable us to trace certain important developments.

The organization of book 5, title 6 demonstrates how the linkage of Jews and Muslims initiated in the second half of the twelfth century had gained acceptance in the legal thinking of

[58] Emil Friedberg ed., *Corpus Iuris Canonici*, 2 vols. (Leipzig, 1879–1881; repr. Graz, 1955). The *Decretales* of Gregory IX are found in vol. 2. The notes follow the form of citation used by the *Bulletin of Canon Law*.

the first half of the thirteenth century. Although a considerable portion of this legislation dealt only with relations to Jews, there is no effort to distinguish between Jews and Muslims. This is surprising in light of references to Muslims as *pagani* and the incorporation of crusade legislation directed against the sale of military materials to Muslims. One might expect that some effort to differentiate Christian relations with the two communities would have emerged. After all, one was clearly an enemy, the other a community enjoying a special status by divine injunction. One had come increasingly to be regarded as pagan, while the other preserved the sacred books of the Old Testament. The answer to this failure lies in the nature of the legislation, which made no effort to move beyond the status of converts and the relations of Christians to these communities.

Conversion worked a fundamental change in status on those who accepted baptism. The question that arose from this change was the manner in which it affected previous relationships of the convert: marriage, rights of inheritance, offspring before conversion, and personal freedom. Marriage was the most intimate and difficult of these relationships. Several decretals responded to problems arising from the differing marriage practices of non-Christian communities. One problem was the different regulations regarding consanguinity. Innocent III dealt with the validity of marriages after baptism of those infidels who had earlier been married within forbidden degrees of relationship. His decision made clear that it applied not merely to Jews but also to other non-Christians, including Muslims. The use of the term "Infidels" (unbelievers) in the letter makes this clear.[59] He maintained that those who followed their own law or traditions were validly married. This subject came up again in a letter from the bishop of Tiberias, which drew a response from Innocent in the decretal, "Gaudemus in Domino."[60] Again, he affirmed the validity of marriages contracted

---

[59] X, 4, 14, 4. But see Benjamin Z. Kedar, "Muslim Conversion in Canon Law," *Proceedings of the Sixth International Congress of Medieval Canon Law, Berkeley, 1980*, eds. S. Kuttner and K. Pennington (Citta del Vaticano, 1985), pp. 321–32, esp. p. 323, n. 7.

[60] X, 4, 19, 8.

prior to the baptism of one or both of the parties, within the prohibited decrees, arguing that "quum sacramentum coniugii apud fideles et infideles existat," and marriages within these degrees were permitted to pagans by their laws, the convert could remain married "quum per sacramentum baptismi non solvantur coniugia sed crimina dimmitantur."

Marriage gave rise to other problems, such as that posed in a decretal of Celestine III, regarding the validity of marriages contracted after the death of a husband in a conflict between Christians and Muslims, and the subsequent marriage of a widow to her husband's killer.[61] This decretal, clearly arising from the circumstances of combat along the frontier, permitted such marriages where there was no conspiracy to murder the husband, but forbade them where there was. The conduct of the war in itself did not prevent former belligerents from marrying even in these unusual circumstances. In yet another instance, Pope Gregory IX favored converts over their unconverted spouses by awarding offspring to the converted party.[62] Moreover, Innocent III declared that the progeny of marriages of converts, where the parties were related within the prohibited degree, were to be considered legitimate. This measure ensured protection for their inheritances.[63] The Third Lateran Council had already granted converts protection for those possessions they held at the time of their conversion.[64] But Christianity was not able to accommodate the Muslim practice of polygamy. In "Gaudemus in Domino," Innocent III recalled that the patriarchs and other just men had many wives at the same time, but not even conversion could make it possible for a Muslim to have more than one wife at a time.[65] Nevertheless, canon law favored the rights of the convert against those of the community to which he or she had belonged. However, its prescriptions with respect to inheritances often ran into conflict

---

[61] X, 3, 33, 1.
[62] X, 3, 33, 2.
[63] X, 4, 17, 1.
[64] *COD*, p. 224.
[65] Cf. X, 4, 17, 15 and 4, 19, 8. Kedar has discussed this problem in "Muslim Conversion in Canon Law," p. 323.

with secular law. Further potential for such conflicts with secular authorities emerged from the effort in canon law to maintain a separation between Christians and Muslims.

Efforts to limit contacts between Christians and Jews had a long history in the church. Prohibitions against the construction of new synagogues went back to the first centuries following recognition of Christianity as a legal religion in the Roman Empire. Likewise, from a very early date, Jews were forbidden to keep Christian slaves. These restrictions were often repeated and augmented, particularly after the middle of the twelfth century. The Fourth Lateran Council went further by requiring the wearing of an identifying badge not merely by Jews but also by Muslims. Moreover, it contained further restrictions of the public activities of these groups during the season of the Passion of the Lord.[66] The council also revived earlier prohibitions against Jews' holding of public office, making clear that they were to be applied also to pagans. Gregory IX specifically mentioned Muslims in his decretal on this subject.[67] At the end of the century, Boniface VIII declared that Christians who converted to Judaism or who returned to Judaism after their conversion to Christianity were to be regarded as heretics.[68] It is unclear whether this legislation was meant to apply to Islam. At the Council of Vienne, within a decade of the "destruction" of Lucera, the pope and council called on secular rulers to prevent Muslim communities from calling on the name of the prophet in public, that is, to forbid the muezzins' call to prayer.[69] The small Muslim communities reestablished by Charles II after 1302 in the region around Lucera were already in conformity with this requirement. This legislation was specifically aimed at Muslims. Limited though this measure was, it was a cause of concern to Muslims and to their Christian lords. By the early fourteenth century, despite intense interest in conversion of subject Muslims by Raymond Lull and others, the papacy and the hierarchy of the church remained chiefly con-

[66] COD, p. 226.
[67] X, 5, 6, 18.
[68] VI, 5, 2, 13.
[69] COD, 380.

cerned to isolate them from their Christian neighbors. Expulsion, already underway in Sicily, loomed as the solution to the Muslim problem along the frontiers. One can only wonder how much contemporary expulsions of Jews were influenced by this climate.[70]

The views of St. Bernard and Peter the Venerable, that seemed to suggest that the conversion of subjugated Muslims was to be regarded in the same manner as that of the Jews—thereby placing both in the same eschatological framework—were increasingly eroded in the thirteenth century by fears that their presence would endanger the faith of neighboring Christians. These fears provided a significant motivation for the increasing emphasis on the conversion of Muslims. Expulsion or isolation could be justified on this basis. The concerns of the

[70] Oldradus da Ponte takes up the expulsion of the Jews and Saracens in *consilium* 87 (Oldradus, *Consilia* [Rome, 1472], 87; Clm 3638, 41r–41v; Clm 5463, 124r–124v [204]) where he states: "Et sic cum iuste possideant bona eis auferri non debent." However, he modifies this view in keeping with contemporary experience to permit their expulsion on two grounds. First, Jews may be expelled by secular rulers because they are serfs of the king. Second, both Jews and Saracens must live quietly and give no scandal to the faith. Further, in *consilium* 91 (ibid. [Rome, 1472], 91; Clm 3638, 42v; Clm 5463, 125v [208]) dealing with the obligation of Saracens to pay tithes, Oldradus denies the property rights of Saracens: "Immo totum quidquid circa mare et sic ex quo recuperata debet redire ad pristinam naturam." He does not discuss expulsion here, but this view does raise the question whether expulsion might not be legitimate. In *consilium* 264 (ibid. [Rome, 1472], 264; Clm 3638, 151v–152v) he returns to the subject of the expulsion of Jews and Saracens. Here he takes the view that rulers cannot expel Jews and Muslims without cause. Although he bases his argument on natural rights and Christian love, he may, in fact, have in mind similar limits to those expressed above. In his third reason, he argues "non debemus Iudaeos et paganos *pacificos* rebus suis spoliare, eadem ratione nec eorum habitaculis in *terra native* privare" (emphasis added). Their continued presence depends on living quietly and not deceiving "simplices Christianos." Oldradus was no friend to those arguing for expulsion, but he was a very cautious lawyer. The value of his consilia lies in the way in which they reflect the contemporary debate over the question of expulsion. Oldradus had no real answer to the charge that Jews and Muslims were a danger to the faith, but he enunciated a strong defense of their rights and, as a good lawyer, attempted to limit the cases in which they might be subject to expulsion. Cf. Muldoon, *Popes, Lawyers, and Infidels*, pp. 18–21. The above summary differs from that given on these pages.

papacy for the faith of simple Christians narrowed its capacity to recognize the burdens placed upon Muslim and Jewish communities. Only the mediation of secular rulers persuaded the popes to mitigate some of the restrictions placed on them by Lateran IV.

Though canonists, like Oldradus da Ponte, might defend the rights of minorities to their property, the price was that they must not disturb or give scandal to the faith of Christians. *Utilitas* provided the real basis for the continued existence of these communities. In the case of Muslims, once their utility to their secular masters declined, the only alternatives were expulsion or assimilation. This is not to say that the popes ceased to be interested in efforts to convert Muslims and Jews. Quite the contrary, there was even an increased urgency to such efforts because of the danger that these groups posed to Christians. Conversion was, after all, the route to gradual assimilation. But, by the late thirteenth century, the difficulties in that direction were very evident.

CONCLUSIONS

A COMPARATIVE NOTE

James M. Powell

BY THE END OF THE THIRTEENTH CENTURY, Latin rule in the kingdom of Acre had drawn to a close. In southern Italy, the Muslims of Lucera had been dispersed; in Sicily only remnants of the earlier Muslim communities survived. Only in Spain, particularly in Valencia, did Muslims continue to dwell in substantial numbers under Christian rule. For those who remained, there were increased pressures toward conversion and restrictions on public prayer, particularly of the muezzin's summons. Slavery and the slave trade assumed a somewhat greater importance as a means of providing household servants and agricultural labor, as indigenous communities of Muslims declined.

The main reasons for this decline lay in changing conditions within each region. Aside from the loss of the crusader states, the chief factor seems to have been the growth of Christian communities through immigration. Certainly, the early decline of Muslim communities in Sicily is largely accounted for by the deliberate colonization policy of the Normans and their successors, which brought large numbers of immigrants from both the mainland and northern Italy to the island. Similarly, immigration played a role in the decline of Muslim communities in Catalonia and the Balearic islands, to name only two examples. On the other hand, the lack of sufficient numbers of Latin Christian cultivators provides at least a partial explanation for the persistence of Muslim communities in some parts of Spain down to the seventeenth century.

The concern of the church over the danger posed by Muslim minorities to the faith of simple Christians found its expression chiefly in efforts to limit contacts between Christians and Muslims. In those instances where the danger aroused the greatest fears, as in the instance of Lucera during the second half of the thirteenth century, the papacy went so far as to advocate expulsion. Yet even the strongest opposition of the papacy had only a limited impact. The strictures of canon law were most effective when applied in local ecclesiastical courts in cases involving sexual and marital conduct. Though it would be correct to describe the effects of these efforts as anti-Muslim, their intent was clearly aimed at the protection of the Christian community from contamination by alien religious ideas and practices. Even the severely critical descriptions of Muslims by preachers reflect more their effort to prevent curious Christians from investigating Islam or to condemn apostates than any direct enmity toward Muslims. Not that such feelings did not exist. However, historians would be well advised to look for their causes in local tensions and conflicts. Only after examining these factors may they turn to broader religious and ideological considerations that served to provide support and context to local grounds for dispute.

Such a view does not minimize the role of religious belief as a cultural factor defining the differences between the Latin Christian and Muslim communities along the frontier. Rather, it defines the role of Christian religious ideas toward Muslims more precisely and thus places a limit on the tendency to overgeneralize from statements found in the polemical literature of the time. The comparative approach taken in these essays advances a multicausal explanation for the various patterns of behavior found in Spain, Sicily, and the East. Under these circumstances, it becomes impossible to discuss Christian-Muslim relations within the narrow context of religious toleration in its modern meaning or even in its medieval Christian meaning alone. Indeed, medieval Christian ideas of toleration, accommodating the alien community, are themselves in conflict with concerns over the preservation of religious orthodoxy. Separation of the two communities results from an effort to reconcile this conflict. Likewise, efforts at conversion of Muslim minorities proceed within a framework that tries to mediate between the prohibition against the use of force and the desire to protect the Christian community. Both of these elements were present, as well as a basic desire to propagate Christianity. The difficulties in reconciling these divergent needs are well illustrated in the writings of the period, perhaps nowhere better than in the *consilia* of Oldradus da Ponte.

What makes the thirteenth-century Muslim-Christian experience particularly interesting is not the emergence of a coherent body of legislation, secular or ecclesiastical, to regulate this relationship, but the evidence that the search for solutions constantly raised new questions and problems and forced reassessment of fundamental principles. The divergence of secular and ecclesiastical views should not occasion surprise; they proceeded from very different concerns, even though canon law did exercise some influence on secular legislation, as, for instance, in the prohibition of the muezzin's call to prayer. In secular law, the principle of *utilitas* occupied the most prominent place in justifying the continued toleration of the Muslim minority, but it also found a lesser place in the views of the canonists and of the papacy. This interaction further increased the tension between the secular and spiritual authorities even as it forced them to try to reconcile their differences.

In large measure, the story told here is marked by numerous failures, most notably the failure to find long-term ways in which small Muslim communities might live equitably, as semi-states, under Christian rule. However, these failures are not without their long moments of success, in which the two groups lived together in peaceful and even fruitful relations. The Muslim experience under Christian rule was not really so different from that of minority Christians under Muslim rule. The lot of minorities cannot really be reduced to simplistic tales of oppression on either side.

The long-term impact of this experience must also be viewed in rather mixed terms. Attempts to reduce the "Spanish character" to the peculiar impact of the *Reconquista* receive a rather considerable blow from the discussions presented here. There is little to support the view of a common Spanish experience so fondly presented by earlier scholars. On the other hand, the

Muslim-Christian relationship did provide something of a laboratory in which numerous experiences yielded their results. It becomes rather easier to understand the sixteenth-century debate over the enslavement of the Indians if we move beyond the traditional arguments over slavery and see the Spaniards in roles not terribly different from those their ancestors had faced vis-à-vis Muslim minorities in the thirteenth century. Northern Europeans had no similar fount of experience on which to draw in forging relations with native Americans. The point here is not that Spaniards or Portuguese found better solutions than did the Dutch or Englishmen, but that they tended to form their solutions against the background of their previous experience with Muslim minorities. Consciousness of this fact has already contributed to a more perceptive reading of the history of the *conquistadores*, but much remains to be done.

Finally, we must deal with persecution and repression as phenomena that especially mark the period subsequent to our own. It is all too easy to yield to the temptation to find the rather obvious trends in the thirteenth century that lead toward an intensification of pressures on minorities, Jews, and Muslims. But such straight-line causal analysis ignores numerous important changes that took place in the demographic, social, and political structures of Europe after the early fourteenth century. Certainly, many of the same factors that influenced attitudes in the thirteenth century continued to play their part in shaping attitudes and practices later. On the other hand, the route to repression was marked by a much greater hesitation and was limited to less direct measures than might have been the case without the long experience of living with Muslim subjects. Muslim-Christian relations were interlaced with seeming contradictions that can best be understood if we look at them within a comparative context. Their complexity begs for the kind of meticulous analysis that has marked these essays.

NOTES ON THE CONTRIBUTORS

David S. H. Abulafia is University Lecturer in History and Fellow of Gonville and Caius College, Cambridge. He is the author of *The Two Italies: Economic Relations between the Norman Kingdom of Sicily and the Northern Communes* (1977), *Italy, Sicily, and the Mediterranean* (1987), and *Frederick II: A Medieval Emperor* (1988).

Robert I. Burns, S.J., professor of history at the University of California, Los Angeles, is a fellow of the Medieval Academy of America and holder of its distinguished Haskins Medal, as well as numerous other offices, honors, and awards, including the Creu de Sant Jordi (1989). Among his numerous important books are *The Crusader Kingdom of Valencia*, 2 vols. (1967), *Islam under the Crusaders* (1973), *Medieval Colonialism* (1975), *Jaume I i els valencians* (1981), *Muslims, Christians and Jews in Crusader Valencia* (1983), *Society and Documentation in Crusader Valencia* (1985), and *The Foundations of Crusader Valencia* (1990).

Benjamin Z. Kedar is professor of history at the Hebrew University of Jerusalem and the author of several works, including *Merchants in Crisis: Genoese and Venetian Men of Affairs and the Fourteenth Century Depression* (1976) and *Crusade and Mission: European Approaches toward the Muslims* (1984).

Joseph F. O'Callaghan is professor of medieval history at Fordham University and former director of its Center for Medieval Studies (1980–1986). He is author of *A History of Medieval Spain* (1975), *The Spanish Order of Calatrava and Its Affiliates. Collected Studies.* (1975), and *The Cortes of Castile-Leon, 1188–1350* (1988).

James M. Powell is professor of medieval history at Syracuse University and author of numerous studies, including *Anatomy of a Crusade, 1213-1221* (1986), which was awarded the John Gilmary Shea Prize of the American Catholic Historical Association in 1987. He was a member of the Institute for Advanced Study, 1989/1990.

INDEX

'Abbāsid caliph, 140
"Abcocon," 'Alī and Muḥammad, 97
'Abd Allah b. Aḥmad, 93
'Abd Allāh, *rey de los moros del Arrixaca*, 35
'Abd al-Haqq al-Bayasī, 16, 36
'Abd al-Māssīh, 113
'Abd ar-Rahmān, 109
Abulafia, Abraham, 118
Abulafia, David S. H., 6, 7
Abū' l-Hassam 'Ali b. Abialī, 93
Abū Muḥammad 'Ubayd Allah, 142
Abū-l-Qasim, 46
Abu' l-Qāsim al-Rumaylī, 144
Abu' l-Qāsim b. Ḥammd, 159
Abū Ṣalt Umaiya, 91
Abū Zayd, governor of Valencia, 16, 79
Acre, 135, 138, 139, 145, 146, 149, 150, 153, 162, 205
Adelaide, countess of Sicily, 107, 158
Afonso I, king of Portugal, 15, 25, 26, 36, 40
Afonso II, king of Portugal, 25, 35
Afonso III, king of Portugal, 18, 25, 26, 36, 37, 40, 44
Agrigento, 107
Aguilar, 21
Aḥmad, 'Azīz, 102
Aḥmad b. Muḥammad b. Qudāma, 151–52, 170, 173
Aidone, 107
Alandroal (castle), 27
Albalat, Andreu. *See* Andreu Albalat
Albanians, 128
Albigenses, 63
Alcácer, 25, 36, 40
Alcalá de Guadaira, 17, 21
Alcalá del Río, 21

Alcalde, 36, 37
Alcañiz, 65
Alcántara, 35
Alcaudete, 21
Alcerius, archbishop of Palermo, 180
Aledo, 23, 28
Alentejo, 18, 20
Aleppo, 147
Aleramico family, 107
Alexander II, pope, 180
Alexander III, pope, 188
Alexandria, 112
Alfonso, son of Fernando III, 17
Alfonso IV, king of Argon, 95
Alfonso VI, king of Léon-Castile, 14, 20, 43, 46, 178, 182
Alfonso VII, king of Léon-Castile, 14, 29, 37
Alfonso X, king of Léon-Castile, 21–56, 90, 101; law codes, 25
Alfonso XI, king of Léon-Castile, 22
Algarve, 15, 18, 20, 25, 26, 120
'Alī al-Harawī, 150, 159
Alicante, 26, 27, 37, 40, 41, 45
Aljama, 24, 26, 33, 34, 35, 36, 41, 48, 62, 63, 66, 71, 73, 76, 77, 80, 86, 95, 101
Almada, 25, 36, 40
Amari, Michele, 100
Almodóvar, 21, 45
Almogàvers, 86
Almoguera, 19, 41
Almohads, 15, 27, 49, 70, 73, 74, 79, 80, 108
Almoravids, 14
Almusafes, 80
Amalfi, 107
Amalfitans, 106
American Historical Association, 3
Amīn, 62, 77

Anastasius (monk), 48
Anatoli, Jacob, 121, 126
Al-Andalus. *See* Andalusia
Andalusia, 15–56, 73, 120, 132, 149
Andreu Albalat, bishop of Valencia, 91
Andújar, 16
Antioch, 135, 142, 146, 155, 172
Antist, Gillem d', 97
Apostate, 45, 78
"Apostolic legation," 183–84
Apulia, 104
Al-Aqṣa Mosque, 161, 162
Arabic, 82–85, 91, 99, 101–2, 114, 117, 126, 174; books, 93
Arabic language school, 50, 51, 80
Aragon, 3; kingdom, 6, 43, 60–74, 94, 133
Architecture, Mudejar, 65–66, 98
Arcos, 17, 21, 22
Arian, 70
Arjona, 21
Arnau de Villanova, 90–91
Arsuf, 145
Arrixaca, 24, 33, 35
Ascalon, 145, 150, 156
Asinara, 115
Asmectus (Aḥmad) Bursarius, 132
Assises of Ariano, 111
Assises of Jerusalem, 154
Assisi, 107
Asturias, 19, 27
Athārib, 147, 156
Avila, 19, 41, 45
Ayamonte, 20
'Ayn al-Baqar, 139

Badajoz, 35
Baena, 21
Baeza, 15, 16
Baldwin I, king of Jerusalem, 146–47, 156, 158
Baldwin II, king of Jerusalem, 162, 163, 171

Baldwin IV, king of Jerusalem, 155
Baldwin of Ibelin, 151
Balearic islands, 61, 68, 205
Banu Sulayḥa, 157
Barceló Torres, M. C., 76, 83, 93
Barcelona, 61, 91, 107
Basileus, 123
Al-Bayasī. *See* 'Abd al-Haqq al-Bayasī
Baybars, sultan of Egypt, 153, 158
Beatriz, widow of Manuel, 34
Bedouin tribes, 151, 164
Beirut, 143, 171
Beja, 37
Bejar, 39
Bella Antiochena, 168
Benquerencia, 35
Benvenuto of Pistoia, 107
Benvenutus of Jerusalem, 160
Berber, 71, 74
Bernard, abbot of Clairvaux, 202
Bernard, archbishop of Toledo, 43, 48, 136, 182
Bernat, Mestre. *See* Mestre Bernat
Bertranninus, 160
Bevere, R., 197
Bilbays, 143
Black Death, 65, 76, 94, 95
Boccaccio, 106
Bohemond III, of Antioch, 141, 142
Bolognese, 107
Boniface VIII, pope, 197, 201
Book of King Roger, 122
Boswell, John, 3, 65, 76, 82, 84, 87, 94
Braga, archbishop, 15, 49
Bresc, Henri, 3, 101–2, 131
Brescia, 107
Brodman, James W., 29
Brown, Thomas, 121
Burchard, bishop of Strassburg, 115
Burgos, 19, 26, 37, 41
Burns, Robert I., 3, 6, 50, 176
Burriana, 75, 87

INDEX   213

Buscetta family, 112
Byzantium, 123

Cabra, 21
Caesarea, 135, 143, 161
Cagigas, Isidro de las, 11
Cahen, Claude, 143, 167
Cairo, 93
Calabria, 127, 177
Calatayud, 65
Calatrava, 14
Campania, 104
Campo de Calatrava, 15, 20
Canon law, 7, 35, 56, 130, 174, 193, 198–203, 206
Cantigas de Santa Maria, 46, 53
Capella Palatina, 103
Carmona, 17, 21, 22
Cartagena, 17, 20, 38, 41, 43, 45
Castellón, 87
Castile, 6, 11, 13–50, 60, 84, 94, 102, 118, 153
Castration, 166
Castro, 45
Castro, Américo, 78
Castro del Río, 21
Catalan, 84–85; settlement, 106
Catalonia, 6, 60–64, 67–68, 72, 74, 94, 107, 130, 153, 161, 205
Cauncis (?), 19
Cazalla, 21
Cefalù, 107
Celano, 115
Celestine III, pope, 200
Ceuta, 17
Charles I, of Anjou, 73, 101, 130, 196
Charles II, of Anjou, 130, 131, 197, 201
Christianization, Sicily, 103–4
Clement IV, pope, 197
Coimbra, 13
Community, 4–9, 58–59, 100–101, 185–86, 190–92, 196–97, 205–8; Christian, 73, 77; Jewish, 25, 41–42, 58, 77, 92, 176; Muslim, 6, 7, 33–34, 41–42, 68, 73, 86, 90–91, 94–99, 164, 176
Compostella. *See* San Diego di Compostella
Constantina, 22, 41
Constantinople, 123
Constanza, queen of Léon-Castile, 43
Constitutions of Melfi, 120
Contra Gentiles, 80
Conversion, 5–7, 46–53, 62–63, 78–79, 81–82, 89, 101–2, 109, 111, 116, 130, 153–56, 162–63, 186–87, 189, 195, 198–203, 205–6
Convivencia, 7, 78, 103
Córdoba, 16, 20, 22, 37, 41, 43; Caliphate, 13; diocese, 40; kingdom, 21, 34
Coria, 14, 19, 41; *fuero*, 20
Corleone, 107
Council of 1330 (Aragon), 95
Cour de la Fonde, 164
Court of Burgesses, 164–65
Craftsmen, Muslim, 18, 26, 40, 65, 71, 93, 101, 153
Crevillente, 91
Crimes and penalties, 39–40
Crusade, First, 149, 185
Crusade, Third, 148
Crusade, Fifth, 3
Crusade and Mission, 176
Crusades, 6, 74, 75, 90, 143, 144–45, 146, 151–52, 161, 189; against the Hohenstaufen, 129–30; Frederick II, 112, 193–95; James I, 74
Cuenca, 19, 42; *fuero*, 20, 29, 30
Cusa, S., 100
Cyprus, 107
Cyrenaica, 120, 131

Dallesium Maltesium, 115
Damascus, 152

Damietta, 194
Dante, 115
Daroca, 65
De Iudaeis, Sarracenis, et eorum servis, 198
Decarreaux, Jean, 175
Decretales, 193, 198
Déer, Josef, 175
Desclot, Bernat, 86
Dhimma, 70, 83, 168
Diyā' al-Dīn. *See* al-Mugaddasī
Dome of the Rock, 161
Dominicans, 50, 52, 80, 91, 128, 195
Donation of Constantine, 178–80
Doxapatrios, Neilos, 122–23
Dress, Jews, 190–91; Muslim, 30–32, 79, 81, 166, 190–91, 201
Dubrovnik, 60
Dufourcq, Charles, 67

Ebles de Roucy, 181
Ebro river, 66
Écija, 21, 38
Edessa, 149
Elche, 24, 34, 91
Entella, 113
Epalza, Míkel de, 72–73, 101–2
Erice, 119
Ernoul, 148
Escalona, *fuero,* 35
Espéculo, 38
Eudes de Sully, bishop of Paris, 191
Eudes of Châteauroux, 154
Eugenius, admiral of the kingdom of Sicily, 125
Eustache of Boulogne, 144–45
Évora, 25, 26, 36
Extravagantes Communes, 193
Extremadura, 19, 35

Faenza, 126
Falconry, 126
Fallamonica, Uberto, 125
Faqīh, 90

Farmers, Muslim, 18, 65, 71, 72, 93
Faro, 20, 25, 36, 40
Fatima (slave), 28
Fatima, wife of Asmectus, 132
Fatimid, 144
Ferdinand and Isabella, 184
Fernández y Gonzales, Francisco, 11
Fernando I, king of Léon-Castile, 13, 14
Fernando III, king of Castile-Léon, 15–16, 17, 23, 33, 34, 54
Fernando IV, king of Castile-Léon, 24, 54
Ferrer i Mallol, M. T., 94, 95, 96
Feudal overlordship, 177–81
Fibonacci, Leonardo, 126
Flanders, 105
Florence, 107
Fodale, Salvatore, 184
Francis of Assisi, 49
Franciscan rule, 49
Franciscans, 80, 99
Frederick II, Holy Roman emperor and king of Sicily, 100–101, 103, 107, 112–29, 193–97
Freemen, Muslim, 26–30
Freixo, *foral,* 47
French invasion of 1285, 86
Fuero Real, 29, 45
Fueros, 30, 37; municipal, 25, 29, 47
Fulcher of Chartres, 146, 150, 155, 163, 171

Gaeta, 107
Galicia, 14, 19
"Garbum," 120
García, Ballester, Luis, 90–91
"Gaudemus in Domino," 199–200
Gautier, chancellor of Antioch, 168
Gaza, 150
Gelasius, pope, 178, 182
Genizah texts, 105, 144
Genoa, 60, 64
Genoese, 104, 107, 114, 146
Genoese-Sicilian treaty of 1156, 104

Geoffrey Malaterra, 183
Geography, Arabic, 122
George of Antioch, 121
Gerons, 86
Gharb, 157
Giacomo da Lentini, 127
Gibraltar, 27, 54
Gilbertus Anglicus, 160
Glick, Thomas, 87
Godfrey of Bouillon, 156
Goitein, S. D., 169
González Jiménez, Manuel, 11, 22, 34, 54
Gonzalez, Julio, 20
Gothic architecture, 98
Goyo, 116, 119
Granada, 93; Invasion of 1302, 94; kingdom, 19–27, 54, 74, 92, 184
Greeks, 103, 106, 108, 118, 122, 174; in southern Italy and Sicily, 121–25, 128, 133
Green Mosque, Ascalon, 162
Gregory I, pope, 50
Gregory VII, pope, 48, 136, 178–81
Gregory IX, pope, 74, 154, 163, 193, 195, 198, 200
Grosseteste, Robert, bishop of Lincoln, 192
Grousset, René, 165, 167
Guadalquivir River, 18, 21
Guadiana River, 20
Gualterius de Garrexio, 107
Guide for the Perplexed, 126
Guido delle Colonne, 127
Guillena, 21
Guiral-Hadziiossif, Jacqueline, 95, 96

Ḥadīth, 144, 151
Haifa, 143, 146
al-Ḥākim, 158
Hamdān b. ʿAbd al-Raḥīm al Athāribī, 137, 143, 156–57
Ḥanbalīs, 7, 138, 140, 151, 161
Ḥaṭṭīn, 139

Hebrew, 83, 91; script used for Arabic, 117
Hebron, 144, 150
Henricus de Morra, 115
Henry IV, Holy Roman emperor, 180
Henry, count of Malta, 115
Historia orientalium principum, 137
History of the Five Patriarchates, 123
History of the Franks who came forth to the Land of Islam, 137
Holy Land, 79, 185
Holy war, 173
Honorius III, pope, 193–95
Hornachos, 35
Huesca, 65
Hugh, abbot of Cluny, 48
Hugh of *Jubiletum*, 160
Hugh of St. Victor, 48
"Hugo Falcandus," 125
Humbert de Romans, 80
Humbert of Moyenmoutiers, 177
Hungary, 3

Iacopo Mostacci, 127
Ibn ʿAbbad, 113
Ibn al-Aḥmar, king of Granada, 16, 17, 18, 22
Ibn al-ʿArabī, 149
Ibn al-Athīr, 141, 150
Ibn al-Qalānisī, 150
Ibn ʿAmmar of Tripoli, 142
Ibn Ḥammūd, 110, 112, 113
Ibn Hūd, 16, 18; family of, 17; Ibrāhim Abū Isḥaq, 36
Ibn Jubayr, 111–13, 138–39, 149, 152, 155, 159, 162–70
Ibn Khaldūn, 54, 90, 115
Ibn Maḥfūṭ, king of Niebla, 18, 21
Ibn Rashīq, 52
Ibn Sabah, *alcayde de Moros*, 34, 36
Ibn Sab ʿīn, 125
Ibn Tasīr, 152
Ibn Timmons family, 121, 126
Idrīsī, 122

'Imād al-Dīn, 139–40, 149, 153, 155, 161–63
Innocent III, pope, 45, 78, 163, 190, 199, 200
Irrigation, 87
Italian language, 128

Jabal Bahrā, 155
Jabala, 141–42, 155, 163–64
Jaén, 16, 17, 20, 21; kingdom, 21, 34, 43
Jaime. *See* James I, king of Aragon
James I, king of Aragon, 23–24, 43–101, 197; autobiography, 98–99
James II, king of Aragon, 95
Jammā'īl, 152, 169, 170, 173
Játiva, 69, 80, 88–89, 93
Jaume. *See* James I, king of Aragon
Jazr, 157
Jerba, 116, 120
Jerez, 17, 22, 54
Jerusalem, 143, 144, 149, 150, 151, 153, 156, 161; kingdom, 139, 148, 176
Jerusalem school, 3
Jews, 8, 9, 22, 25, 31, 35, 41–44, 50–51, 56, 63, 70, 80, 103, 117–21, 143–44; in canon law, 189–92; sale of property to, 34
Jihād, 167
Joan de Cámera, 97
Joan de Puigventos, O. P., 80
João, archbishop of Braga, 49
Jodar, 21
John XIII, pope, 177
John XXII, pope, 95, 193
John of Gorze, 48
Jordan River, 170
Juan Manuel, Infante, 50, 56
Júcar River, 80
Judah ha-Cohen, 126
Jurj b. Ya'qūb, 157

Kafr Kāna (Cana), 171
Kamāl al-Dīn, 147

Kashrut, 119
Kedar, Benjamin Z., 3, 176, 187
Khuṭba, 140
Khwarezmians, 155–56
Knights Hospitaller, 165, 171
Knights Templar, 161
Koran, 49, 50, 52, 53, 77, 90, 93, 140, 151

Ladero Quesada, Miguel Ángel, 11, 19–20, 22, 43, 54
La Mancha, 20
Lamego, 13
Lampedusa, Giovanni de, 133
Landulph, bishop-elect of Pisa, 180
Languedoc, 96
Laodicea, 141–42
Lapeyre, Henri, 76
Las Navas de Tolosa, 15, 73
Lateran Council, Third, 18–89; Fourth, 190–92, 201, 203
Latin, 83, 91, 103; script used for Arabic, 117
Latinization, 102, 132–33
Law, 36–40, 42; Castilian, 25; Islamic, 26, 65; Valencian, 79, 91
Lebrija, 21, 22
Leo IX, pope, 177, 178, 179
León, 13; city, 19, 41; kingdom, 19, 42
Leonine wall, 177
Leopard, 133
Lērida, 61, 62, 63
Levant, 6, 104, 135–74
Leyes de moros del siglo XIV, 26
Leyes del estilo, 39
Libro del repartimiento de Jerez, 22
Liguria, 104, 107
Linehan, Peter, 175
Lisbon, 15, 25, 26, 33, 36, 40, 44, 49
"Lombardi," 108, 128
Lorca, 17, 20, 23, 35, 37
Louis IX, king of France, 73
Loulé, 20, 25, 36

INDEX 217

Lucera, 7, 100–117, 125, 128–30, 187, 193–98, 201, 205, 206
Luis, brother of Alfonso X, 34
Lull, Ramon, 79, 80, 101, 201
Luque, 21
Luttrell, Anthony, 115
Lyons, council, 192, 196

Ma'arrat al-Nu'mān, 143, 157
McVaugh, Michael, 91
Madrid, 19, 41
Magacela, 35
Maghieb, 112, 120, 121, 152
Mahdia, 108
Maimonides, 126
Majorca, 7, 61, 63, 67, 89, 130
Malagón, 15
Maleinoi, 121
Malta, 114, 115, 116, 117, 119, 127
Mamluks, 171
Manfred, king of Sicily, 196
Manises, 98
Manṣūr b. Nabīl, 16, 141–42, 164
Manuel, brother of Alfonso X, 24, 34
al-Maqrīzī, 153, 162
Mār Būniya, 156
Marchena, 21, 22
Mark of Toledo, 50
Marsala, 107
Marseilles, 60
Martí, king of Aragon, 95
Martī, Ramon, 80
Mawdūd (of Mosul), 155
Mayer, Hans Eberhard, 159, 169
Mayor Petrez (nun of San Clemente), 28
Mazzeo di Ricco of Messina, 127
Mdina-Notabile, 119
Mecca, 38
Medical licensing, 92
Medicine, 90–93, 159–60
Medina Sidonia, 17, 22
Mercedarians, 97
Merchants, Muslim, 18, 26, 61, 93, 96; Tuscan wine merchants to Tunis, 105
Messina, 6, 104, 106, 107
Mestre Bernat, 92
Meyerson, Mark, 71, 96
Michael Scot, 125–26
Milan, 107
Military orders, 35, 88, 161; Alcántara, 20; Avis, 20, 27; Calatrava, 20; Santiago, 20, 41
Minnesinger, 127
Minorca, 7, 67
Moamyn, 126
Mondego River, 14, 19
Mongolia, 81
Monreale, 109, 120
Montesa castle, 88
Montpellier, 61; University, 91
Moors, 13–51, 80
Morería, 19, 22, 33, 34, 63
Moriscos, 61, 95, 102; Valencian, 112
Morocco, 22, 49, 81, 123
Morón, 21, 34, 36
Moses ben Solomon of Salerno, 121
Moura, 35
Mozarabic Christians, 12, 26, 48
Mudajjan, 13, 59
Mudejar revolt of 1264, 34
Mudejars, 12, 13, 18, 34, 42–48, 53, 59, 64, 68, 70–73; Andalusia, 11, 18, 22, 54; Aragon, 64–66, 82, 92; Castile, 11, 38, 41; Catalonia, 61–62; Murcia, 11, 22, 23, 43; Portugal, 11, 25; Sicily, 100–134; Valencia, 68–69, 74–97; culture, 90–94; population, 18–25, 75–76, 148; social status, 25–26
Muezzin, 44, 62, 95, 197, 201
Muḥammad, 14, 16, 38, 42, 44, 52, 53, 177
Muḥtasib, 97
Mujīr al-Dīn, 150
Mula, 17
Muldoon, James, 175

Al-Muqaddasī, Diyā' al Dīn, 138, 140, 151, 152, 158, 169, 170
Murcia, 15–24, 33–37, 50–51, 89
Muret, 73
Murviedro, 80
Muslims, Hungary, 3
Al-Mu'tamid, king of Seville, 46

Nablus, 7, 135, 139, 140, 144, 149, 151, 155, 159; council, 165–66
Najera, *fuero*, 39
Names, 47–48; Christian, 32, 157–58; Muslim, 158; Romance, 84
Naples, 126
Narbonne, 15
Nasrids, 16
Naval, 65
Navarre, 33
Nicodemus, archbishop of Palermo, 180
Nicosia, Cyprus, 160; synod of 1298, 154
Nicosia, Sicily, 107
Niebla, 18, 21
Normands, papes, et moines, 175
Normans in Italy, 177–78, 205; kings, 103, 108
North Africa, 19, 24, 49, 54, 64, 74, 75, 105, 108, 112, 116, 119, 121
Novara di Sicilia, 107
Nuṣayrī, 155

Obbertus of Savona, 107
Oberto Manayra, 107
O'Callaghan, Joseph F., 6
Oldradus da Ponte, 9, 203, 207
Oriental Christians, 149, 157, 168
Orihuela, 33, 41
Osuna, 21
Orvieto, 107
Otto the Great, Holy Roman emperor, 48
Oviedo, 47

Palencia, 19, 41
Palermo, 6, 103, 105, 108, 109, 119, 121, 131, 132, 140, 159
Palma, 45
Palma del Río, 21
Palmela, 25, 36, 40
Pantelleria, 114, 132
Papacy, 175–203
Papacy and the Levant, 175
Paper mills, 69, 88–89
Papsttum und Normannen, 175
Partidas. See *Siete Partidas*
Paschal II, pope, 184–85
Paterna, 98
Patronato real, 184
Peire Vidal, 127
Peñafiel, council, 51
Pere the Ceremonious, king of Aragon, 95
Perez, de Isco, Eximeno, 97
Peter, king of Aragon, 78, 90
Peter Crassus, 180
Peter of Blois, 121
Peter the Venerable, abbot of Cluny, 49, 202
Peter of Mahdia, 111, 121, 159
Philip of Montfort, 158
Piacenya, 107
Piedmont, 107
Pietro del fu Vitale, 107
Piracy, 71
Pisa, 107
Pisans, 104, 106
Pita Mercé, Rodrigo, 61, 62
Plasencia, 19, 42
Porcuna, 21
Portugal, 6, 13–28, 37, 50
Prawer, Joshua, 3, 176
Provence, 74; poetry, 127
Pugio Fidei, 80

al-$q\bar{a}$'id, 36, 61, 101, 195, 196
al-$q\bar{a}d\bar{\imath}$, 36, 61, 101, 140, 141, 142, 155, 163

Quesada, 16
Qur'āns, 112

Rabat, 119
Ramla, 151, 156
Ramon de Penyafort, 51, 80, 198
Ramon Muntaner, 84
Ravello, 106
Reconquista, 207
Reilly, Bernard F., 43
Religious freedom, 42–46, 62
Repartiment (Valencia), 74
Rinaldo d'Aquino, 127
Robert, bishop of Messina, 183
Robert Guiscard, 180
Robert of Ketton, 49
Rodrigo, archbishop of Toledo, 43, 49–50
Roger, bishop of Syracuse, 183
Roger I, count of Sicily, 136, 182–85
Roger II, king of Sicily, 103, 107, 110–11, 121–24, 132–33, 159, 184
Roger of Howden, 155
Roger Sclavus, 108
Roman Rite, 178–79, 181
Romance, 82, 83, 102, 104, 174
Romanesque-Gothic architecture, 98
Romuald, archbishop of Salerno, 110–11
Rosso Rosso, 127
Rota, 22
Rubiera, Maria Jesús, 85
Rute, 21

Sa'īda, 152
St. Paul outside the Walls, 177
St. Peter's Cathedral, Caesarea, 161–62
St. Peter's, Rome, 177
Saladin, 138, 139, 141, 153, 155
Salado, 22
Salem de Messana, 132
Salerno, 183

Samuel b. Manasseh, 86
Sancho II, king of Portugal, 18
Sancho IV, king of Léon-Castile, 35, 37, 41, 43, 52–53, 54
Sancho IV, king of Navarre, 178
Sancho Ramirez, king of Aragon, 179
San Clemente (convent), 28
Sancta Maria Viridis, 162
San Diego di Compostella, 16
San Gil, 19
Sangimignano, 106
San Isidro, 21
Sanlúcar, 21, 22
San Pedro, 21
San Salvador, 21
Santa Catalina, 21
Santaella, 21
Santa Olalla, 19, 41
Santarém, 15, 37
Sasanian, 70
Savona, 107
Scuola siciliana, 127
Sebaste, 153
Segovia, 19, 41
Sepúlveda, *fuero*, 28, 35, 38
Serpa, 35
Setton, Kenneth, 175
Seville, 16–26, 33, 43, 49, 54; archdiocese, 43–44; Cortes, 30, 31, 41, 44, 50; kingdom, 21, 34
Sexual relations, 31–32, 45, 166, 199–200, 206
al-Shafra al-Qirbilyanī, Muḥammad, 91–92
al-Shāṭibī, 93
Shiite, 74
Sibylline oracles, 125
Sicily, kingdom, 6, 100–133, 135, 139, 159, 161, 177–78, 205
Sidon, 139, 146, 147, 150, 156
Siete Partidas, 25, 28, 31, 33, 38, 42, 45, 50, 51
Silibar, 21, 34
Silves, 25, 36

Simon, son of Roger I of Sicily, 183
Sivan, Emanuel, 143
Slavery, 7, 26–30, 71, 79, 101, 152–54, 208
Slaves, Christian, 189; Greek, 131; Muslim, 7, 26–30, 47, 61, 67, 77, 79, 81, 111, 131–32, 163; slave trade, 131; Tatar, 131
Sobrado (monastery), 47
Soto Company, Ricardo, 67
Song of Roland, 5
Spanish Church and the Papacy, 175
Sunnite, 74
Syracuse, 127

Tagus River, 15, 18, 20, 23
Talmud, 91
Tancred, 144–45, 146, 147, 151
Tarazona, 65
Tarifa, 54
Tarragona, 177, 182
Tavira, 25, 36
Taxation, 40–42, 71, 89, 98–99, 101, 161, 168–71
Tejada, 21
Templar of Tyre, 157, 158
Templum Domini, 161
Teruel, 65
Thaddeus de Suesa, 196
Theodore of Antioch, 126
Thomas Aquinas, 80, 126
Thoros, king of Armenia, 148–49
Tiberias, bishop of, 199
Tibnīn, 149
Toledo, 14, 15, 18, 26, 28, 33, 46, 126, 182; archdiocese, 19, 42, 43, 49, 50; *fuero*, 29, 37; kingdom, 20
Toleration, 4, 5, 8, 9, 12, 72, 102, 103, 206–8
Torah, 119
Torres Fontes, Juan, 11, 24
Tortosa, 61, 63; synod, 95
Trapani, 112, 113, 130
Treaties, 7, 13–23, 61, 75, 83, 104, 185

Trinitarians, 97
Tripoli, 108, 145, 146
Tudejen, 33
Tudela, 65
Tunis, emir of, 17
Turin, 107
Turkish lands, 118
Turmeda, Anselm, 99
Tuscany, 104, 106
Tyre, 135, 138, 139, 146, 150, 162

Úbeda, 15, 16
'Ulamaā, 62
Urban II, pope, 48, 136, 182–85
Urban IV, pope, 196
Urvoy, Dominique, 80
Usāma b. Munqidh, 155, 162, 163
Usury, 188
Utilitas (usefulness), 6, 7, 189, 203, 207

Valencia, 35, 67, 80, 87–89; aljamas, 86; kingdom, 6, 59, 61–97, 131, 153, 187, 205; university, 91
Vall de Uxó, 86
Valladolid, 19; cortes, 31
Vejar, 22
Venetians, 104, 146
Venice, 60
Verlinden, Charles, 166
Vich, 177
Vienne council, 95, 201
Vinyolesi Vidal, Teresa, 61
Viseu, 13
Visigothic Code, 12
Vocabulista, 80

Waqf, 93
Water Court, 87–88
Water mills, 88–89
William I, king of Sicily, 188
William II, king of Sicily, 109, 111, 129
William of Tyre, 137, 159
Women, Christian, 31–32; Jewish,

31; Muslim, 33, 110, 199–200; Physicians, 92

Yaḥyā b. Uthmān, 151
Yolande, 193

Zafadola, Moorish king, 14
Zag de la Maleha (Jewish tax farmer), 35
Zaida, daughter-in-law of king of Seville, 46
Zambra, 21
Zaragoza, 48, 65
Zengi of Aleppo, 157
Zorita, fuero, 39
Zuheros, 21

GPSR Authorized Representative: Easy Access System Europe - Mustamäe tee
50, 10621 Tallinn, Estonia, gpsr.requests@easproject.com